I0816310

STEP-BY-STEP

# COOKING FOR KIDS

STEP-BY-STEP

# COOKING FOR KIDS

Delicious ideas for 5–12 year olds, from lunch boxes and picnics to quick and easy meals, snacks, sweet treats, desserts, drinks and party food

150 irresistible recipes for kids to cook, with easy-to-follow instructions and more than 1000 fantastic photographs

**Nancy McDougall**

LORENZ BOOKS

This edition is published by Lorenz Books
an imprint of Anness Publishing Ltd

info@anness.com

www.lorenzbooks.com; www.annesspublishing.com

If you like the images in this book and would like to investigate using them for publishing, promotions or advertising, please visit our website www.practicalpictures.com for more information.

Publisher: **Joanna Lorenz**
Senior Editor: **Lucy Doncaster**
Text Editors: **Nancy McDougall** and **Glynis McGuinness**
Designer: **Lisa Tai**
Photography: **William Lingwood**
Food Stylists: **Lucy McKelvie** and **Fergal Connolly**
Prop Stylist: **Helen Trent**
Models: **Freddie, Cressida, Lucas, Eve, Gus, Kit, Scarlett** and **Lavina**
Production Controller: **Ben Worley**



Manufacturer: Anness Publishing Ltd
For Product Tracking Go To:
www.annesspublishing.com/tracking
Batch: 8151-25598-1127

**Notes**
For all recipes, quantities are given in both metric and imperial measures and, where appropriate, in standard cups and spoons. Follow one set of measures, but not a mixture, because they are not interchangeable.

Standard spoon and cup measures are level. 1 tsp = 5ml, 1 tbsp = 15ml, 1 cup = 250ml/8fl oz. Australian standard tablespoons are 20ml. Australian readers should use 3 tsp in place of 1 tbsp for measuring small quantities of gelatine, flour, salt, etc.

Electric oven temperatures in this book are for conventional ovens. When using a fan oven, the temperature will probably need to be reduced by about 10–20°C/20–40°F. Since ovens vary, check with your manufacturer's instruction book for guidance.

The nutritional analysis is calculated per portion (i.e. serving or item), unless otherwise stated. If the recipe gives a range, such as Serves 4–6, then the analysis will be for the smaller portion size, i.e. 6 servings.

Medium eggs are used unless otherwise stated in the text.

**Publisher's Note**
Although the advice and information in this book are believed to be accurate at the time of going to press, neither the authors nor the publisher can accept any legal responsiblity or liability for any errors or omissions that may be made nor for any inaccuracies nor for any harm or injury that comes about from following instructions or advice in this book. All children need to work with adult guidance and supervision and it is the parent or carer's responsibility to ensure the child is working safely.

# Contents

# Getting started

Cooking is both fun and very rewarding, whatever your age or previous experience in the kitchen. As with most things, there are some basic guidelines that should be followed, but once these have been learned, you will be able to make a fabulous range of tasty treats.

► *Learning to cook at a young age will stand you in good stead for the rest of your life.*

Making food you can eat and share is really fun, and there is nothing better than seeing your friends or family enjoy the food that you've cooked. What's more, cooking teaches you important skills, such as weighing, measuring, counting and understanding time, which are useful both in and out of the kitchen. Mixing, stirring, sprinkling and spreading will help your co-ordination, and things like decorating cakes and biscuits (cookies) are a great way to be creative.

Although cakes and biscuits aren't the healthiest of foods, home-made ones, made with good quality ingredients and no artificial additives or colourings, are far better for you than most store-bought snacks, and also taste so much better.

Once you have been cooking for a little while you will feel confident enough to try out new foods. You can then start substituting ingredients and creating your own recipes – discovering new combinations of flavours and textures and coming up with some really exciting dishes of your own.

► *Children of all ages will enjoy helping in the kitchen.*

## Cooking safely

Children develop at different rates and only parents or guardians will know when their kids are ready to be introduced to using specific tools or are able to help with certain jobs in the kitchen. Working alongside an adult and trying new cooking methods (with close guidance) is a good way for children to learn safe practices and to gain the skills needed for greater independence, although adult supervision is always recommended when children of any age are cooking.

Many of the projects in this book use knives, scissors, graters, electronic equipment or heat. Adult supervision is always required when using these, no matter how old or experienced the child, and help will be required for younger children. Pictures showing how to do something dangerous, which will require adult help or supervision, have been highlighted with icons, shown below:

(!) = the task being shown uses sharp or dangerous implements or electronic equipment, such as knives, graters, food processors or blenders. Adult help may be required to do the step or, at the very least, supervise children very carefully.

(oven glove icon) = the task being shown involves heat. Adult help may be required to do the step or, at the very least, supervise children very carefully. Gloves (mitts) should be worn when using an oven. Adults should always drain hot foods, such as pasta, and put dishes or tins (pans) in the oven and remove them when the food is cooked.

## Choosing a project

When selecting a project, first check the coloured strip across the top of the page to see how long it might take to make and cook. These don't include any food rising, chilling, resting or freezing time – instead they are a guide to how long you will need to be in the kitchen for.

In order to help you see how easy or difficult a recipe is we've also added a simple star rating, which works as follows:

★ = the project is '**easy as ABC**'. All children from 5 to 12 should be able to tackle these, with supervision, and there is only a small amount of cutting or electronic equipment use involved. Adults should help with any steps requiring heat or dangerous implements.

★★ = you should '**give it a try**'! There might be some more cutting or manual dexterity involved. With close parental supervision, most children will be able to enjoy them.

★★★ = the project is '**nice and challenging**'. These are designed for older children and perhaps kids who already have some cooking experience and are ready to try some more advanced techniques. Adult supervision will still always be required for any steps involving dangerous implements or heat.

## Getting organized

In addition to the star rating, and cooking and preparation times shown in the coloured strip at the top of the page, a list of tools is also included for every recipe. It is sensible to check you have everything you need before you start making the recipe, as there is nothing worse than getting halfway through and realizing you can't complete the dish. Child-sized equipment should be used where appropriate, and it is important that everything is clean before you start. The same applies to ingredients, and you should make sure you do any preparation listed in the ingredients list, such as chopping or peeling, before you start, so you are completely ready to do the recipe. You could also measure out everything into small bowls, like they do on television, so everything is ready to be combined and you are sure you have all the ingredients.

## General rules

**1** Recipes are given in metric, imperial and cup measurements. Whichever you decide to use, you must stick to it for the whole of the recipe. Never mix different measurements in the same recipe.

**2** Spoonfuls are all level. Always use proper measuring spoons instead of normal cutlery. They usually come in sets, and measure from a tablespoon down to a quarter of a teaspoon. To make sure the top is level, run the flat side of a round-bladed knife across the top.

**3** Ovens should be preheated to the specified temperature at least 10 minutes before you cook the dish. If you have a fan-assisted (convection) oven, follow the manufacturer's instructions for reducing the time and temperature. As a rough guide, reduce the temperature by 20°C/68°F or the cooking time by 10 minutes. Try not to open the oven during the cooking time.

**4** Although average cooking times are given for foods such as pasta and rice, you should always check on the packet and follow what is says there, as different brands and different types of ingredients cook in different amounts of time.

**5** Always check that meat and fish are completely cooked through before serving. Cooking times can vary slightly depending on how thick the meat or fish is, so it is better to be safe than sorry.

**6** Only reheat food once and make sure it's piping hot all the way through before serving.

▲ *Younger children should stick to the easier recipes in this book, and should always be supervised by an adult.*

# Safety in the kitchen

Kitchens can be dangerous places if you are not careful, so it is important that you follow a few basic rules about hygiene and about using equipment such as sharp knives and ovens, to ensure your cooking experience is both fun and safe.

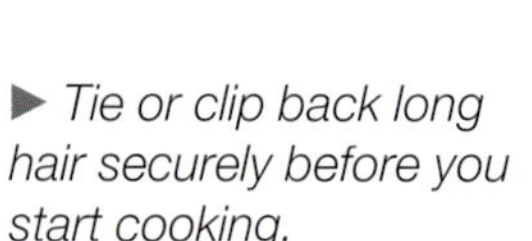

► *Tie or clip back long hair securely before you start cooking.*

### Before you start

Proper preparation in a kitchen is essential, and if you follow these simple guidelines, then you will not only be safe but the recipes are more likely to work, too.

**1** Check with an adult that it's okay for you to cook.

**2** Read the recipe all the way through and make sure that you've got enough time to make and cook it without rushing. There's nothing worse than running out of time before you've finished cooking. Ask for help if you need it.

**3** Shut pets out of the kitchen before you start to cook. You don't want animal hairs in the food – ugh! And they may get under your feet, which can be very dangerous.

**4** Get out all the ingredients that you need. Measure the ingredients and put them in bowls. It's much easier to make a recipe if everything is ready to add when you need it and it means you won't forget to add an ingredient.

**5** Get out all the equipment that you'll need.

**6** Line any cake tins (pans) needed.

▼ *Get out any equipment before you start.*

### Hygiene in the kitchen

**1** Always wash your hands before you start cooking.

**2** Tie back long hair.

**3** If you handle raw meat or fish, or dirty fruit or vegetables, wash your hands again before you carry on cooking.

**4** If possible use separate chopping boards for raw meat and fish, cooked meat and fish, and fruit and vegetables. If you like, use a different coloured board for each type of food. Alternatively, wash knives and chopping boards before using them to prepare different types of food.

**5** Make sure meat and fish are cooked right through before serving. If necessary, cut a piece open in the middle to check.

## Safety first

### general care in the kitchen

✔ If you drop or spill anything on the floor, mop it up immediately. If you leave it until later, you may forget and someone may slip on it.

✔ Handle sharp knives with care. When chopping and slicing make sure you keep your fingers well away from the blade. Chop on a board and keep the blade pointing downwards. Keep sharp knives out of reach of young children.

✘ Never touch plugs, electrical equipment, sockets (outlets) or switches with damp hands – you could get an electric shock.

✔ If very young children can't reach the work surface easily stand them on a sturdy chair, making sure it is totally steady. Supervise them closely all the time.

► *It is very important that you wash your hands thoroughly with hot water and soap before starting cooking. You must also wash them again immediately after touching raw fish or meat, or handling chillies.*

## Using dangerous implements

1 Adult supervision is always required when you are using dangerous implements.
2 The blades in food processors and blenders are extremely sharp, so never put your hands in to move anything and ask an adult to help.
3 Always make sure the lid of a blender or the stopper on a processor is firmly on before you press the start button. Adult supervision is required.
4 Allow hot soups and sauces to cool slightly before putting them in a blender or processor.
5 Keep your fingers well away from the beaters of electric mixers while they are whizzing around. Adult supervision is required.
6 Always make sure the beaters of an electric hand mixer are touching the base (bottom) of the bowl before you switch it on. If you don't, the mixture will fly all over the kitchen when you switch on.
7 When grating, hold food with your hand, away from the cutting edge. Adult supervision is required.
8 Put a damp dish towel under the bowl before beating ingredients to prevent it slipping about.

▲ *Take care when grating. Hold the grater firmly in one hand, and grip the food with the other hand, away from the cutting edge.*

## Safety first
### for ovens, stoves and microwaves

✔ Turn pan handles to the sides of the stove, so they can't be accidentally knocked over.

✔ Make sure that the pan you are using is big enough so that the food doesn't boil over or spill over. Only adults should drain hot foods.

✔ Stir pans carefully, making sure that hot food doesn't slop over the edges. Adult supervision is required.

✔ Always use oven gloves to get food out of the microwave because some dishes get hot when microwaved. Remove the lid or clear film (plastic wrap) covering the food very carefully so you don't get burnt by steam. Adult supervision is required.

✔ Ask an adult, wearing oven gloves, to take dishes and tins out of the oven.

✔ Make sure you turn off the stove as soon as you've finished using it. If you leave it on you may touch it or put something on to a hot burner that will break or melt with the heat.

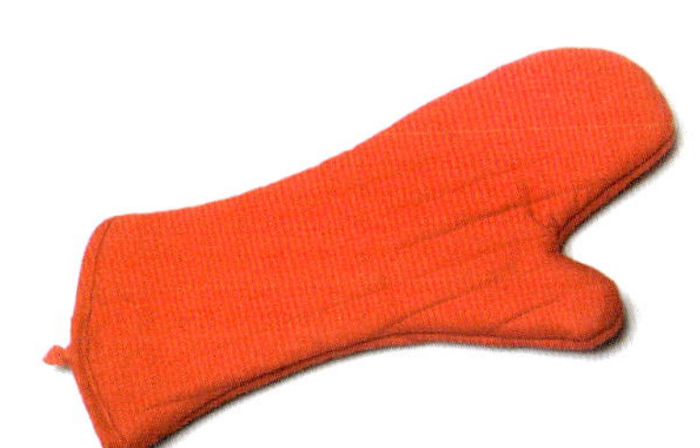

◀ *Adults should remove hot pans and dishes from the oven, wearing oven gloves.*

✔ Take great care when frying and NEVER leave a hot frying pan unattended. Stir-frying and shallow-frying should be done only by older children. Deep-frying must be done only by adults.

✔ Food must be dry if it will be placed in hot fat – otherwise, it will spit and even burn. If food is damp, pat it dry with kitchen paper. When frying food, stand back from the pan and lower food in gently, one piece at a time. Adult supervision is required.

✔ Steam burns really badly, so keep your hands away from steaming kettles and pans and take care when removing the lid from a pan containing boiling water.

✘ Never put foil, metal dishes or dishes with metal paint rims in the microwave.

# Healthy eating

Cooking at home is a really fun way to find out about ingredients and try out a wide range of different foods that you may not have had before. Making meals from scratch is also much healthier and tastier than eating ready-prepared and takeaway meals.

Cooking is the perfect way of learning why we need to eat a healthy diet, what certain foods do for our bodies and how to judge if food is fresh, ripe and good quality. Ask lots of questions, such as why certain foods are good for you.

Mealtimes are the best opportunity to show off your new skills, so whenever possible try and gather everyone together around the table. Weekends are often the best time to try more complex dishes as there is generally more time to cook.

▼ *This diagram illustrates how much of each type of food you should try to eat during a day.*

▶ *Cooking your own food encourages you to try new things, such as this fresh home-made pasta.*

## A balanced diet

Children of all ages need a balanced diet with at least five portions of fruit and vegetables a day, plus two to three portions of protein (meat, fish, eggs, nuts or pulses/beans) and two to three portions of dairy produce (milk, yogurt and cheese). They also need some starchy carbohydrates (bread, rice, pasta, breakfast cereals and potatoes) with each meal.

**FOOD WHEEL**

*Carbohydrates, such as bread, potatoes, pasta and rice*

*Fresh fruit, vegetables and salads*

*Protein, such as meat, poultry, fish, eggs, dairy, nuts and pulses*

*Natural fats, such as oily fish, avocados and nuts*

*Only eat a small amount of fatty or sugary foods, such as cakes, biscuits, crisps and sweets*

▲ *Eating a rainbow of different coloured fruit and vegetables every day ensures you get all the vitamins and minerals you need.*

An easy way to check you are eating the right balance of foods over a day is to imagine a dinner plate and divide it into several sections. One third should be taken up by carbohydrates, one third with fresh fruit, vegetables or salad, and the remaining third divided into three smaller sections containing protein, natural fats and a very small amount of added fat or sugar, such as crisps (potato chips), chocolate or biscuits (cookies). This is often called a food wheel, and it is shown in the diagram opposite.

It is also extremely important that you eat three meals a day, since children require a lot of energy for rushing around and for growing. Breakfast is especially vital for enabling concentration at school and providing energy to see you through until lunch. It also provides a good opportunity to eat high-fibre fortified breakfast cereals and a dose of vitamin C in the form of a glass of orange juice.

In order to ensure you eat a good range of foods across a week, you should sit down and plan your meals. This not only gives you the chance to have your say, but it also means you can plan ahead and check you have all the ingredients.

## Five a day

Children and adults need at least five portions of fruit and vegetables a day, of which half should be vegetables and half should be fruit. These should be as varied in colour as possible – think of the foods as a rainbow and have five different colours each day. A medium apple, orange, banana, pear or peach is one portion. Fruit juice counts as only one portion of fruit. If you don't like eating large pieces of fruit, make them into smoothies or cut them into bitesize pieces.

## Maximum vitality

In order to get the best from the food you eat, lightly cook vegetables or serve them raw in salads – overcooking destroys many of the nutrients, especially vitamin C. Sticks of raw carrot, celery, red (bell) pepper and cucumber are great served with a dip, and grated raw carrot mixed with raisins and roasted cashew nuts makes a tasty snack.

## Menu must-haves

Although everyone needs to eat a balanced diet, children do have a few special requirements. The following should be included on a weekly basis:

1. Calcium-rich foods are essential for strong teeth and bones, so foods such as milk, cheese, yogurt, soya beans, tofu and nuts are very important. Fortified breakfast cereals, margarine and oily fish contain dietary vitamin D, which ensures a good supply of calcium in the blood.
2. Vitamin A, found in milk, margarine, butter, leafy green vegetables, carrots and apricots, promotes good vision and healthy skin. So although carrots may not make you see in the dark, they will help you have eagle eyes!
3. Iron is very important for healthy blood and energy levels. Good sources include red meat, liver, fish, beans, lentils, green vegetables and fortified breakfast cereals.
4. In order to be able to absorb all that iron, your body needs vitamin C. As well as being found in citrus fruits, such as oranges and lemons, it is also present in tomatoes and potatoes.
5. Oily fish, such as mackerels and sardines are a good source of protein, vitamins and minerals, and they also contain omega 3 fatty acids, which have many heart-friendly properties. Omega 3 is also found in seeds and walnuts, as well as in some products that have been enriched with the fats, such as milk and eggs.

◀ *Dairy and eggs are high in calcium and packed with vitamins.*

## Eat your greens!

Fussy eating is actually quite common in small children. If they refuse a few foods but still eat a balanced diet it's probably best not to make a fuss about it. No one food is essential. So if, for instance, they won't eat Brussels sprouts and cooked cabbage but will eat raw cabbage in home-made coleslaw, then it's best not to nag them. Food should be a pleasure not a battle. Just keep encouraging them to try a tiny amount of new foods – experts say that sometimes it takes up to eight tries before a small child will accept something different. However, if a child will only eat a very small range of foods, and these are mostly unhealthy, then you will need to resort to disguising healthy food in soups and sauces. Vegetables are one of the most common foods that children are fussy about.

Making home-made vegetable soup is a good way of encouraging children to eat more vegetables – butternut squash and carrot soup always seem popular. You can also add chopped vegetables to casseroles and curries and pasta sauces. If it is meat that they won't eat you can blend cooked chicken into a vegetable soup. If older children have made a decision to become vegetarian, however, you should try to respect their choice and make sure that they get adequate protein from other sources.

Going foraging or fruit picking is another good way of encouraging them to try new foods as well as teaching them where it comes from. If they select and handle the food themselves, they will be more inclined to try it.

► *Fresh vegetables can be used in many dishes.*

## Special diets

Food allergies and intolerance are on the increase, especially in children under five. The most common foods that can cause an adverse reaction are cow's milk, eggs, peanuts, soya, other nuts and wheat. Allergic reactions are also known to have been caused by citrus fruit, chicken, goat's milk, sesame and other seeds and exotic fruits, such as mango.

After the age of five many, but not all, children outgrow their allergies, so it is worth consulting your doctor and, if so advised, trying them with a very small amount of the food. Some children, however, have a severe, immediate reaction to certain foods, called anaphylaxis, which can be lethal. Peanuts are the most common cause of this, so great care needs to be taken not to expose children to any food that may have been in contact with nuts. If you are cooking for other children or giving a children's party, it is best to ask the parents well in advance if any of the children have special requirements.

▲ *Going fruit picking is tons of fun and will teach you a lot about where different foods, such as apples, come from.*

▲ *Many children are intolerant or allergic to foods, such as eggs, dairy products and nuts, so check before feeding other children.*

## Staying healthy

There is an ever-increasing problem with childhood obesity in the Western world and we need to make sure that children have a healthy diet and don't eat too much sugar and fat in the form of sweets and fatty snacks, such as crisps (potato chips). However, that needs to be balanced by making sure that growing youngsters have enough calories to give them energy, especially when they have a growing spurt or do a lot of exercise. Energetic, growing teenagers need more calories than their parents.

All children are different, even in the same family, so you need to watch them and treat the diet of each one individually. If you think a child is becoming obese, gently encourage him or her to cut out some of the treats and replace them with healthy snacks, such as fruit and low-fat, low-sugar yogurts. But be tactful and don't make an issue of it – the last thing you want to do is make the child self-conscious and anxious. If a child is growing it's best to keep their weight even and let them 'grow into it' rather than try and lose weight.

Encourage children to drink more water and cut out sugary drinks – this alone can make a huge difference. Sugar in drinks is empty calories that have no nutritional value and don't help to satisfy the appetite. Water is best, but if they won't drink plain water give them low-calorie squashes (soft drinks). Avoid drinking lots of fruit juice as a thirst quencher. A glass of freshly squeezed orange juice a day is a good source of vitamin C, but if they drink several glasses the calories will mount up.

◀ *Home-made fruit smoothies are a much healthier choice than commercial fizzy drinks (sodas) or milkshakes.*

Milkshakes made with anything other than fruit and milk should only be enjoyed on special occasions. These are fattening and because they're drinks, they slip down without being considered as food. Don't cut out milk altogether (unless they have a dairy allergy) as it's a valuable source of calcium and protein. Children under five should have full-fat (whole) milk. Older children can have semi-skimmed (low-fat) milk.

Many experts think the main cause of childhood obesity is lack of exercise, so encourage your children to walk more and do more sport. Take them swimming, go for country walks and cycle rides – it will do you good, too.

▲ *Low-fat yogurt served with home-made fruit purée and topped with granola makes a tasty dessert or snack.*

▲ *Milk makes a delicious and nutritious drink, and is very important for the development of strong, healthy bones.*

# Cooking terms explained

Although some cooking terms, such as rinse or chop, may be familiar, there are some words that may be new to you. This easy-to-use directory explains some of the basic terms that will appear in the recipes and should make them easier to follow.

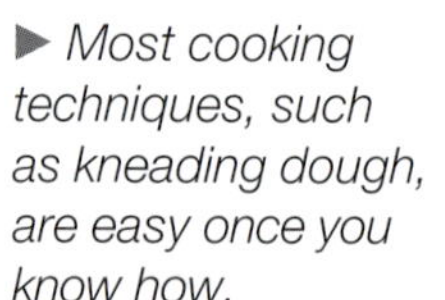

► *Most cooking techniques, such as kneading dough, are easy once you know how.*

**Bake** To cook food in the oven.

**Beat** To mix and soften ingredients with a spoon, whisk, fork or electric mixer (adult supervision is required).

**Blend** To mix ingredients until the mixture looks smooth. This is done in a bowl with a whisk, spoon or electric mixer, or in a blender. Adult supervision is required when using electrical equipment.

**Brown** To fry meat in a hot pan until it goes brown. Adult supervision is required.

**Chop** To cut food into pieces. Use a sharp knife and a chopping (cutting) board. Adult supervision is required.

**Drain** To pour off the water, often by pouring it through a colander or sieve (strainer). To drain fried food, lift it using a fish slice (spatula) or draining spoon and transfer it to a plate lined with kitchen paper. Adults should drain anything hot.

**Drizzle** To sprinkle drops of liquid on to food.

**Flake** To break drained cooked or canned fish into pieces using a knife and fork. As you do it remove any bones carefully with your fingers.

**Fold** To carefully mix flour or other ingredients into a cake mixture. Always use a metal spoon and be careful not to knock the air out of the mixture.

**Fry** To cook food in hot oil or fat. Frying is for older children only and adults must always supervise. There are different types of frying:

- ***Deep-frying*** is done in a pan or a deep-fat fryer so that the food is completely submerged in oil. Only adults should do this.
- ***Shallow-frying*** is done in a frying pan or skillet, usually in about 5mm/¼in of oil.
- ***Stir-frying*** is best done in a wok. The food is cut into even-size small pieces and is constantly moved around the pan as it cooks over a high heat.
- ***Dry-frying*** is done in a non-stick frying pan without added fat. The fat in the food melts and comes out as it cooks, so the food cooks in its own fat.

**Garnish** To decorate dishes with food such as herbs, slices of lemon, grated chocolate or berries.

▲ *Cake ingredients are often beaten together.*

▲ *There are many different ways of chopping food.*

▲ *Tuna and other fish can be easily flaked with a fork.*

▲ *Olive oil is often drizzled over foods before or after cooking.*

▲ Shallow-frying is usually done in a frying pan.

▲ Cream is often whipped until it is quite stiff.

▲ When a liquid is simmering you will see small bubbles.

▲ Sifting flour or other dry ingredients removes any lumps.

**Grate** To shred food by sliding it from the top to the bottom of a grater. Most graters have different-size holes on each side. Use the biggest ones for foods such as cheese and the smallest ones for lemon zest and nutmeg. Adult supervision is required.

**Grease** To brush or rub a baking tin (pan) or a dish with oil or butter so that cooked food doesn't stick.

**Knead** To make dough smooth by working the mixture with your hands on a floured surface. Bread dough must be kneaded vigorously for at least 5 minutes, but scone (biscuit) and pastry dough should be handled gently just until the dough forms a smooth ball, or it will become tough.

**Line** To put non-stick baking parchment in the base or base and sides of a cake tin (pan) so that the mixture doesn't stick. For small cakes or muffins put a paper case in each hole of a bun tray (shallow muffin pan) or muffin tray (pan).

**Mash** To pulp foods such as cooked potatoes or bananas until they form a smooth paste. This can be done with a potato masher or a fork.

**Melt** To heat a solid food, such as butter or chocolate, and make it liquid. Chocolate needs to be melted slowly in a heatproof bowl set over a pan containing a small amount of barely simmering water (known as a *bain marie*). The water should not touch the bottom of the bowl, or the chocolate may burn. Adult supervision is required.

**Purée** To squash fruit or cooked vegetables to make them smooth and sauce-like. Use a blender or food processor (adult supervision is required), or put the food in a sieve (strainer) set over a bowl and push it through with a wooden spoon.

**Sift** To push fine ingredients such as flour and icing (confectioners') sugar through a sieve or sifter into a large bowl to get rid of lumps.

**Simmer** To cook liquid so slowly that small bubbles just come to the surface. Adult supervision is required.

**Whisk or whip** To beat food using an electric mixer (adult supervision is required) or a whisk until it becomes stiff, in the case of cream or egg whites, or lump-free, in the case of sauces.

▲ Kneading should be done on a lightly floured surface.

▲ Take your time when melting chocolate.

▲ Line bun tins with colourful paper cases.

▲ Pushing fruit through a sieve creates a purée.

# Some useful equipment

There is an almost endless selection of gadgets and gizmos available for the kitchen, but many of these are not actually necessary for making the recipes in this book. This directory lists those that are most useful and will help you understand their uses.

► *Tools such as graters are vital for many recipes.*

### Scales and cups

There are three main types of kitchen weighing scales – balance scales, spring-loaded scales and electronic digital scales. Balance scales are the old-fashioned ones where you use a set of weights at one side and a bowl for the food at the other side. You put the correct amount of weights on one side and then put enough food in the bowl until both sides balance evenly.

▲ *Spring-loaded weighing scales*

Spring-loaded scales have a bowl to put the food in on top and a dial below that goes around as you add food. Always make sure that the pointer is at zero when the pan is empty. Then add the food to the pan until the pointer reaches the correct place and is steady. Electronic digital scales are accurate, even when you're weighing tiny amounts. Put a bowl on the scales, then press a button and add the food until it registers the correct amount.

Solid ingredients such as flour, rice, peas or chopped celery can be measured in a set of standard measuring cups from ¼ cup to 1 cup. Use the back edge of a knife to level off the ingredient in the cup.

### Measuring jug (cup)

Used for measuring liquids, a heatproof glass jug is better than plastic because it can hold hot liquids. A 600ml/1 pint/2½ cup jug is the most useful size. Crouch down so that your eyes are level with the jug, then pour in the liquid until you have the right amount. If you look from above the jug you'll end up with the wrong amount.

▼ *Measuring jug*

### Measuring spoons

These are used for measuring small amounts accurately, especially baking powder and spices. Spoonfuls in recipes are always level. To measure a level teaspoon accurately fill it and then run your finger or the back of a blunt knife across the top.

▲ *Measuring spoons*

### Bowls

▲ *Mixing bowls*

You need bowls in several sizes, including at least one large bowl, for mixing cakes and bread doughs, plus a medium one and a small one. Before you start a recipe make sure your bowl is going to be large enough to mix all the ingredients easily, without spilling food over the edge. This is especially important for mixing cakes and batters. Pyrex bowls are good because they are heatproof and fairly sturdy and you can see through them. The best bowls have rounded bottoms so that you can get to every bit of the mixture with your whisk, spatula or spoon.

### Sieve (strainer)

Used for sifting dry ingredients, such as flour, a sieve removes any lumps and helps add air into the mixture to make cakes lighter. You can also use a sieve to sieve (strain) sauces and purées to make them smooth, or drain small ingredients, such as rice or peas.

▲ *Metal sieve*

### Colander

This is essentially a large bowl with holes in it used for draining foods such as pasta or cooked vegetables, or for rinsing fruit and vegetables. Only adults should strain hot liquids. Always remember to put the colander in the sink or over a bowl or pan before you pour liquid through it.

▲ *Colander*

### Chopping boards

It's best to have several plastic chopping boards in different colours so that you can use different ones for each type of food. This means that any bacteria that is in raw meat or fish, or any strong odours, don't get passed on to other foods, such as fruit. There's nothing worse than a fruit salad tasting of onion! Ideally you should have a separate board for each of the following: raw meat, raw fish, cooked meats and cheeses, vegetables and fruit. Plus you need a wooden bread board for cutting bread and cakes. Always wash boards really thoroughly, especially after using them for raw meat or fish. Never cut food, using sharp knives, directly on a table or work surface or you'll cut and spoil it.

▲ *Chopping boards*

### Knives

If you're old enough to use sharp knives you will need at least two: a medium-size one, called a cook's knife, for chopping – about 25cm/10in long, with a 15cm/6in blade – and a small one with a serrated edge for cutting foods with smooth skins and cucumber. Always handle knives very, very carefully with an adult present. Ask an adult to sharpen them if they are blunt. It's actually safer to use a sharp knife than a blunt one because it will cut through food easily, so that you won't have to press hard before it will cut, and it won't slip.

▲ *Sharp knives*

### Peeler

Use a peeler to peel vegetables such as carrots and potatoes and fruit such as apples and pears. They are great for removing just the thin peel and not a thick layer of the fruit or vegetable. There are two main types of peeler, straight ones and Y-shaped ones. Most people find the Y-shaped type easier to use. Ask an adult to show you how to use the one in your kitchen but remember to always hold the piece of fruit or vegetable in one hand and peel with the other, making sure you keep your fingers well away from the sharp edge. You can peel away from you or towards you. Adult supervision is required.

▲ *Y-shaped peeler*

### Grater

Most graters have at least two cutting surfaces, but some special ones, called microplanes, only have one. Use the side with big holes for grating cheese and carrots and the side with fine holes for lemon zest, ginger and nutmeg. It's easiest to use a box grater, which has a handle on top and sits on a chopping (cutting) board, so that it doesn't slide about as you grate. Graters can cut fingers as well, so keep your fingers away from the edge. Adult supervision is required.

▼ *Box grater*

### Garlic crusher

A really handy tool for crushing garlic cloves without using sharp knives or getting your hands smelly, a crusher is easy to use – simply put a clove of garlic in the space in the crusher and press the handles together so the garlic comes out through the holes.

▲ *Garlic crusher*

### Cookie cutters

These metal or plastic shapes are used for cutting out biscuits (cookies) and scones. You need at least one round cutter to make biscuits but if you have lots of shapes and sizes you can make different shapes. They are also useful for cutting shapes out of slices of bread.

▲ *Cookie cutters*

## Rolling pin

A long, smooth, round, heavy bar, usually made of wood, a rolling pin is used for rolling out pastry or biscuit (cookie) dough, as well as for bashing biscuits to crumbs and flattening meat.

▲ *Rolling pin*

## Wooden spoons

Use a wooden spoon to stir food in pans and for beating cake mixtures. You will need two or three different sizes, so that you can use a small one in a small pan or bowl and a long one in a large pan or bowl. Some spoons have one straight edge, which is useful for getting right into the corners of pans when you're making sauces that get thicker as they cook.

▲ *Wooden spoons*

## Slotted spoon

A large metal spoon with holes in it, a slotted spoon is used to lift pieces of solid food out of pans, leaving the liquid behind in the pan.

## Ladle

A big spoon with a deep bowl and a long handle, a ladle is used for scooping soup, stews or sauces out of a pan or bowl.

▲ *Slotted spoon and ladle*

## Fish slice (metal spatula)

This metal tool has a flat end with holes in it and a long handle. It is used for lifting things off baking trays and sheets and out of frying pans and roasting tins (pans), so that any fat drains off through the holes. Fish slices are made in different shapes and sizes.

◄ *Fish slices*

## Spatula

Bendy rubber or plastic spatulas are used for scraping the sides of a mixing bowl to get all the mixture out so nothing is wasted. They are also useful for pushing food down into blenders.

▲ *Spatula*

## Tongs

Useful for turning pieces of food or removing them from a frying pan or skillet or from under the grill (broiler), tongs have long handles to keep your hands away from spitting fat. The easiest ones to use have scalloped edges on the gripping heads, which grip food well while you hold them safely.

▲ *Tongs*

## Wire whisk

There are two types of wire whisk – a balloon whisk where the wires make a round shape, and a coil whisk which has a sturdy wire shaped into a loop at the end, with a fine wire coiled all the way around it. Use for whisking eggs, cream or other liquids.

◄ *Balloon whisk*

## Citrus juicer

There are different types of juicer. The easiest one to use has a bowl underneath to collect the juice and a filter with holes in to catch the seeds. They can be glass or plastic. You can also get a wooden juicer on the end of a short handle. You insert the squeezer end into the halved fruit and twist so the juice flows out into a bowl underneath.

▼ *Lemon squeezer*

## Cooling rack

A large, flat wire rack on short legs, this is used to cool cakes and biscuits (cookies). With cakes, remove the lining paper before you put it on the rack, or it can be hard to remove. You can get cooling racks that stack on top each other, which are useful in a small kitchen or if you have more than one batch of food to cool.

▲ *Wire rack*

## Timer

This device is a great help because it's easy to forget how long things have been cooking when you're having fun in the kitchen. Always set the timer when a recipe gives a specific time. It counts backwards and pings when the time is up.

▲ *Timer*

## Food processor

This multi-functional machine has a main bowl with a lid and a variety of attachments, some of which are supplied with the original purchase, while others can be bought separately. It is very useful for finely chopping raw ingredients, such as onions, as well as for quickly combining ingredients. Adult supervision is required.

▲ *Food processor*

## Blender

This has a plastic or glass jug (pitcher) placed on a motorized base, which powers blades inside the jug. It is sometimes part of a food processor, but is also available as a stand-alone machine. Blenders can be used to purée fruits and cooked food. Adult supervision is required.

▲ *Blender*

## Electric mixer

Extremely useful for mixing cakes or whisking cream or eggs, hand-held electric mixers come with detachable whisks (beaters) and different speed settings. Adult supervision is required.

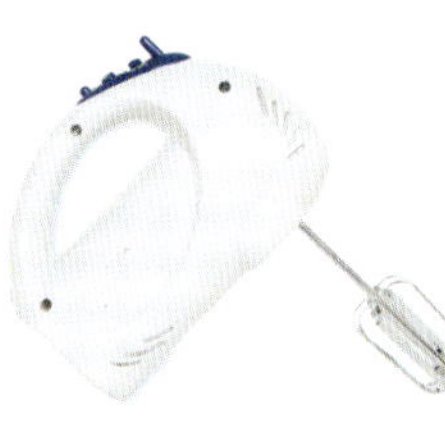

▲ *Electric mixer*

## Cake tins (pans)

There are many different types and sizes of cake tin (pan). Spring-loaded cake tins have a clip on the side and a removable base, while sandwich tins (layer cake pan) are shallower and in one whole piece.

## Bun and muffin tins (pans)

These are baking trays (sheets) with dents in them. Bun tins (shallow muffin pans) are used for cooking tarts, little cakes, mince pies and small Yorkshire puddings. Muffin tins (pans) have bigger, deeper holes. You can line them with paper cases. They are mostly metal, but you can also get bendy silicone ones.

▲ *Types of cake tin and a muffin tin.*

## Frying pans

Non-stick frying pans or skillets are best because food doesn't stick to them. You need a small frying pan, about 16cm/6¼in across at the base (bottom), for making omelettes or pancakes and a large one for frying foods such as vegetables and eggs. Always check with an adult that the tools you use for turning food won't damage the surface. Adult supervision is required when using heat.

◀ *Frying pans*

## Wok

A large, deep pan with rounded edges, this pan is used for stir-frying vegetables, meat and fish. A wok must be large so that there's plenty of room to move the food about. A flat base sits safely on the stove without moving around. Adult supervision is required.

▲ *Wok*

## Griddle irons (grills) or griddle (grill) pans

A flat, heavy metal plate that is part of some stoves, sometimes with a ridged base, is called a griddle iron. A griddle (grill) pan is a heavy frying pan with a ridged base. Flat griddle irons can be used for some scone (biscuit) recipes, while ridged ones are for fish or meat. Adult supervision is required.

▲ *Griddle pan*

## Pans

Used for heating and cooking all kinds of foods, pans are available in many sizes and materials. Ones with lids are best, because they let you control how quickly the food cooks and how much water evaporates during cooking. Adult supervision is required.

▲ *Saucepan with a lid*

# Some useful ingredients

There is an almost endless range of foods on sale in supermarkets and grocery stores. When buying ingredients for a recipe, it is important that you get exactly the right thing, so it is worth making a list. This directory covers some of the more commonly used foods.

► Chopping up fresh vegetables and fruit for different dishes is very satisfying.

## Fruit

There are loads of different types of fruit available in supermarkets and greengrocers, some of which you can buy all year, while others, such as strawberries, are only available at certain times of the year. Most are delicious simply chopped up and eaten raw, or they can be used to make a wide range of mouth-watering cakes, desserts, jams and other scrummy treats.

### PEELING AND CORING AN APPLE

1 Hold the apple in one hand and peel it with the other hand, using a vegetable peeler, starting from the stem end and peeling all the way round. Adult supervision is required.

2 Put the apple on a chopping (cutting) board, set a sharp knife in the middle and cut in half. Put each half on the board, cut-side down and halve again. Adult supervision is required.

3 Turn each quarter, flat-side down, and carefully slice away the core. Cut each quarter into three or four slices or into bitesize cubes, depending on what the recipe says.

**Apples** There are many types of apples and you probably have your own favourite, but for cooking purposes there are two types – eating apples and cooking apples. Despite their name, eating apples are often used in cooking, especially where you want the pieces to stay whole when they're cooked. Some of the nicest varieties of eating apples are Granny Smith, Gala, Braeburn and Cox's. Bramleys are cooking apples and they are great for making apple sauce, apple crumble and other dishes where you want the apple to become soft and pulpy. They have a sharper flavour than eating apples so you may need to add a little sugar.

▲ Granny Smiths

**Bananas** As bananas ripen they go from green to yellow and eventually get small brown spots on the skin. If you want to make a banana cake, let them sit in the fruit bowl until they've got lots of little brown spots on the skin. This will mean that they're riper, softer, sweeter and have a stronger banana flavour.

▲ Bananas

**Berries** From strawberries, raspberries and blackberries to blueberries and gooseberries, berries can be used in all manner of dishes. Eat them mixed with yogurt or on cereal, or you can stir them into hot porridge (oatmeal). They're also great added to muffins, crumbles or pies. You can also often buy dried or frozen berries if you can't find fresh ones.

▼ Raspberries

▲ Red cherries

**Cherries** Sweet and juicy, there are many different varieties of cherry, which vary in colour from yellow to bright red to dark red. They're at their best eaten raw, but they're also good in cooking.

You can buy a special gadget to pit cherries easily or you can use a small, sharp knife – although this is fussy and very messy. So if you don't have a gadet for pitting, it's easiest to cook them whole and let everyone spit the pits out. For cooking you can also buy frozen or canned pitted cherries.

**Stone fruits** Apricots, peaches, nectarines and plums are a real seasonal treat. These sweet fruits have a wonderful flavour and scent and are yummy eaten as they are, made into fruit salads, or baked on their own or as pies and tarts. The best way to remove the stones (pits) is to cut the fruits in half, twist to separate and then pull out the stone. When fresh ones are out of season, you can buy ready-to-eat dried types. These can be nibbled for a healthy snack or cut into pieces and added to cakes and other bakes. They can also be poached until soft in apple juice or syrup, then puréed.

▲ Peaches and nectarines

**Citrus fruits** From tangy lemons and sour limes to juicy oranges and aromatic grapefruits, citrus fruits are really useful in the kitchen. Lemons and limes are especially good, because the juice can be used for flavouring sweet and savoury dishes, for making salad dressings and for marinating meat and fish. The juice also stops chopped fruits, such as apples and pears, from going brown.

The zest (the coloured part of the rind) of lemons, limes and oranges contains oils that are full of flavour and can be used in cakes, puddings and marinades. Grate it off the fruit using the finest side of a grater. Unwaxed fruits are best if you're going to use the zest.

▲ Lemon

▲ Kiwi fruit

**Kiwi fruit** About the size and shape of an egg, kiwi fruit have a rough, hairy, skin. Inside, the sweet, soft flesh is a bright green colour flecked with little black seeds, which you eat.

**Lychees** These tropical fruits have a rough, pink, papery skin that you can't eat. Peel it off and inside you'll find a shiny, silky white fruit with delicious, exotic smelling flesh. Inside that is a large black stone (pit) that you can't eat.

▲ Lychees

**Mangoes** Juicy, large oval fruits with a big stone (pit) in the middle, mangoes are widely available. They are lovely in fruit salads or made into ice creams, and they're great added to savoury salads, especially with chicken or prawns (shrimp). The skin colour varies with the type of mango – it can be green or an orange colour with a pink blush. The flesh is a deep orange colour. To test if it's ripe, hold it in the palm of your hand and squeeze it very gently. If it gives slightly, it's ripe.

▲ Mango

## PREPARING MANGOES

1 Put the mango on a chopping board, on its side. Using a sharp knife, cut from top to bottom, either side of the stone (pit), so that you have two halves. Adult supervision is required.

2 Put one half on a board, cut-side up, and cut parallel lines, about 1cm/½in apart, cutting almost all the way through the flesh. Make similar cuts the other way to make little squares.

3 Holding the half in both hands, push the skin side upwards so the mango flesh opens up. Cut the flesh off the skin and it will come away in cubes. Repeat with the other half.

**Passion fruits** These tropical fruits are egg-shaped with a hard, inedible skin. Cut them in half and scoop out the pretty, delicious seeds and scented juicy flesh – it's lovely served on ice cream or stirred into Greek (US strained plain) or natural (plain) yogurt. Passion fruit are ripe and ready to eat when the skin is wrinkled.

▲ *Passion fruit*

**Pineapples** To test if a pineapple is ripe, smell it – if it smells sweet and fruity it will taste good. If it doesn't smell it won't have much taste and may be a bit dry. Alternatively, try plucking out one of the spiky leaves – if it comes out easily it's ripe. To prepare a pineapple ask an adult to help you cut off the skin and core because you need a large, sharp knife. It is delicious raw or sliced and barbecued.

▲ *Pineapple*

## Vegetables

Wonderfully versatile, tasty and healthy, there is a huge range of vegetables just waiting to be transformed into delectable dishes. Many, such as potatoes and carrots, will be familiar to you, while others, such as squashes, may be new.

**Potatoes** Filling and cheap, potatoes can be cooked in many different ways. If you are going to bake or boil them in their skins, ensure that you scrub them well with a brush first. They can also be peeled and boiled, mashed, fried, roasted, sautéed or used to thicken soups. There are lots of different varieties, and it usually says on the packet what they are suitable for. Waxy ones are best for salads, while fluffy types are best for mashing, roasting and baking.

▲ *Potatoes*

**Squashes** These vegetables come in different shapes and sizes and include courgettes (zucchini), butternut, acorn and spaghetti squashes, pumpkins and marrows (large zucchini). Except for courgettes, all need peeling and their seeds removing before use. They can be cut up, baked or boiled, or used to make soups or pies.

▲ *Pumpkin*

### CHOPPING AN ONION

1 Put the onion on a chopping board and cut it in half, from the top down to the hairy root end. Peel off the skin with your fingers. Cut off the root. Adult supervision is required.

2 Put one half on the board, cut-side down, and make parallel cuts, quite close together, right through to the board, going almost all the way to the top end, but leaving the top intact.

3 Turn the onion round and cut across these cuts in parallel lines all the way along the length, so that the onion is cut into small cubes. Repeat with the other half of the onion.

**Onions** One of the cornerstones of cooking, onions are infinitely versatile in the kitchen and crop up in a whole range of dishes, from soups, salads and pickles to casseroles and sauces. There are lots of types available, including small, sweet shallots, standard white onions, red onions, tender leeks, long, mild spring onions (scallions), and thin green chives.

▲ *Red, yellow and white onions*

**Garlic** Famous for its strong smell and flavour, garlic is one of the most frequently used flavourings in cooking. It can be roasted whole, or peeled and finely chopped or grated to be added raw to dips or cooked in other dishes.

▼ *Garlic*

**Broccoli** Bright green, tasty and very good for you, broccoli can be eaten in a number of ways – lightly steamed, raw and chopped in salads, or cooked and blended with a range of ingredients such as cream or cheese to make a nourishing soup.

▲ *Broccoli*

**Cabbage** There are many different types of cabbage, from small Brussels sprouts and mild white cabbage to leafy Savoy cabbage, vibrant red cabbage and Chinese pak choi (bok choy). All can be steamed, stir-fried or boiled. The white and red types are ideal for shredding and eating raw, while the softer green-leafed types are best cooked.

▲ *Brussels sprouts*

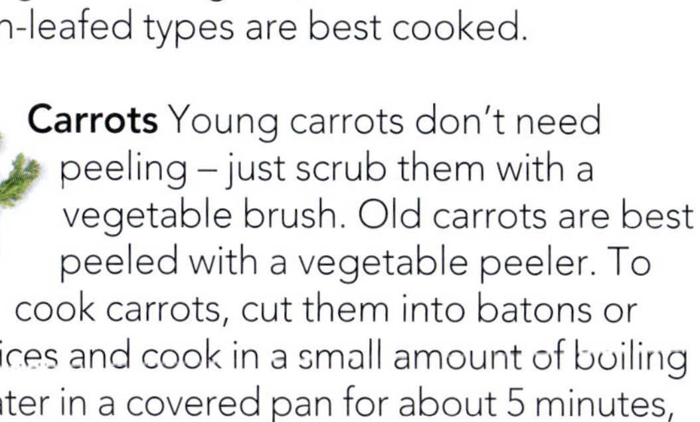

**Carrots** Young carrots don't need peeling – just scrub them with a vegetable brush. Old carrots are best peeled with a vegetable peeler. To cook carrots, cut them into batons or slices and cook in a small amount of boiling water in a covered pan for about 5 minutes, until just tender. Baby carrots can be cooked whole. Raw carrots can be grated and added to salads or cut into sticks and served with dips.

▲ *Carrots*

**Celery** Crunchy and flavoursome, celery is one of the vegetables that is used as the base for many stews, casseroles and soups. It is also tasty eaten raw with dips, such as hummus, for a healthy snack.

► *Celery*

**Peas** One of the few vegetables that is often better from frozen, green peas make an ideal accompaniment to most main dishes, or can be added to favourites such as shepherd's pie or lasagne for extra flavour. Sugar snaps and mangetouts (snowpeas) can be eaten whole and raw, or very lightly steamed for just a minute.

▲ *Mangetout, sugar snaps and peas*

**Beans** There are lots of types of beans, including French (green) beans, runner beans and broad (fava) beans. They are best eaten as fresh as possible.

▲ *Broad beans*

**(Bell) Peppers** Available in jewel-bright colours that make food look good, peppers are also very tasty. Red, yellow and orange peppers have a sweeter flavour than green ones, so they're the nicest to use in most recipes. Peppers are good eaten raw, in salads or with dips, or cooked in stir-fries, casseroles and sauces. To prepare them, cut them in half lengthways (lengthwise) and cut out any white pith and all the little white seeds.

▼ *Assorted peppers*

**Aubergines (eggplants)** Large, oval, glossy dark purple vegetables with cream coloured flesh, aubergines are always eaten cooked. They are good halved, stuffed and baked or sliced and then griddled, grilled or fried, or cut into chunks, drizzled with oil and baked.

▲ *Aubergines*

## MASHING POTATOES

1 Ask an adult to drain cooked potatoes, then return to the pan over a low heat for 30 seconds – this will help to drive off any excess water. Remove from the heat and mash the potatoes by crushing them under a potato masher until soft. Make sure all the potatoes are mashed.

2 Add a little milk and keep mashing until you have lovely, fluffy mashed potatoes. Season to taste with salt and ground black pepper. For a change, you could also add a heaped teaspoon of mustard, some grated Cheddar cheese or some chopped chives.

▲ Spinach

**Spinach** If you're using spinach in a recipe, you'll be surprised by how much the recipe says you need. This is because a large amount of fresh spinach reduces to a really small amount when it's cooked. Fresh spinach needs to be washed well before you cook it. Put it in a large bowl of cold water and swish it around with your hands to rinse it. Then lift it out and put it in your largest pan. Don't add any water – you can cook it with just the water that clings to the leaves. Put the lid on the pan, cook for 2 minutes, then give it a stir and cook for another 2 minutes or until it's wilted and soft. Baby leaf spinach is lovely in salads. You can buy it already washed in bags.

**Salad leaves** There are many salad leaves, including a variety of lettuce, peppery rocket (arugula), lamb's lettuce (mâche), watercress and Asian leaves, such as mizuna. They make wonderful salads or can be added to sandwiches.

*▲ Rocket and lamb's lettuce*

**Tomatoes** There are many types of tomato – tiny, medium and huge ones, round ones and oval ones. You can even get yellow tomatoes as well the usual red ones. But for most of the recipes in this book, you can use whatever tomatoes you happen to have. Cherry tomatoes are tiny and sweet and make a great snack. Vine-ripened tomatoes have the best flavour. Plum tomatoes are the oval-shaped ones, which are wonderful for cooking because they have less seeds and juice than other tomatoes and loads of flavour. Beef tomatoes are the huge round ones – they're great sliced in salads or hollowed out, stuffed and baked.

*▲ Clockwise from left: beef tomatoes, vine-ripened tomatoes, cherry tomatoes and standard tomatoes*

Canned tomatoes are cheap and very versatile, and because they're picked and canned when they're ripe they often have a better flavour than fresh ones. For cooking it's easiest to buy canned, chopped or whole tomatoes.

### PEELING TOMATOES

Put the tomatoes in a large heatproof bowl and ask an adult to cover with boiling water. Leave for exactly one minute (count to 60), then lift out of the water and pierce the skin of each tomato with a small sharp knife. You should be able to peel the skin off easily.

## Herbs

All sorts of herbs can be used in recipes. Among the most commonly used are rosemary, thyme, sage, mint, oregano, coriander (cilantro), parsley and basil. Some, such as rosemary and sage, need to be cooked in a dish, while others, especially basil, are delicious raw in salads or on pizzas.

*▲ Basil*

## Spices

It is difficult to have every spice, but some, such as black pepper, cumin seeds, coriander seeds, paprika, ground mixed spice (allspice), nutmeg, ground ginger and cinnamon are essential for any cook. In order to prolong their flavour, keep them in airtight containers.

*▲ Cinnamon sticks and ground mixed spice*

## Meat, poultry and fish

There are too many types of meat, poultry and fish available to list them all here, but in general it is important that you use the type specified in the recipe as the cooking time will have been calculated for that variety. It is worth paying a little extra for good-quality foods, as both the flavour and the texture will be better.

*▼ Selection of fish and other seafood*

## Dairy and eggs

There are many types of milk, cream, yogurt and eggs available, and they are used in all kinds of recipes.

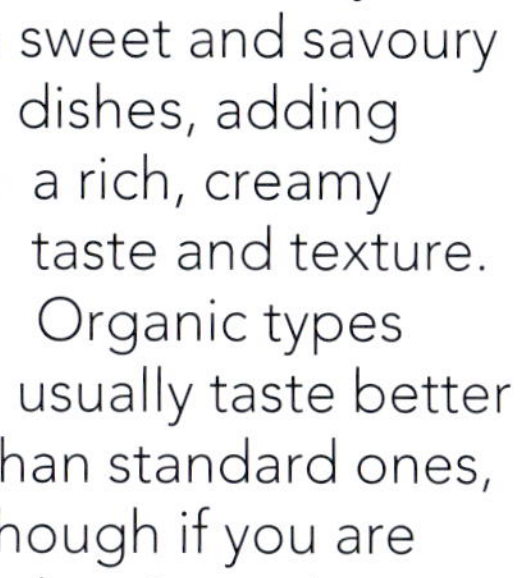

▲ Clockwise from left: milk, whipped cream and single cream

**Milk, cream and yogurt** These everyday ingredients are widely used in sweet and savoury dishes, adding a rich, creamy taste and texture. Organic types usually taste better than standard ones, although if you are cooking with them then it won't matter too much which you use. Full-fat (whole) versions will be creamiest, although semi-skimmed or low-fat types are perfectly acceptable for cooking. There are three main types of cream: single (light) cream, for pouring; whipping cream, for whipping; and double (heavy) cream, for pouring or whipping. Use whichever is listed in the ingredients.

**Butter** There are two main types of butter – salted and unsalted. Unsalted butter is often best for cakes and biscuits (cookies), while the salted type is best for spreading.

▲ Butter

▲ Parmesan cheese

**Cheese** From hard, strong varieties, such as Cheddar, and Parmesan to soft, mild ones, such as brie or creamy marscarpone, cheese can be used in all kinds of savoury and sweet dishes. Some, such as Cheddar or mozzarella, are perfect for melting, while others, such as feta or halloumi, are better crumbled or sliced and served raw or just lightly cooked. Use whichever type is recommended in the recipe.

**Eggs** Boiled, poached, fried, scrambled, baked or beaten and used in all kinds of recipes, eggs are a mainstay of every kitchen. Most of the recipes in this book use medium (US large) hen's eggs, but duck and quail eggs are also delicious, especially when hard-boiled and used in salads.

▲ Quail's eggs

### GRATING CHEESE

Use a box grater that will sit on a board without wobbling. Hold it in your left hand (right if you're left-handed) and the cheese in the other hand. Rub the cheese down the side with the biggest holes, keeping your fingers away from the cutting edge. Adult supervision is required.

## Nuts

From cashew nuts, peanuts, pine nuts and walnuts to brazil nuts, hazelnuts, almonds and macadamia nuts, most types of nut are delicious eaten raw as a healthy snack, or they can be chopped up and incorporated in a wide range of sweet and savoury dishes, including stir-fries, crumbles, brownies and flapjacks (cereal bar).

▲ Pine nuts and hazelnuts

## Seeds

▲ Sunflower seeds

A great addition to breakfast cereals, biscuits (cookies), salads, stir-fries and breads, there is a wide range of seeds that can be used in the kitchen. Common types include sunflower seeds, pumpkin seeds, poppy seeds and sesame seeds.

## Noodles

Made from either egg and wheat (egg noodles) or rice flour (rice noodles) and available fresh or dried, noodles are a great accompaniment to stir-fries or can be added to soups for extra texture. There are various thicknesses available, and wholemeal (whole-wheat) types, but all are quick and easy to cook. Simply follow the method in the recipe and read the packet instructions.

▲ Different types of egg noodles

▲ Dried penne

## Pasta

One of the quickest and easiest things to cook, there are two main types of pasta – fresh and dried, and these can be standard or wholemeal (whole-wheat). They come in many shapes and sizes, from small macaroni to large conchigliette. Most fresh pasta is made with egg yolks, making it richer, so you need less. Cook all types according to the packet instructions, in a large pan of lightly salted boiling water. Then simply add your favourite sauce and enjoy!

## Rice

There are several different types of rice, including long grain rice, easy-cook rice, brown rice, basmati rice, paella rice, risotto rice, jasmine rice and pudding (short-grain) rice. It's important to use the one mentioned in the recipe, because they look, taste and feel different when cooked, and also take different amounts of time to cook. If in doubt read the information on the pack – it will tell you what the rice is best for.

▲ Jasmine rice

## Flour

There are four main types of flour and it's important to use the correct type. Plain (all-purpose) white flour is sometimes called 'soft' white flour. It is used for making shortcrust pastry, biscuits (cookies), sauces, muffins, batter and some cakes.

Strong white bread flour is made from wheat that has a high gluten (a protein in wheat) content. This means that when it's mixed with water and kneaded it becomes stretchy and elastic, so it's ideal for making bread, pizza, yeast buns and puff pastry.

Self-raising (self-rising) flour is plain white flour with a raising (rising) agent, such as baking powder, added. The proportion of raising agent is the same in all brands of self-raising flour, and is the correct amount to make many types of cake, such as fairy cakes (cupcakes) and sponge cake. If a recipe needs more or less raising agent it will use plain flour and baking powder or self-raising flour with added baking powder.

Wholemeal (whole-wheat) flour is made from the whole grains of wheat, and is brown, higher in fibre and healthier than white flour. It is used to make bread, scones (biscuits) and cakes.

▲ Wholemeal flour

## Raising (rising) agents

Baking powder is a raising agent that is added to cakes with the flour to make them rise well. It is made of an alkaliusually bicarbonate of soda (baking soda) and an acid-reacting chemical, such as cream of tartar, plus some dried starch or flour to bulk it out. When it is mixed with liquid and heated in the oven it forms tiny air bubbles, which make the cake mixture expand and rise. You only need tiny amounts so it's vitally important to measure it accurately. Some recipes call for bicarbonate of soda and cream of tartar instead of baking powder, or in addition to it.

▲ Baking powder and bicarbonate of soda

## Sweet things

There are lots of different types of sweet sugar. They can taste different, and the way they mix into recipes and react to cooking varies, so use the correct type.

**White sugar** There are three main types of white sugar: granulated, caster (superfine) and icing (confectioners') sugar. Granulated sugar is the ordinary type that you add to tea. In cooking it's used for making syrups and in recipes where it is dissolved in hot water. You can use golden (unbleached) or white granulated sugar.

▲ Granulated and caster sugar

Caster sugar has finer grains that dissolve more easily in mixtures than the coarser grains of granulated sugar. It is used in cakes, biscuits (cookies) and puddings. You can use golden caster sugar or ordinary white caster sugar in these recipes. Icing sugar is ground to a fine powder. As its name suggests, it is used to make all types of icing.

**Brown sugars** Unrefined brown sugars have fine grains and a caramel flavour. They can be light brown, dark brown, muscovado or demerara. Soft dark brown has a stronger flavour than soft light brown sugar. If you don't have this type, replace it with caster (superfine) sugar. Muscovado is considered to have the best flavour, while raw demerara, with its large crystals, is used to give a crunchy topping.

▲ Muscovado and demerara sugar

▲ Clear honey

**Honey** The world's oldest sweetener, honey is a totally natural product, made by bees. Clear, runny honey is best for cooking because it mixes in more easily. Set, cloudy honey is best for spreading on bread because it is thicker. You can buy a huge range of special honeys, such as heather honey and orange blossom honey. These are named after the flowers from which the bees collected the nectar and each one has its own special flavour. For cooking it is a waste to buy expensive honey – any clear, runny honey is fine.

**Golden (light corn) and maple syrup** Sweet golden syrup is a by-product from sugar manufacture. Maple syrup is made from the sap of the sugar maple tree. Both are used as sweeteners on porridge (oatmeal), pancakes and ice cream, as well as in recipes, such as gingerbread.

▲ Golden syrup

▲ Black treacle

**Black treacle (molasses)** Dark, thick treacle is another by-product of sugar manufacturing. It has a stronger flavour and a dark, almost black colour. It is used in gingerbread and fruit cakes.

**Chocolate** The ultimate treat for those with a sweet tooth, chocolate can be used to make many luscious puddings, tarts, cakes and biscuits (cookies). It is worth using the best-quality you can find, because it will taste much better. If using dark chocolate, look out for packets that say '70% cocoa solids', because it will have the best flavour. Milk chocolate is less strong and tends to be creamier. White chocolate is very sweet. All are available in blocks or as drops, and can be melted and used in recipes.

▲ White, milk and dark chocolate drops

▲ Cocoa powder

**Cocoa powder** Used for making hot chocolate and for flavouring cakes, biscuits (cookies) and desserts, cocoa has a strong flavour and is not sweetened, so you usually need to use it with some added sugar.

## MELTING CHOCOLATE

1 Break the chocolate into squares and put into a heatproof bowl that is the right size to sit on top of a pan.

2 Quarter fill the pan with water and put the bowl on top.

3 Heat gently until simmering. The water should never touch the bottom of the bowl. Stir occasionally until the chocolate has just melted. Immediately remove the bowl from the pan. Adult supervision is required.

## Oils

Used for most types of frying, drizzling and in salad dressings, oil is a key ingredient in the kitchen. Olive oil has a strong flavour that is great for salad dressings and for cooking dishes from Mediterranean countries. Some types are very expensive. These are called virgin and extra virgin olive oils, and they are made from the first pressing of the olives. For most of the recipes in this book, ordinary oil is fine.

Sunflower and vegetable oils are all-purpose oils without much flavour. They are great for dishes such as roast potatoes and chips (fries).

Sesame oil has a strong flavour that is good in Asian cooking, while walnut oil has a nutty flavour that is lovely for salad dressings.

▲ Olive oil

▲ Rice and malt vinegar

## Vinegars

There are lots of different types of vinegar. Malt vinegar is the brown type. There's an all-purpose white vinegar. Others include cider, red wine, white wine, balsamic and flavoured vinegars, which are used for salad dressings, and there are also rice vinegar and sherry vinegar, used in Asian cooking.

# Basic techniques

A range of skills is required in the kitchen. Most of these are easy, and all of them will become easier as you practise. This section explains how to do some of the most useful techniques, helping you to make a range of delectable treats!

▶ *Knowing how to do simple tasks, such as beating, will enable you to make all sorts of dishes.*

## Measuring fluids

Accurate measuring is essential for really successful cooking, especially with baking. For tiny amounts use proper measuring spoons – you can buy them cheaply from supermarkets or hardware stores. They come in a set and should have spoons that measure out 1.25ml/¼ tsp, 2.5ml/½ tsp, 5ml/1 tsp and 15ml/1 tbsp. If a recipe says a dessertspoon it means 10ml/2 tsp.

For large amounts use a see-through measuring jug (pitcher), which can be made from plastic or a special glass called Pyrex, which is heatproof. You need to make sure the jug is on a level surface, then squat down until your eye is level with the markings on the side and pour in the liquid slowly until it reaches the right level. If you pour it in and look down into the jug, you'll find that a measurement that looks right from above is different when you look at it from eye level. Try with some water and see! You can now get special sloped measuring jugs that give you accurate readings from above that are easier to use.

▲ *Measuring jug and spoons*

## Measuring dry ingredients

In some countries, dry ingredients, such as flour and sugar, are measured by weight using scales. In others, such as the USA and Australia, they are measured using special measuring cups. These are very easy to use: simply scoop up the dry ingredients and shake until the surface is level, then check the amount against the gauge on the side. All the recipes will work perfectly using metric or imperial or cup measurements, but you must use only one type for the whole of a recipe.

Small amounts, such as spices and baking powder, need to be measured with measuring spoons. Unless a recipe says otherwise, the spoonfuls must be level. Run the blunt side of a knife along the top to level it. Do this over a sheet of kitchen paper (paper towel) so you can tip any excess back into the jar.

▲ *Measuring cups and spoons*

### MEASURING SPOONFULS

Fill the correct size measuring spoon right to the top. For sticky things such as golden (corn) syrup, lightly grease the spoon with a little butter first. Then the syrup or honey will just slide off.

### USING SCALES

Make sure the pointer is at zero when the pan is empty – there will be a screw or dial that you can use to adjust it. Then add the food to the pan until the pointer reaches the correct place and is steady.

## Breaking an egg

Have a mixing bowl ready to catch the egg. Hold the egg with both hands and tap it firmly in the centre on the rim of the bowl so that the shell cracks all the way through. Holding the egg over the mixing bowl, carefully enlarge the crack by pulling the halves apart until the shell is almost in two pieces. Let the egg yolk and white fall into the bowl positioned below and discard the egg shell. Repeat the process with more eggs as many times as necessary.

*▲ Breaking an egg is easy once you know how, and is an invaluable skill in the kitchen.*

## Whipping cream

The only creams that you can whip successfully are double (heavy) cream and whipping cream. Single (light) cream won't whip. Make sure the cream and bowl are chilled before you start. Use a balloon or coil whisk or an electric hand mixer (on the slowest speed and with adult supervision) and whip until the cream is just floppy and holds its shape. Don't over-whip or it will start to separate and look grainy, and if you keep over-whipping you'll end up with butter!

## Grinding in a mortar and pestle

Put the ingredients in the mortar (bowl) and grind by pressing and rolling firmly with the pestle (stick), until you have a coarse powder. If you don't have a proper pestle and mortar you can cheat by putting the spices in a small bowl and grinding them with the end of rolling pin.

*▲ Pestle and mortar*

### SEPARATING AN EGG

1 Have two mixing bowls ready. Carefully tap the egg on the side of a bowl and gently pull the two halves apart over the bowl, so that just the egg white starts to fall into the bowl.

2 Tip the yolk from one half of the egg shell to the other several times so that the yolk stays whole and all of the white falls into the bowl. Tip the yolk into the other bowl.

**Top tip:** If you're separating more than one egg, you need three bowls. One for the yolks, one for the separated whites and one to break the egg over. This way if the yolk breaks and you get a bit of yolk in the white, you only spoil one egg (you can use it for scrambled egg). Egg whites won't whisk successfully if they have any yolk in with them.

### WHISKING EGG WHITES

1 Put the egg whites in a spotlessly clean, completely dry, large bowl and make sure the whisk is clean and dry as well. Holding the bowl firmly with one hand, tilt the bowl slightly and start whisking, using a circular motion, with the other hand.

2 Whisk the whites until they form stiff peaks. If using an electric mixer, start at slow speed for the first minute, then increase the speed to high. If you're brave, you can test if they are done by turning the bowl upside-down. If they're whisked enough they'll stay in the bowl.

**Top tip:** You can use a balloon whisk, rotary whisk (beater) or electric mixer, but if you're whisking more than two egg whites at a time it's best to use an electric mixer – for this adult supervision is required.

## Zesting a lemon, lime or orange

The zest is the coloured part of the rind of the lemons, limes and oranges and it's full of flavour. To remove the zest, wash the fruit under cold running water and then dry it thoroughly with kitchen paper (paper towels). Grate it on the finest side of a grater, taking care to remove only the coloured zest and not the white pith below it, which tastes slightly bitter. Sharp graters grate flesh as well as food, so take care to keep your fingers away from the cutting edge! Adult supervision is required.

Sometimes a recipe mentions a strip of zest. This is usually added to syrups while they are simmering to flavour them and then taken out before eating. To peel off a strip of zest, run a vegetable peeler along the length of the fruit, using just enough pressure to remove the coloured zest. Adult supervision is required.

## Creaming butter and sugar

It's important that butter or margarine is soft before you start. Put them in a large bowl and beat together with a wooden spoon or electric mixer, until the mixture is smooth with a soft, light, creamy texture. A wooden spoon is fine for small amounts, but for large amounts it will be hard work and it's easier with an electric mixer. Adult supervision is required.

When you cream a mixture really well the sugar grains look smaller and the mixture becomes much lighter in colour. If you use caster (superfine) sugar, it makes the mixture change from yellow to a pale cream colour. This is because there will be lots of tiny air bubbles trapped in it. These air bubbles expand as the cake cooks and help to make the cake light.

Keep stopping and scraping down the sides of a bowl with a spatula, so any mixture that gets stuck on the sides of the bowl goes back into the main mixture and it gets creamed together evenly.

► *Creaming can be done with a spoon or an electric mixer.*

### RUBBING IN FLOUR AND BUTTER

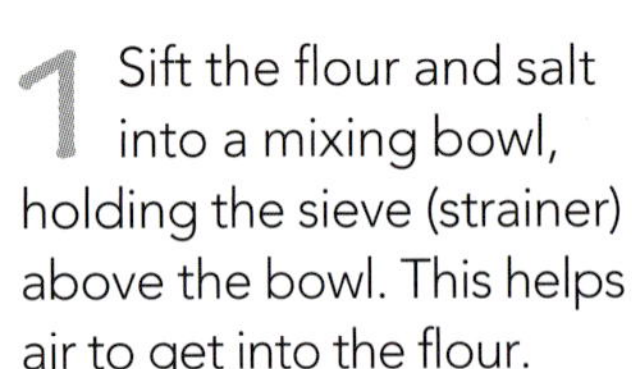

1 Sift the flour and salt into a mixing bowl, holding the sieve (strainer) above the bowl. This helps air to get into the flour.

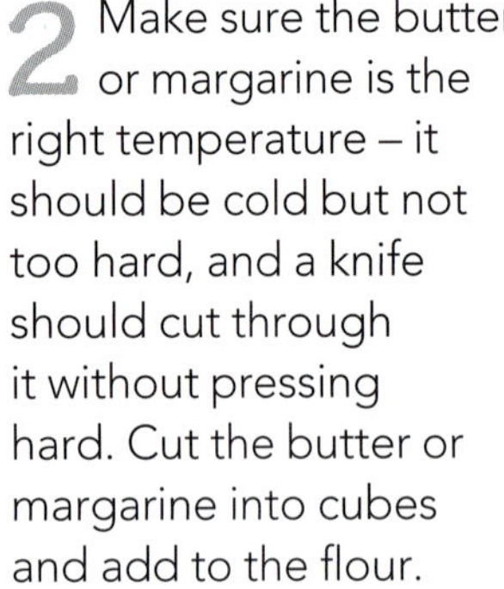

2 Make sure the butter or margarine is the right temperature – it should be cold but not too hard, and a knife should cut through it without pressing hard. Cut the butter or margarine into cubes and add to the flour.

3 Lift a little flour and butter out of the bowl and rub between the tips of your fingers and thumbs, letting it fall back into the bowl. Keep doing this until the pieces of butter get smaller and smaller and look like crumbs.

**Top tip: You need cold hands to rub in well. If your hands are warm, put them under cold running water for 1 minute.**

## Folding in ingredients

Always use a large metal spoon (tablespoon size) to fold in. You need to gently cut the spoon down through the mixture and then bring it back to the top, folding it over as you do. Be as gentle as possible so you don't knock out the air in the mixture. Stop as soon as it's evenly mixed.

## All-in-one cakes

You can make great fairy cakes, cup cakes, sponge cakes and light fruit cakes using a very easy all-in-one method. First, sift the flour and baking powder into a large bowl, holding the sieve (strainer) above the bowl. This ensures the flour and baking powder are evenly mixed and adds air to the flour. Add all the other ingredients (butter or margarine, sugar and eggs plus any flavouring, such as vanilla, if used) and beat with a wooden spoon or an electric mixer (adult supervision is required), on slow speed, until everything is thoroughly mixed. Then STOP.

## GATHERING PASTRY DOUGH TOGETHER

1 After rubbing the flour and fat together sprinkle a little very cold water evenly over the surface and mix with a round bladed knife until it starts to come together in clumps.

2 Add about 15–20ml/1–1½ tbsp ice cold water for every 115g/4oz/1 cup flour. Start by adding 15ml/1 tbsp and then add a tiny bit more if necessary.

3 Gather the dough together with your fingertips and thumb – you should have a firm dough that leaves the sides of the bowl clean. Shape into a smooth ball.

4 Wrap the dough in clear film (plastic wrap) and, if you have time, chill for at least 30 minutes. This isn't essential if you're in a hurry, but it makes the pastry easier to roll.

## KNEADING DOUGH

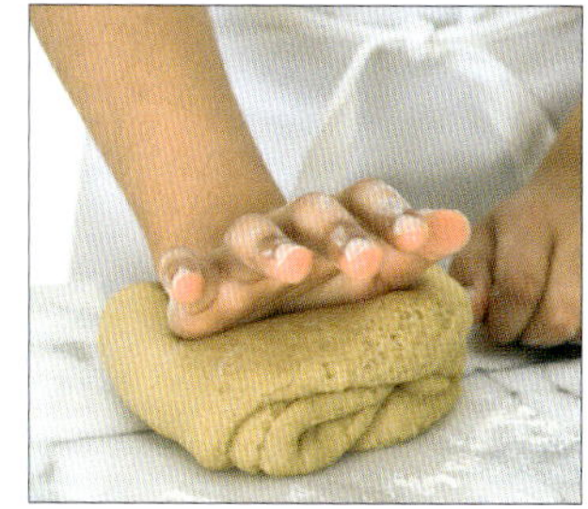

1 Put the dough on a lightly floured surface and lightly dust your hands and the surface of the dough with flour. Flatten the dough slightly then fold it over towards you.

2 Press the heels of your hands into the dough and push it away from you to stretch it. Turn the dough a quarter of the way around and push and stretch again.

3 Turn it another quarter way around and repeat again. Keep doing this, dusting the work surface with a little more flour if necessary, for 5–10 minutes until the dough feels elastic and smooth.

4 Depending on what type of dough it is, you may need to leave it to rise, shape it into balls or roll it out with a rolling pin.

## Rolling out dough

Lightly dust a clean, dry work surface and a rolling pin with flour or, if rolling out icing, use icing (confectioners') sugar. Put the ball of pastry, dough or icing on the surface and flatten it slightly with the rolling pin. Roll the pin over the pastry away from you, pressing just enough to make the dough longer, but not to squash it. Then give the dough a quarter turn and roll it away from you again.

Carry on doing this, lightly dusting the work surface and rolling pin with more flour or icing sugar when necessary, until the dough is slightly thicker than a coin. By turning the dough a quarter way around between rolls you should end up with a round shape.

If you want a square shape, pat the dough into a square with your hands before you start rolling. For an oblong pat it into a square and then roll twice away from you, turn and roll once, then turn again and roll twice.

► *Rolling out pastry, biscuit (cookie) dough or fondant icing is easy if you know how.*

## LINING A PASTRY DISH

1 Roll out the pastry to the correct thickness and until it is about 5cm/2in larger than the dish you want to line. Check by placing the dish on top of the pastry occasionally as you roll.

2 Put the rolling pin in the middle of the round, then gently lift one end of the pastry and fold it over the rolling pin. Move it on the rolling pin to fit over the top of the dish.

3 Using your fingers, press the pastry into the dish to line the base and the sides, easing it right into the corners. Let any excess hang over the edge. Roll the rolling pin over the top to cut off the excess.

4 Prick the base of the pastry with a fork. Cover with clear film (plastic wrap) and chill for 20 minutes to help to stop it shrinking as it cooks. Preheat the oven to 200°C/400°F/Gas 6.

5 Cut out a large piece of baking parchment and place it on top of the pastry. Cover with baking or dried beans or rice and bake for 10 minutes. Uncover the pastry and ask an adult to return to the oven for 5 minutes.

► *Try to stamp out as many shapes as you can from a piece of rolled-out pastry or dough, then re-roll the leftovers and stamp out more shapes.*

## Stamping out shapes

Once you have rolled out your pastry or biscuit (cookie) dough, you may want to stamp out different shapes. To do this, dip the chosen cutter into flour, tap to knock off any excess, then position the cutter on the rolled-out dough. Press down firmly with the palm of your hand, but do not twist or move the cutter if you can help it. Lift up the cutter, remove the shape and place it on a baking tray (sheet). Repeat all over the dough, stamping out as many shapes as possible. Gather the remaining dough together, then roll it out again and stamp out more shapes. Continue until you have used all the dough.

## Greasing and lining a tin

If the recipe just says to grease a tin (pan), you simply need to smear the inside with butter or oil. You can use a small piece of baking parchment, a pastry brush or your fingers. Make sure you go right into the corners.

To line the base and sides of a cake tin, cut a strip of baking parchment a little wider than the height of the tin and long enough to go all the way around the tin. Make a fold all the way along the long side, 1cm/½in in, and then make small cuts all the way along the folded part, about 1cm/½in apart – like a frill (fringe). Put the tin on a sheet of baking parchment and draw around the outside with a pencil. Cut out with scissors. Lightly grease the inside of the tin. Put the strip of paper inside the edge to line the sides, with the frill at the bottom and the fold in the corner. Put the paper base shape in to cover the snipped bit.

## Piping icing

Once you have cooked your biscuits (cookies) or your cake, you may want to decorate the top with icing. You can buy special icing pens from cake decorating shops, but it is very easy to make your own icing and use a piping (pastry) bag, which you can either buy or make. Whichever you use, you will need special icing nozzles (tips), which fit into the smaller pointed end of the icing bag. Ensure these are securely in place before you start.

Spoon a few tablespoons of icing into the bag, and gently squeezing the open end until the icing is pushed down to the nozzle end. Over a piece of baking parchment, gently squeeze a bit harder until some of the icing comes out. Have a practice go on to the paper before you start decorating, then pipe squiggles, lines, words, flowers or whatever you like on to the surface. Refill the bag as and when needed.

▼ *Let your imagination run wild when decorating biscuits and cakes.*

### LINING THE BASE OF A CAKE TIN

1 Put a small piece of butter in the tin (pan) and, using either a piece of scrunched up baking parchment or your fingers, rub it all over the inside surface of the tin to coat.

2 Put the tin on a piece of baking parchment and draw around the outside edge with a pencil to mark the shape. Carefully cut out the parchment circle, with adult supervision.

3 Place the parchment circle in the base of the tin, pushing it down, right into the edge so that the bottom is fully covered and there are no gaps. Pour in the cake mixture.

### MAKING A PAPER PIPING BAG

1 With adult supervision, cut a square piece of non-stick baking parchment 23cm/9in x 23cm/9in. Fold in half diagonally. Cut along the fold so that you have two triangular pieces.

2 Place the triangle flat with the longest side facing you. Mark the centre of the longest side by pinching the paper. Take one corner edge of the longest side up to fit on to the top corner.

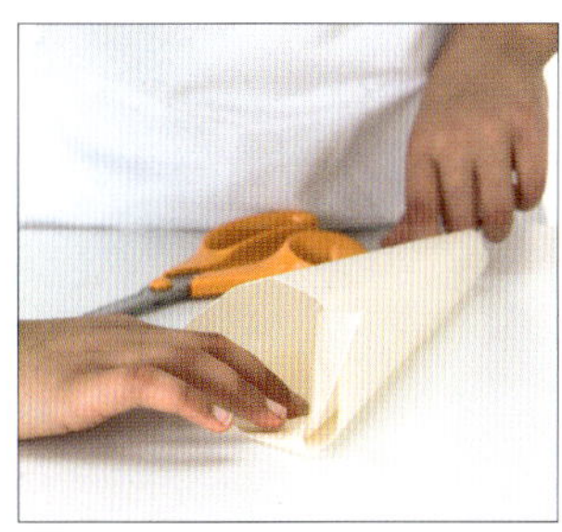

3 Hold it there while you do the same with the other corner, wrapping it right around. You will now have a cone shape with a narrow end. Secure with tape. Slip the icing nozzle inside.

# Menu ideas

Whether you want a quick bite after school or to try your hand at creating a feast for your family, there is a recipe in this book to suit the occasion. These sample menus show what sort of recipes may go together to make up a tasty meal, but you can easily adapt them yourself.

## Winter warmer

- Tomato and bread soup
- Fish and cheese pies
- Rice pudding
- Vanilla milkshake

▲Tomato and bread soup p123

▲ Fish and cheese pies p137

▲ Rice pudding p157

## Light summer meal

- Hummus
- Tuna pasta salad
- Banana and toffee ice cream
- Ruby red lemonade

▲ Hummus p40

▲ Tuna pasta salad p85

▲ Banana and toffee ice cream p162

## After-school fast feast

- Ham and pineapple pizza
- Chunky veggie salad
- Baked bananas
- Totally tropical

▲ Ham and pineapple pizza p95

▲ Chunky veggie salad p82

▲ Baked bananas p161

## Picnic

- ✱ Ciabatta sandwich
- ✱ Speedy sausage rolls
- ✱ Apricot and pecan oaty bars
- ✱ Banana muffins
- ✱ Fresh orange squash

◀ Speedy sausage rolls p41

◀ Banana muffins p194

▶ Ciabatta sandwich p67

▶ Fresh orange squash p176

## Barbecue

- ✱ Thai pork patties
- ✱ Cheesy burgers
- ✱ Colourful chicken kebabs
- ✱ Lemony couscous salad
- ✱ Pineapple sorbet on sticks
- ✱ Fruit punch

◀ Cheesy burgers p153

◀ Lemony couscous salad p55

▶ Colourful chicken kebabs p108

▶ Pineapple sorbet on sticks p163

## School cake sale

- ✱ Gingerbread people
- ✱ Stripy biscuits
- ✱ Peanut and jam cookies
- ✱ Luscious lemon cake
- ✱ Pecan squares
- ✱ Creamy fudge

◀ Gingerbread people p226–7

◀ Luscious lemon cake p201

▶ Stripy biscuits p241

▶ Pecan squares p204

# Party ideas

One of the best things about parties is that it gives you a good excuse to indulge in all your favourite treats. Instead of making all the food yourself, you could ask a few of your friends to come round and help you – getting the party going early!

## Birthday bonanza

- Crazy rainbow popcorn
- Sandwich shapes
- Mini ciabatta pizzas
- Jolly jellies
- Balloon cake
- Rainbow juice and fruit slush

### BIRTHDAY PARTY THEMES

- Wild animals
- Clowns
- Pirates
- Fairies
- Witches and wizards
- Dragons and monsters

◄ Sandwich shapes p215

▲ Crazy rainbow popcorn pp212–13

◄ Balloon cake pp234–5

◄ Mini ciabatta pizzas p218

► Jolly jellies p230

## COOK'S TIPS

► It is always best to write down your party ideas well in advance and talk them through with a parent or guardian. That way you can ensure you have all the right ingredients ready.

► Cut food up quite small so that everyone can try a bit of each food and less gets wasted.

► Pack up any leftovers and pop them into goody bags.

► Decorate paper tablecloths yourself, following the theme of the party.

## Halloween

- Tortilla squares
- Chicken mini-rolls
- Spooky cookies
- Chocolate witchy apples
- Jack-o'-lantern cake
- What a smoothie

◀ *Tortilla squares p219*

◀ *Spooky cookies p236*

▶ *Chocolate witchy apples p237*

▶ *Jack-o'-lantern cake pp238–9*

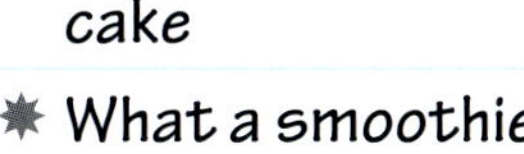

## Midnight feast

- Cheese and ham tarts
- Eggstra special sandwich selection
- Sweet toast toppers
- Butterscotch brownies
- Strawberry shake

◀ *Cheese and ham tarts p46*

◀ *Eggstra special sandwich selection pp42–3*

▶ *Butterscotch brownies p60*

▶ *Strawberry shake p185*

## Breakfast party

- Cantaloupe melon salad
- Ham and tomato scramble
- Buttermilk pancakes
- French toast
- Strawberry and apple cooler

▶ *Cantaloupe melon salad p171*

▶ *Ham and tomato scramble p75*

◀ *French toast p193*

◀ *Strawberry and apple cooler p181*

# Packed lunches and picnics

Whether you are at school, going on a day trip or simply want something delicious to enjoy outside in the park, portable food should be easy to eat, tasty and able to withstand travel. This selection of savoury and sweet treats will provide you with plenty of inspiration, so roll up your sleeves and get cooking!

# Hummus

Originally from the Middle East, hummus is perfect for a packed lunch or picnic, served with pitta, crusty bread (which you could toast in advance) or vegetable sticks.

*serves* 4

## ingredients

- **chickpeas**, 400g/14oz can, drained
- **garlic cloves**, 2
- **sea salt**, a pinch
- **tahini** (see Cook's Tip) or **smooth peanut butter**, 30ml/2 tbsp
- **olive oil**, 60ml/4 tbsp
- **lemon**, juice of 1
- **cayenne pepper**, 2.5ml/½ tsp, plus a little extra for sprinkling
- **sesame seeds**, 15ml/1 tbsp

## tools

- **Colander or sieve (strainer)**
- **Blender or food processor**
- **Spoon or spatula**
- **Small non-stick frying pan**

1 Put the chickpeas in a colander or sieve and rinse under cold water.

2 Put the chickpeas in a blender or food processor with the garlic and a pinch of salt. Blend until almost a paste. Adult supervision is required.

3 Add the tahini or peanut butter and blend until fairly smooth. Very carefully, with the motor running, pour in the oil and lemon juice. Adult supervision is required.

4 Stir in the cayenne pepper. If the mixture is too thick, stir in a little water.

5 With adult supervision, heat a frying pan.

6 Add the sesame seeds. Cook for 2–3 minutes, shaking the pan, until golden. Adult supervision is required. Sprinkle some cayenne over the hummus. Serve, or spoon into a plastic container.

## COOK'S TIPS

▸ The hummus will keep in a sealed plastic container in the refrigerator for 2–3 days.

▸ Tahini is a paste made from sesame seeds traditionally used in hummus. It has a thick, creamy texture very similar to peanut butter.

*tahini*

# Speedy sausage rolls

Instead of being covered in pastry, these sausage rolls are wrapped in slices of bread, brushed with butter then baked until crispy. They make perfect picnic food.

makes 18

## ingredients

- **multigrain white bread**, 8 slices
- **cocktail sausages**, 225g/8oz
- **butter**, 40g/1½oz/3 tbsp
- **carrot** and **cucumber sticks**, to serve

## tools

- Chopping board
- Large serrated knife
- Non-stick baking sheet
- Small pan
- Pastry brush
- Oven gloves

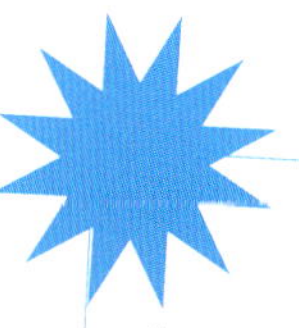

## COOK'S TIPS

▶ Spread a little tomato relish, tomato ketchup or mild mustard over the bread before wrapping it around the sausages, to give a sharper flavour.

▶ Melt butter in the microwave on Full Power (100%) for 30 seconds. Adult supervision is required.

1 Preheat the oven to 190°C/375°F/Gas 5.

2 On a chopping board, trim the crusts off the bread. Cut into slices that are a little shorter across the width than the length of the cocktail sausages. Adult supervision is required.

3 Wrap each piece of bread around a sausage, with the ends of the sausage sticking out. Place on a baking sheet.

4 Put the butter or margarine in a pan and heat gently until just melted. Adult supervision is required.

5 Brush the melted butter or margarine over the sausage rolls.

6 Bake in the oven for 15 minutes, until the bread has browned and the sausages are cooked through. Ask an adult to remove them from the oven.

7 Cool, then serve with some carrot and cucumber sticks or pack into a sealable plastic container to transport.

# Eggstra special sandwich selection

A delicious sandwich makes a convenient and quick packed lunch, picnic or after-school snack. Egg is always a favourite, so why not learn the basics with these two great fillings.

serves 6

## ingredients

- **white** or **brown (whole-wheat) bread**, 12 thin slices
- **butter**, 50g/2oz/¼ cup, at room temperature

*for the egg and cress filling*

- **small eggs**, 2
- **mayonnaise**, 30ml/2 tbsp
- **cress**, ½ carton
- **salt** and **ground black pepper**

*for the egg and tuna filling*

- **small eggs**, 2
- **canned tuna in oil**, 75g/3oz, drained
- **paprika**, 5ml/1 tsp
- **lemon juice**, a squeeze
- **salt** and **ground black pepper**
- **cucumber**, 25g/1oz piece, peeled and thinly sliced

eggs

cress carton

### COOK'S TIP

▶ Cress is easy to grow and is great to add to any sandwich filling. Look for cress seeds (or if you prefer a more peppery flavour look for mustard and cress seeds) in supermarkets and garden centres. Sprinkle the seeds on to wet kitchen paper (paper towels) and leave in a light, warm place to grow. They will sprout within a few days.

## tools

- ✱ Large pan
- ✱ Large metal spoon
- ✱ Chopping board
- ✱ Large sharp knife
- ✱ 2 mixing bowls
- ✱ Wooden spoon
- ✱ Fork
- ✱ Serrated bread knife
- ✱ Butter knife

1 To make the **egg and cress filling**, fill a pan with water and bring up to the boil. Carefully lower the eggs into the water on a large draining spoon. Bring the water back up to the boil and boil the eggs for 8 minutes. Adult supervision is required.

2 Ask an adult to place the pan under cold running water for a few minutes, until the eggs are cool.

3 Remove from the water and leave until completely cold, then tap on a hard surface to crack the shell and peel it away.

4 Put the eggs on a chopping board and use a large knife to finely chop the eggs. Adult supervision is required.

5 Place the eggs in a bowl and add the mayonnaise, cress and salt and pepper. Mix well.

6 To make the **egg and tuna filling**, cook the eggs in the same way as for the egg and cress filling.

7 Put the tuna in a bowl and flake with a fork. Mix the chopped eggs with the tuna, paprika, lemon juice, salt and pepper.

 = Watch out! Sharp or electrical tool in use. (!) = Watch out! Heat is involved.

**8** **To make the sandwiches**, remove the crusts from the bread using a serrated knife on a chopping board. You can keep the crusts on, if you like. Adult supervision is required. Spread the butter over the bread, then lay half of the slices on the board.

**9** Spread the egg and cress filling over one half of the bread slices and the egg and tuna filling over the other half, topping with the cucumber. Top with the remaining bread slices and press down gently. Cut into triangles. Adult supervision is required.

**10** If eating immediately, arrange all the sandwiches on a plate and garnish with tomato wedges and parsley. Alternatively, if you have made them for a lunch box or picnic, wrap the sandwiches tightly in clear film (plastic wrap) and chill in the refrigerator until required. The sandwiches will keep fresh for 4–5 hours.

# Ham and mozzarella calzone

A calzone is a kind of 'inside-out' pizza – the dough is on the outside and the filling on the inside. It's a great way of making pizzas for picnics or packed lunches. They travel well wrapped in paper or clear film.

*serves* 2

## ingredients

- **pizza dough mix**, 1 packet
- **ricotta cheese**, 115g/4oz/½ cup
- **freshly grated Parmesan cheese**, 30ml/2 tbsp
- **egg yolk**, 1
- **chopped fresh basil**, 30ml/2 tbsp
- **salt** and **ground black pepper**
- **mozzarella cheese**, 75g/3oz, cut into small cubes
- **cooked ham**, 75g/3oz, finely chopped
- **olive oil**, for brushing

## tools

- **2 non-stick baking sheets**
- **2 mixing bowls**
- **Wooden spoon**
- **Rolling pin**
- **Metal spoon**
- **Pastry brush**
- **Small knife**
- **Oven gloves**
- **Palette knife**
- **Wire rack**

1 Preheat the oven to 220°C/425°F/Gas 7. Lightly oil two non-stick baking sheets.

2 Make the dough according to the packet instructions. Knead briefly until smooth on a lightly floured surface, then shape into a ball.

3 Divide the dough in half and place on a floured surface. Using a rolling pin, roll out each piece to an 18cm/7in round.

4 Mix together the ricotta and Parmesan cheeses, egg yolk, basil, salt and pepper in a large bowl with a spoon.

5 Spread the cheese mixture over half of each round, leaving a 2.5cm/1in border. Sprinkle the mozzarella and ham on top.

6 Brush the edges of the dough with water and fold the uncovered dough over the filling.

7 Press the edges to seal. Carefully lift on to baking sheets. Brush with oil and make a small hole in the top of each. Bake for 15–20 minutes, until golden.

8 Ask an adult to remove the calzone from the oven and lift it on to a wire rack with a palette knife. Serve warm, or leave until cold and wrap in clear film (plastic wrap) to transport.

*basil leaves*

★★ give it a try | time to cook: **30–35 minutes** | preparation: **20 minutes**

# Tomato and cheese pizza

This yummy pizza is easy and great fun to make. It is delicious warm or cold, making it a great choice for a tasty, portable packed lunch.

*serves* 2–3

## ingredients

- **pizza base (crust)**, 1, about 25–30cm/10–12in diameter
- **olive oil**, 30ml/2 tbsp
- **mozzarella**, 150g/5oz, thinly sliced
- **ripe tomatoes**, 2, thinly sliced
- **fresh basil leaves**, 6–8
- **freshly grated Parmesan cheese**, 30ml/2 tbsp
- **ground black pepper**

*mozzarella*

### for the tomato sauce

- **olive oil**,15ml/1 tsp
- **onion**, 1, finely chopped
- **garlic cloves**, 2, peeled and finely chopped
- **chopped tomatoes**, 400g/14oz can
- **tomato purée (paste)**, 15ml/1 tbsp
- **chopped fresh herbs**, such as **oregano**, **parsley**, **thyme** or **basil**, 15ml/1 tbsp
- **sugar**, a pinch
- salt and **ground black pepper**

### tools

- Chopping board
- Medium knife
- Large pan
- Wooden spoon
- Non-stick baking sheet
- Pastry brush
- Oven gloves

1 To make the tomato sauce, heat the oil in a large pan, add the onion and garlic and fry for 5 minutes. Add the tomatoes, tomato purée, herbs, sugar and seasoning. Stir to combine, then simmer for 15–20 minutes, until thick. Remove from the heat. Adult supervision is required.

2 Preheat the oven to 200°C/400°F/Gas 6. Place the pizza base on a baking sheet and brush with 15ml/1 tbsp of the oil.

3 Spread over the tomato sauce, leaving a small gap around the edge. Put the mozzarella and tomato on top.

4 Roughly tear the basil leaves and sprinkle over the pizza with the grated Parmesan cheese. Drizzle over the remaining olive oil and season with plenty of black pepper.

5 Bake in the oven for 15 minutes, until crisp and golden.

6 Ask an adult to remove the pizza from the oven. Leave to cool slightly, then cut into wedges. Eat warm or leave to cool completely, then wrap in clear film (plastic wrap) or put in a plastic container to transport.

COOK'S TIP

▶ Make double the quantity of the sauce and freeze it.

# Cheese and ham tarts

These tasty little tarts are a clever twist on ham and cheese sandwiches, and will make a welcome change.

*makes* 12

## ingredients

for the pastry

- **plain (all-purpose) flour**, 115g/4oz/1 cup
- **chilled margarine**, 50g/2oz/4 tbsp, cubed

for the filling

- **mild cheese**, 50g/2oz/½ cup
- **ham**, 2 thin slices, chopped
- **frozen corn**, 75g/3oz/½ cup
- **egg**, 1
- **milk**, 120ml/4fl oz/½ cup
- **salt** and **ground black pepper**
- **paprika**, a pinch
- **carrot** and **cucumber sticks**, to serve

## tools

- Mixing bowl
- Palette knife or wooden spoon
- Rolling pin
- 7.5cm/3in round fluted cookie cutter
- 12-hole non-stick bun tin (muffin pan)
- Grater
- Whisk or fork
- Oven gloves

1 **To make the pastry**, place the flour in a bowl and add the margarine. Using your fingertips, rub the margarine into the flour until the mixture resembles breadcrumbs. Gradually add 20ml/4 tsp cold water and mix to a smooth dough with a palette knife or wooden spoon.

2 Form the dough into a ball, then wrap in clear film (plastic wrap) and chill for 20 minutes.

3 Preheat the oven to 200°C/400°F/Gas 6. Put the pastry on to a floured surface and lightly knead. Using a rolling pin, roll out the pastry until thin.

4 Stamp out 12 circles with a cookie cutter, re-rolling the pastry trimmings as necessary. Press into the holes of a bun tin. Chill for 30 minutes.

5 **To make the filling**, grate the cheese. Adult supervision is required. Mix with the ham and corn.

6 Divide the cheese mixture among the tarts. Beat together the egg, milk and seasoning with a whisk or fork. Pour into the tarts and sprinkle the tops with paprika.

7 Cook in the oven for 12–15 minutes, until risen and browned. Ask an adult to remove from the oven and cool slightly before loosening and sliding out with a palette knife.

8 Serve warm or cold with carrot and cucumber sticks, or wrap in foil or clear film to transport.

 = Watch out! Sharp or electrical tool in use. (!) = Watch out! Heat is involved.

# Spicy sausage tortilla

This chunky Spanish omelette is a meal in one pan and is delicious eaten warm or cold. Colourful and filling, it is perfect for a lunchtime treat.

*serves* 4–6

## ingredients

- **chorizo** or **spicy sausages**, 175g/6oz
- **olive oil**, 75ml/5 tbsp
- **potatoes**, 675g/1½lb, peeled
- **onions**, 275g/10oz, peeled and halved
- **eggs**, 4
- **chopped fresh parsley**, 30ml/2 tbsp
- **grated Cheddar cheese**, 115g/4oz/1 cup
- **salt** and **ground black pepper**
- **chopped tomatoes** and **basil**, to serve (optional)

## tools

- ✱ Chopping board
- ✱ Medium sharp knife
- ✱ 20cm/8in non-stick frying pan with an oven-proof handle
- ✱ Draining spoon
- ✱ Mixing bowl
- ✱ Fork
- ✱ Spoon
- ✱ Palette knife
- ✱ Oven gloves

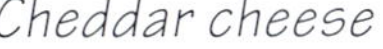

*Cheddar cheese*

1 Thinly slice the sausages on a chopping board. Heat 15ml/1 tbsp of the oil in the frying pan. Add the sausage and fry until golden brown and cooked through. Adult supervision is required.

2 Lift out with a draining spoon, drain on kitchen paper. Set aside.

3 Thinly slice the potatoes and onions. Adult supervision is required.

4 Add 30ml/2 tbsp oil to the pan. Fry the potatoes and onions for 2–3 minutes, turning frequently. Cover and cook for 30 minutes, turning occasionally, until softened. Adult supervision is required.

5 In a mixing bowl, beat the eggs with a fork then mix in the parsley, cheese, sausage and seasoning. Gently stir in the potatoes and onions.

6 Wipe out the frying pan with kitchen paper, add the remaining 30ml/2 tbsp oil and heat on high. Add the potato and egg mixture and cook over a very low heat, until the egg begins to set. Adult supervision is required.

7 Meanwhile, ask an adult to preheat the grill (broiler) to hot.

8 When the base of the tortilla has set (check by lifting up one side), place under the grill for 2 minutes, until golden. Adult supervision is required.

9 Cut into slices. Serve with tomatoes and basil, if you like. Or, cool and wrap in clear film (plastic wrap) to transport.

# Popeye's pie

serves 4

Popeye was a famous cartoon character who ate lots of spinach to make him really strong. Tuck into this crunchy layered pie at lunchtime and you too can have bulging muscles!

## ingredients

- **oil**, for greasing
- **fresh spinach**, 900g/2lb, stalks removed, (see Fact File)
- **butter**, 115g/4oz/½ cup
- **mature (sharp) Cheddar cheese**, 50g/2oz, grated
- **feta cheese**, 115g/4oz/⅔ cup, drained
- **salt** and **ground black pepper**
- **filo (phyllo) pastry**, 275g/10oz
- **mixed ground cinnamon**, **ground nutmeg** and **ground black pepper**, 10ml/2 tsp of each

## FACT FILE

### SPINACH

As well as large, slightly tough spinach leaves supermarkets and grocers now sell a tender young leaf variety that is ideal for eating raw in salads. Spinach is very nutritious (especially when it is eaten raw as none of the nutrients are destroyed by cooking) and it contains lots of important vitamins and minerals. It is very easy to prepare and doesn't take very long to cook, and in this recipe you get to squish it in your hands.

spinach leaves

## tools

- **Small, deep-sided roasting pan**
- **Colander**
- **Large, deep frying pan with lid**
- **2 mixing bowls**
- **Grater**
- **Small pan**
- **Pastry brush**
- **Clean, damp dish towel**
- **Fork**
- **Oven gloves**

1 Preheat the oven to 160°C/325°F/Gas 3. Brush the inside of a roasting pan with a little oil. Put the spinach in a colander and wash. Drain. With adult supervision, melt 25g/1oz/2 tbsp of butter in a frying pan.

2 Add the spinach. Season. Cover and cook for 5 minutes, until wilted. Adult supervision is required.

3 Ask an adult to drain the spinach, cool, then squeeze to remove as much liquid as possible.

4 Put the grated cheese in a large bowl, then crumble the feta cheese over it. Add the salt and ground pepper and stir to mix. Gently melt the remaining butter in a small pan. Remove from heat. Adult supervision is required.

5 Unfold the pastry so the sheets are flat. Peel off a sheet and use to line part of the base of the tin.

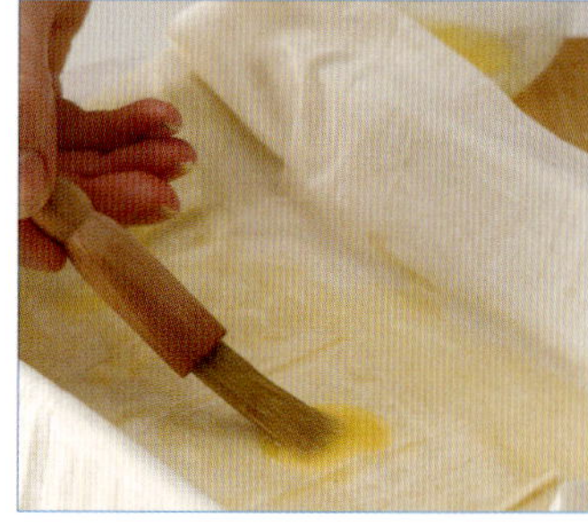

6 Brush the pastry with melted butter. Keep the remaining sheets covered with a damp dish towel.

 = Watch out! Sharp or electrical tool in use.  = Watch out! Heat is involved.

7 Continue to lay filo pastry sheets across the base and up the sides of the tin, brushing each time with butter, until two-thirds of the pastry has been used. Don't worry if the sheets flop over the top edges – they will be tidied up later.

8 Put the cool, squeezed spinach in the mixing bowl and break up any clumps with a fork. Add to the bowl containing the cheeses and mix to combine thoroughly.

9 Spoon the mixture into the pastry-lined tin and spread out. Fold the pastry edges over the filling.

10 Crumple up the remaining sheets of pastry and arrange them over the top of the filling.

11 Brush the pastry with the remaining melted butter and sprinkle the mixed spices over the top.

12 Put in the oven and bake for 45 minutes. Raise the temperature to 200°C/400°F/Gas 6. Cook for 10–15 minutes more. Ask an adult to remove from the oven and leave to cool in the tin for 5 minutes. Cut into squares and serve, or leave to cool and wrap up to transport.

# Tomato and pasta salad

Pasta salads are great for packed lunches, as they are very portable and filling. This one contains roasted tomatoes and peppery rocket for a colourful taste sensation.

serves 4

## ingredients

- **ripe baby Italian plum tomatoes**, 450g/1lb, halved lengthways
- **extra virgin olive oil**, 75ml/5 tbsp
- **garlic cloves**, 2, cut into thin slivers
- **salt**, a pinch
- **dried pasta shapes**, such as **shells**, **butterflies** or **spirals**, 225g/8oz/2 cups
- **balsamic vinegar**, 30ml/2 tbsp
- **sun-dried tomatoes in olive oil**, 2 pieces, drained and chopped
- **sugar**, a large pinch
- **rocket (arugula)**, 1 handful, about 65g/2½oz
- **salt** and **ground black pepper**

## tools

- Chopping board
- Small sharp knife
- Roasting pan
- Large pan
- Colander
- Large mixing bowl
- Large spoon or whisk

1 Cut the tomatoes in half lengthways. Adult supervision is required. Arrange, cut-side up, in a roasting pan. Drizzle 30ml/2 tbsp of the olive oil over them and sprinkle with the slivers of garlic. Season.

2 Preheat the oven to 190°C/375°F/Gas 5.

3 Place in the preheated oven and roast for about 20 minutes, turning once, until the tomatoes are soft and the skin is turning golden. Ask an adult to remove from the oven and set aside to cool.

4 Meanwhile, halfway through the cooking time, two-thirds fill a large pan with water and a pinch of salt. Bring up to the boil. Add the pasta and bring back to the boil. Cook for 8–10 minutes, or according to packet instructions, until just tender (al dente). Adult supervision is required.

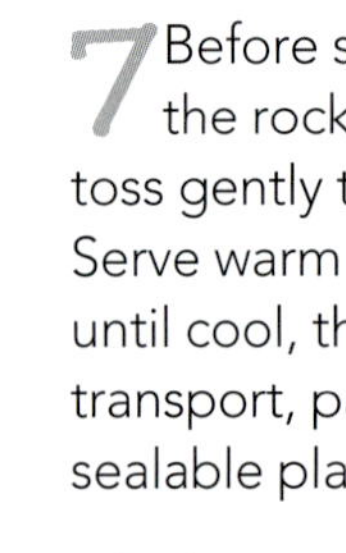

5 Put the remaining oil in a bowl with the vinegar, sun-dried tomatoes, sugar and a little salt and pepper to taste. Stir to mix.

6 Ask an adult to drain the pasta. Add it to the bowl of dressing and toss to mix. Add the roasted tomatoes and mix gently.

7 Before serving, add the rocket leaves and toss gently to combine. Serve warm or leave until cool, then chill. To transport, pack into a sealable plastic container.

### COOK'S TIP

▶ If you are in a hurry, you can make the salad with halved raw tomatoes instead.

 = Watch out! Sharp or electrical tool in use. = Watch out! Heat is involved.

# Chicken pasta salad

Packed with colourful, crunchy veg and juicy chunks of cold roast chicken, this scrummy salad is perfect for using up Sunday's leftover chicken.

*serves* 4

## ingredients

- **salt**, a pinch
- **short pasta**, such as **mezze rigatoni**, **fusilli** or **penne**, 350g/12oz
- **olive oil**, 45ml/3 tbsp
- **cold cooked chicken**, 225g/8oz (see Cook's Tip)
- **small red** or **yellow (bell) peppers**, 2 (about 200g/7oz)
- **spring onions (scallions)**, 4
- **pitted green olives**, 50g/2oz/⅓ cup
- **mayonnaise**, 45ml/3 tbsp
- **Worcestershire sauce**, 5ml/1 tsp
- **wine vinegar**, 15ml/1 tbsp
- **salt** and **ground black pepper**
- **fresh basil leaves**, a few, to garnish

## tools

- Large pan
- Colander
- Mixing bowl
- Wooden spoon
- 2 chopping boards
- Medium knife

1 Two-thirds fill a large pan with water and a pinch of salt. Bring up to the boil. Add the pasta and bring back to the boil. Cook for 8–10 minutes, or according to packet instructions, until just tender (al dente). Drain and rinse. Adult supervision is required. Put in the bowl. Toss with the olive oil.

2 Meanwhile, cut the chicken into bitesize pieces using a knife. Adult supervision is required. Remove any bones, skin or fat. Add to the bowl.

3 On another board, cut the peppers in half and remove the seeds and the membranes; discard.

4 Chop the peppers into bitesize pieces. Trim the spring onions and slice. Adult supervision is required.

5 Add, along with all the remaining ingredients to the bowl, season and mix. Garnish with basil to serve, or pack into a sealable plastic container to transport.

### COOK'S TIP

▶ If you don't have any leftover cooked chicken you can buy some or cook some from raw. With adult supervision, place the chicken in a pan and cover with water. Bring up to the boil, reduce the heat and simmer for 15–20 minutes or until cooked through.

# Mozzarella and avocado salad

This colourful salad is an Italian favourite and it's very quick to make. It can easily be packed in a sealed plastic container, making it great for picnics and packed lunches.

serves 2

## ingredients

- **mozzarella cheese**, 150g/5oz
- **large ripe plum tomatoes**, 4
- **salt**, to taste
- **large ripe avocado**, 1 (see Cook's Tip)
- **fresh basil leaves**, 12, or **fresh flat leaf parsley**, a small handful
- **extra virgin olive oil**, 45–60ml/3–4 tbsp
- **ground black pepper**

## tools

- ✱ Chopping board
- ✱ Large knife
- ✱ Teaspoon

1 Thinly slice the mozzarella and tomatoes. Adult supervision is required. Arrange the cheese and tomatoes on a plate and sprinkle over a little salt.

2 Cut the avocado in half along its length. Adult supervision is required. Hold each half and twist in opposite directions to separate.

3 Carefully lift out the stone (pit) from the middle of one half of the avocado. (You may need to do this by digging under it a little with a teaspoon.)

4 Gently peel away the skin with your fingers. If the avocado is ripe enough, it should come away fairly easily.

5 Slice crossways into half moons. Adult supervision is required.

6 Arrange on the tomatoes, then sprinkle over the basil or parsley. Drizzle over the oil, and add some pepper. Serve immediately, or, to transport, pack into a sealable plastic container.

## COOK'S TIP

► If you are planning to take this salad on a picnic or in a packed lunch, don't slice the avocado until as late as possible because it can turn brown after a while. To avoid this, just sprinkle the avocado with a little lemon juice.

avocado



(!) = Watch out! Sharp or electrical tool in use. (glove) = Watch out! Heat is involved.

# Tuna and bean salad

It's always worth keeping a couple of cans of beans and tuna handy in your store cupboard (pantry) to throw together this fantastic salad for a last-minute picnic. Juicy chunks of tomato and flecks of parsley add colour and extra flavour.

*serves* 4–6

## ingredients

- **cannellini** or **borlotti beans**, 2 x 400g/14oz cans (see Variations)
- **tuna fish**, 2 x 200g/7oz cans, drained
- **extra virgin olive oil**, 60ml/4 tbsp
- **lemon juice**, 30ml/2 tbsp
- **chopped fresh parsley**, 15ml/1 tbsp
- **ripe tomatoes**, 4, cut into chunks
- **spring onions (scallions)**, 3 (optional)
- **salt** and **ground black pepper**
- **fresh parsley**, chopped, to garnish

## tools

- Colander
- Large serving dish
- Medium bowl
- Fork
- Small bowl
- Spoon
- Chopping board
- Small knife

*canned tuna*

1 Pour the canned beans into a colander and rinse well under plenty of cold running water. Drain well. Place in large serving dish.

2 Put the tuna in a medium bowl and break into fairly large flakes with a fork. Arrange over the beans in the dish.

3 Make the dressing by combining the oil with the lemon juice in a small bowl. Season with salt and pepper, and stir in the parsley. Mix well.

4 Pour the dressing over the beans and tuna in the bowl and toss very gently with a fork. Add the chunks of tomato.

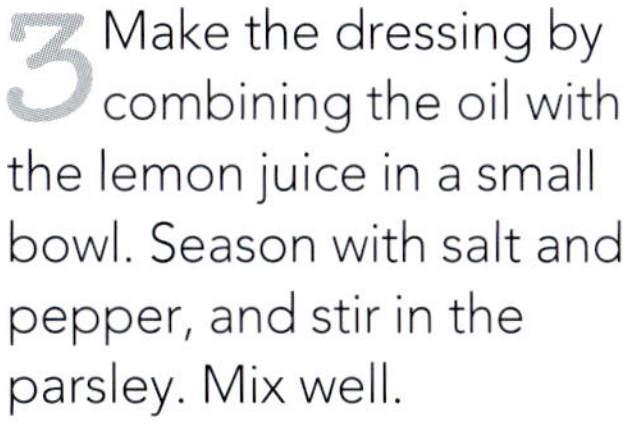

5 Thinly slice the spring onions, if using. Adult supervision is required. Scatter them over the salad and toss well to combine everything.

6 Garnish with parsley, if using, and serve or chill until ready to use. To transport, pack into a sealable plastic container.

## VARIATIONS

- Use any beans you might have handy in the store cupboard, such as mixed beans, chickpeas, butter beans or kidney beans, or a mixture of two or three different types.
- You can replace the tuna with any other canned fish, such as salmon, mackerel or sardines.

# Confetti salad

This salad gets its name from the little pieces of brightly coloured, chopped vegetables that are mixed in with cold rice. Perfect for a tasty meal on the go.

serves 6

## ingredients

- **long grain rice**, 275g/10oz/1½ cups
- **ripe tomatoes**, 225g/8oz
- **green (bell) pepper**, 1
- **yellow (bell) pepper**, 1
- **spring onions (scallions)**, 1 bunch
- **chopped fresh flat leaf parsley** or **coriander (cilantro)**, 30ml/2 tbsp

### for the dressing

- **olive oil**, 75ml/5 tbsp
- **sherry vinegar**, 15ml/1 tbsp
- **strong Dijon mustard**, 5ml/1 tsp
- **salt** and **ground black pepper**

## tools

- **Large pan**
- **Sieve (strainer)**
- **Large heatproof bowl**
- **Small sharp knife**
- **Colander**
- **Chopping board**
- **Medium sharp knife**
- **Whisk**
- **Small bowl**

1 Place the rice in a pan and cover with water. Bring up to the boil and cook for 10–12 minutes, or according to packet instructions, until just tender. Adult supervision is required.

2 Ask an adult to drain the rice. Rinse and drain again. Leave to cool.

3 Meanwhile, place the tomatoes in a heatproof bowl and ask an adult to pour boiling water from the kettle over them to cover. Leave for 5 minutes or until the skins soften and start to split (if they don't split, pierce them with the tip of a sharp knife and they should start to split).

4 Ask an adult to drain them in a colander, cool slightly, then peel away the skin with your fingers.

5 On a chopping board, cut the tomatoes into quarters. Carefully cut out the seeds and discard. Chop into chunks. Adult supervision is required.

6 Cut the peppers in half and cut out the seeds and membranes; discard. Dice the peppers. Trim and slice the spring onions. Adult supervision is required.

7 **To make the dressing,** whisk all the ingredients together in a small bowl.

8 Transfer the rice to a large serving bowl with the tomatoes, peppers and spring onions. Add the herbs and the dressing, season and mix well. Serve or chill until required. To transport, pack into a sealable plastic container.

 = Watch out! Sharp or electrical tool in use.

 = Watch out! Heat is involved.

# Lemony couscous salad

Couscous is a lovely light and fluffy grain that is perfect for making salads as it absorbs all of the delicious flavours. It makes a really quick lunch box treat.

serves 4

## ingredients

- **vegetable stock**, 450ml/¾pt/scant 2 cups
- **couscous**, 275g/10oz/1⅔ cups
- **small courgettes (zucchini)**, 2
- **black olives**, 16–20
- **flaked (sliced) almonds**, 25g/1oz/¼ cup, toasted (optional)

### for the dressing

- **olive oil**, 60ml/4 tbsp
- **lemon juice**, 15ml/1 tbsp
- **chopped fresh coriander (cilantro)**, 15ml/1 tbsp
- **chopped fresh parsley**, 15ml/1 tbsp
- **ground cumin**, a pinch
- **cayenne pepper**, a pinch

## tools

* Small pan or heatproof jug (cup)
* Large heatproof bowl
* Fork
* Chopping board
* Medium sharp knife
* Wooden skewer
* Whisk
* Small bowl

1 With adult supervision, put the stock into a pan and bring up to the boil. Or, put it in a heatproof jug and heat in the microwave for 90 seconds, until boiling.

2 Meanwhile, place the couscous in a large heatproof bowl. Ask an adult to pour over the stock.

3 Stir the couscous with a fork, then set aside for 10 minutes until the stock has been absorbed and the couscous has fluffed up.

4 Meanwhile, trim the courgettes and cut them into pieces about 2.5cm/1in long. Slice into thin strips. Adult supervision is required.

5 If the olives have stones (pits) in them, push them out with a skewer. Cut the olives in half. Adult supervision is required.

6 Fluff up the couscous with a fork, then mix in the courgette strips, pitted black olives and flaked almonds, if using.

7 To make the dressing, whisk the olive oil, lemon juice, coriander, parsley, cumin and cayenne together in a small bowl. Stir into the salad and toss gently. Serve immediately or chill until required. To transport, pack into a sealable plastic container.

*black olives*

# Fabulous fruit salad

Tropical fruit is perfect for picnic and packed lunch fruit salads as it stays firm and fresh for quite a long time and always has a tasty refreshing flavour.

serves 4

## ingredients

- **small pineapple**, 1
- **kiwi fruit**, 2
- **ripe mango**,1
- **watermelon**, 1 slice
- **peaches**, 2
- **bananas**, 2
- **tropical fruit juice**, 60ml/4 tbsp

kiwi fruit

## tools

- ✱ Chopping board
- ✱ Large sharp knife
- ✱ Small sharp knife
- ✱ Mixing bowl
- ✱ Vegetable peeler

1 Ask an adult to help you slice the base and top off the pineapple. Stand upright. Cut away the skin by 'sawing' down. Using the tip of a small, sharp knife, cut out the 'eyes' (dark round pieces). Cut the pineapple in half lengthways, then cut out the core. Chop into bitesize pieces. Put them in a bowl.

2 Use a vegetable peeler to remove the skin from the kiwi. Cut in half lengthways, then into wedges. Add to the bowl.

3 Peel the mango with the peeler, then stand on a board and cut down to create slices. Cut these into smaller pieces. Adult supervision is required.

4 Cut the watermelon into slices, then cut off the skin; discard. Cut the flesh into chunks, then remove the seeds. Adult supervision is required.

5 Cut the peaches in half, remove the stones (pits) and cut into wedges. Peel then slice the bananas. Adult supervision is required.

### COOK'S TIP

▶ To make a coconut cream to serve with the salad, add toasted desiccated (dried) coconut to softly whipped cream.

6 Add all the fruit to the bowl and gently stir in the fruit juice. Cover tightly with clear film (plastic wrap) and chill for 30 minutes before serving. To transport, pack into a sealable plastic container.

 = Watch out! Sharp or electrical tool in use.  = Watch out! Heat is involved.

# Yogurt pots

Spoon some yogurt into a suitable container then create your favourite topping to stir in at school. Make a batch of each so you can mix and match!

*serves* 2

## ingredients

- **natural (plain) yogurt**, 150ml/¼ pint/⅔ cup
- **a topping of your choice**

*for the raspberry and apple purée*

- **eating apple**, 1, peeled and chopped
- **raspberries**, 115g/4oz

*for the apricot compote*

- **ready-to-eat dried apricots**, 3, chopped
- **eating apple**, 1, peeled and chopped
- **nectarine**, 1, stoned (pitted) and chopped

*for the granola*

- **porridge (rolled) oats**, 50g/2oz/½ cup
- **jumbo oats**, 50g/2oz/½ cup
- **sunflower seeds**, 25g/1oz/2 tbsp
- **sesame seeds**, 25g/1oz/2 tbsp
- **hazelnuts**, 25g/1oz/2 tbsp
- **almonds**, 25g/1oz/¼ cup, roughly chopped
- **sunflower oil**, 30ml/2 tbsp
- **clear honey**, 30ml/2 tbsp
- **raisins**, 25g/1oz/2 tbsp
- **dried sweetened cranberries**, 25g/1oz/2 tbsp

## tools

- Peeler
- Chopping board
- Sharp knife
- 2 small pans
- Wooden spoon
- Blender or food processor
- 2 mixing bowls
- Medium pan
- 2 non-stick baking sheets
- Oven gloves

1 To make the raspberry and apple purée, put the apple in a pan with the raspberries and a little water. Cook over a low heat for 5 minutes, stirring until soft. Adult supervision is required.

2 Put in a blender or food processor and blend until smooth. Adult supervision is required. Chill.

3 To make the apricot compote, put the apricots, apple and nectarine in a pan with a little water.

4 Bring up to the boil, reduce the heat and simmer for 10 minutes, until soft. Put in the blender or food processor and blend until smooth. Adult supervision is required. Chill.

5 To make the granola, preheat the oven to 140°C/275°F/Gas 1. Mix together the oats, seeds and nuts in a bowl.

6 Heat the oil and honey in a pan until combined. Add to the oat mixture and stir, then spread out on the baking sheets. Adult supervision is required.

7 Bake the granola for 50 minutes, until crisp, tossing so the mixture does not stick. Ask an adult to remove from the oven.

8 Tip into a clean bowl and stir in the raisins and cranberries. Cool, then store in an airtight container. Serve the yogurt with a topping of your choice.

# Apricot and pecan flapjacks

A tried-and-tested favourite made even more delicious by the addition of maple syrup, fruit and nuts, these juicy bites are a real energy booster at any time of day.

*makes* 10

## ingredients

- **unsalted butter**, 150g/5oz/⅔ cup, diced
- **light muscovado (brown) sugar**, 150g/5oz/⅔ cup
- **maple syrup**, 30ml/2 tbsp
- **rolled oats**, 200g/7oz/2 cups
- **pecan nuts**, 50g/2oz/½ cup, chopped
- **ready-to-eat dried apricots**, 50g/2oz/¼ cup, chopped

## tools

- **18cm/7in square shallow baking tin (pan)**
- **Large heavy pan**
- **Wooden spoon**
- **Medium sharp knife**
- **Oven gloves**
- **Chopping board**

1 Preheat the oven to 160°C/325°F/Gas 3. Lightly grease and line a baking tin.

2 Put the butter, sugar and maple syrup in a large, heavy pan and heat gently, stirring occasionally until the butter has melted. Adult supervision is required.

3 Remove the pan from the heat and stir in the oats, nuts and apricots until well combined.

4 Spread the mixture evenly in the prepared tin and, using a knife, score the mixture into ten bars. Bake for about 25–30 minutes, or until golden.

5 Ask an adult to remove the pan from the oven and cut through the scored lines with the knife.

6 Leave to cool, then turn out on to a board. Cut into pieces along the scored lines. Adult supervision is required. To transport, wrap in clear film (plastic wrap).

## VARIATIONS

- Substitute the pecans with walnuts, brazil nuts, pine nuts, hazelnuts or almonds.
- Leave out the nuts if you like and replace with the same amount of chocolate chips, banana chips or desiccated (dried) coconut.

walnuts

= Watch out! Heat is involved.

# Date slices

These tasty snacks are packed with fruit and seeds, which makes them a healthy choice for lunch boxes.

*makes* 12–16

## ingredients

- **light muscovado (brown) sugar**, 175g/6oz/¾ cup
- **ready-to-eat dried dates**, 175g/6oz/1 cup, chopped
- **self-raising (self-rising) flour**, 115g/4oz/1 cup
- **muesli (granola)**, 50g/2oz/½ cup
- **sunflower seeds**, 30ml/2 tbsp
- **poppy seeds**, 15ml/1 tbsp
- **sultanas (golden raisins)**, 30ml/2 tbsp
- **natural (plain) yogurt**, 150ml/¼ pint/⅔ cup
- **egg**, 1, beaten

*for the topping*

- **icing (confectioners') sugar**, 200g/7oz/1¾ cups, sifted
- **lemon juice**, 15–30ml/1–2 tbsp
- **pumpkin seeds**, 15–30ml/1–2 tbsp

## tools

- 28 x 18cm/11 x 7in shallow baking tin (pan)
- Baking parchment
- Large mixing bowl
- 2 wooden spoons
- Oven gloves
- Small mixing bowl
- Medium sharp knife

1 Preheat the oven to 180°C/350°F/Gas 4. Line a 28 x 18cm/11 x 7in baking tin with baking parchment.

2 In a mixing bowl, stir together all the ingredients, except the icing sugar, lemon juice and pumpkin seeds, with a wooden spoon.

3 Spread in the tin and bake for 25 minutes, until golden brown. Ask an adult to remove from the oven and leave to cool.

4 To make the topping, put the icing sugar in a small bowl and stir in enough lemon juice to make a spreading consistency.

5 Spread the lemon icing over the cooled mixture and sprinkle the top with pumpkin seeds.

6 Leave to set before cutting into squares or bars with the knife. Adult supervision is required. To transport, wrap in foil or clear film (plastic wrap).

VARIATION

- As an alternative try substituting the dates with chopped apricots, figs, pear or soft mango, or try a mixture of your favourites. Instead of sultanas you could try using dried blueberries or cranberries.

# Butterscotch brownies

These gorgeous treats are delicious served warm with whipped cream or vanilla ice cream as a dessert or they make irresistible picnic food.

*makes* 12

## ingredients

- **white chocolate chips**, 450g/1lb
- **unsalted butter**, 75g/3oz/6 tbsp
- **eggs**, 3
- **light muscovado (brown) sugar**, 175g/6oz/¾ cup
- **self-raising (self-rising) flour**, 175g/6oz/1½ cups
- **walnuts**, 175g/6oz/1½ cups, chopped (see Variations)
- **vanilla extract**, 5ml/1 tsp

## tools

- 28 x 18cm/11 x 7in shallow tin (pan)
- Baking parchment
- Small heatproof bowl
- Small pan
- Wooden spoon
- Large mixing bowl
- Electric mixer or whisk
- Large metal spoon
- Sieve (strainer)
- Palette knife
- Oven gloves
- Medium sharp knife

1 Preheat the oven to 190°C/375°F/Gas 5. Grease and line the base of a 28 x 18cm/11 x 7in tin with baking parchment. Lightly grease the sides.

2 Place 90g/3½oz/½ cup of the chocolate chips with the butter in a heatproof bowl. Ask an adult to fill the pan about half full of boiling water from the kettle. Place the bowl over the pan, making sure the water doesn't touch the base of the bowl. Leave until the chocolate and butter have melted. Stir gently, remove from the heat and leave to cool slightly.

3 Place the eggs and sugar in a large bowl and beat until light and foamy. Whisk in the melted chocolate mixture.

4 Sift over the flour and fold in with the metal spoon with the walnuts, vanilla extract and the remaining chocolate chips.

5 Spread out the mixture in the tin with a palette knife and bake for 30 minutes, or until risen and brown.

6 Ask an adult to remove from the oven. Leave to cool. Cut into 12 bars. Adult supervision is required. To transport, wrap in foil or clear film (plastic wrap).

## VARIATIONS

- If you prefer not to use nuts, then why not try adding the same quantity of milk or dark chocolate chips to make double chocolate brownies.
- Alternatively, add raisins or sultanas (golden raisins) or chopped banana chips.

 (!) = Watch out! Sharp or electrical tool in use. (oven glove) = Watch out! Heat is involved.

# Chocolate thumbprint cookies

Chunky, chocolatey and gooey all at the same time, these cookies are filled with a spoonful of chocolate spread after baking – perfect for a mid-morning snack!

cocoa powder

makes 16

## ingredients

- **unsalted butter**, 115g/4oz/½ cup, at room temperature, diced
- **light muscovado (brown) sugar**, 115g/4oz/½ cup
- **egg**, 1
- **plain (all-purpose) flour**, 75g/3oz/⅔ cup
- **unsweetened cocoa powder**, 25g/1oz/¼ cup
- **bicarbonate of soda (baking soda)**, 2.5ml/½ tsp
- **rolled oats**, 115g/4oz/generous 1 cup
- **chocolate spread**, 75–90ml/5–6 tbsp

## tools

- Large non-stick baking sheet
- Large mixing bowl
- Wooden spoon or electric mixer
- Oven gloves
- Wire rack
- Palette knife
- Teaspoon

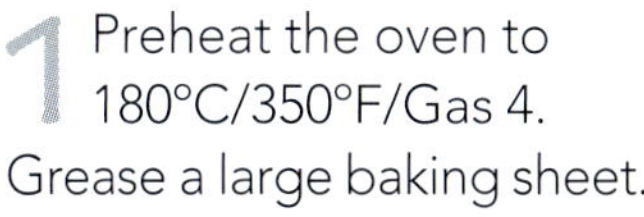

1 Preheat the oven to 180°C/350°F/Gas 4. Grease a large baking sheet.

2 In a large mixing bowl, beat together the butter and sugar for about 10 minutes with a wooden spoon or an electric mixer (with adult supervision) until pale and creamy.

3 Add the egg, flour, cocoa powder, bicarbonate of soda and oats and mix well.

4 Using your hands, roll spoonfuls of the mixture into balls. Place these on the baking sheet, spacing them well apart to allow room for spreading. Flatten slightly.

5 Dip a thumb in flour and press into the centre of each cookie to make an dip.

6 Bake for 10 minutes. Leave for 2 minutes, then transfer to a wire rack to cool. Adult supervision is required. Spoon a little chocolate spread into the centre of each.

### COOK'S TIP

▶ If you like, freeze half of the cookies for another time. Simply thaw, then return to the oven for a few minutes before serving. Alternatively, freeze half of the raw cookie dough then simply thaw at room temperature and continue to cook as in the recipe.

# Peanut butter cookies

These sweet, nutty cookies are an all-time favourite, especially served with a glass of milk. Try sandwiching two cookies together with strawberry jam for a real treat.

*makes* 24

## ingredients

- **butter**, 115g/4oz/½ cup at room temperature, diced
- **soft light brown sugar**, 125g/4½oz/¾ cup
- **egg**, 1
- **vanilla extract**, 5ml/1 tsp
- **crunchy peanut butter**, 225g/8oz/1 cup
- **plain (all-purpose) flour**, 115g/4oz/1 cup
- **bicarbonate of soda (baking soda)**, 2.5ml/½ tsp
- **salt**, a pinch

## tools

- **Large mixing bowl**
- **Electric mixer or wooden spoon**
- **Small mixing bowl**
- **2 forks**
- **Sieve (strainer)**
- **2 non-stick baking sheets**
- **2 metal teaspoons**
- **Oven gloves**
- **Palette knife**

1 Put the butter and sugar in a large bowl. Beat with a wooden spoon or electric mixer (with adult supervision) until pale and creamy.

2 In a bowl, mix the egg and vanilla extract with a fork. Gradually beat into the butter mixture, beating well after each addition.

3 Mix in the peanut butter. Sift together the flour, bicarbonate of soda and salt and stir into the mixture to form a soft dough. Wrap in clear film (plastic wrap). Chill for 30 minutes.

4 Preheat the oven to 180°C/350°F/Gas 4. Grease two baking sheets.

5 Spoon out rounded teaspoonfuls of the dough and roll into balls. Place the balls on the baking sheets.

6 Press flat with a fork into rounds about 6cm/2½in in diameter. Create a criss-cross pattern by pushing down with the fork.

7 Bake the cookies for about 12 minutes or until pale golden brown.

8 Ask an adult to remove them from the oven. Cool for a few minutes, then lift off with the palette knife and cool on a wire rack. To transport, wrap in foil or clear film (plastic wrap).

 = Watch out! Sharp or electrical tool in use.  = Watch out! Heat is involved.

# Blueberry and lemon muffins

This great American favourite makes good use of blueberries, which give a tangy contrast to the sweet muffin mixture. They make a fantastic breaktime snack.

*makes* 12

## ingredients

- **plain (all-purpose) flour**, 175g/6oz/1¼ cups
- **caster (superfine) sugar**, 75g/3oz/scant ½ cup
- **baking powder**, 10ml/2 tsp
- **salt**, a pinch
- **butter**, 50g/2oz/¼ cup
- **eggs**, 2
- **milk**, 175ml/6fl oz/¾ cup
- **vanilla extract**, 5ml/1 tsp
- **grated lemon rind**, 5ml/1 tsp
- **fresh blueberries**, 150g/5oz/1¼ cups

## tools

- ✱ 2 6-hole muffin tins (pans)
- ✱ Paper muffin cases (optional)
- ✱ Sieve (strainer)
- ✱ 2 large mixing bowls
- ✱ Medium pan
- ✱ Fork or whisk
- ✱ Wooden spoon
- ✱ Large metal spoon
- ✱ Oven gloves
- ✱ Wire rack

1 Preheat the oven to 200°C/400°F/Gas 6. Lightly grease two muffin tins, or use paper cases to line them. Coloured ones look best.

2 Sift the flour, sugar, baking powder and salt into a large glass bowl and set aside.

3 Gently melt the butter in a pan. Remove to cool for 5 minutes. Adult supervision is required.

4 In a different bowl, whisk the eggs until blended. Add the melted butter, milk, vanilla extract and lemon rind and stir well until combined.

5 Make a well in the dry ingredients and pour in the egg and butter mixture. Using a large metal spoon, stir until the flour is just moistened and incorporated. It is important not to over-mix the mixture until it is smooth – it should look a bit 'knobbly'.

6 Fold the blueberries into the mixture with a metal spoon. Spoon into the tins or paper cases.

7 Bake for 20–25 minutes until golden. Ask an adult to remove from the oven. Transfer to a wire rack to cool. To transport, wrap in foil or clear film (plastic wrap).

# Snacks and light bites

You are bound to be hungry when you come home after school or a busy day out and about, and this is when quick snacks come into their own. Whether you want something satisfyingly savoury or a sweet energy boost, this chapter provides a wide range of tempting bites that are sure to hit the spot.

# Frankfurter sandwich

This scrummy sandwich is a twist on a hotdog and chips (fries), combining the frankfurter and potatoes with mayonnaise and onions between two slices of bread.

*makes* 2

## ingredients

- **potatoes**, 150g/5oz
- **mayonnaise**, 30–45ml/2–3 tbsp
- **spring onions (scallions)**, 2, chopped
- **salt** and **ground black pepper**
- **butter**, 25g/1oz/2 tbsp, softened
- **wholemeal (whole-wheat) bread**, 4 slices
- **frankfurters**, 4
- **tomatoes**, 2, sliced

*spring onions*

## tools

- ✱ Peeler
- ✱ Medium sharp knife
- ✱ Chopping board
- ✱ Small pan
- ✱ Colander
- ✱ Small bowl
- ✱ Butter knife
- ✱ Large serrated knife

1 Peel the potatoes, then cut into small cubes. Adult supervision is required.

2 Put the potatoes in the pan and cover with water. Cover and bring up to the boil. Cook, uncovered, for about 5 minutes, until the potatoes are soft. Adult supervision is required.

3 Ask an adult to drain the potatoes in a colander. Leave until completely cold, then mix with the mayonnaise and spring onions. Season.

4 Butter the bread and divide the potato salad equally between two slices, spreading it to the edges.

5 Slice the frankfurters into bitesize pieces. Adult supervision is required. Arrange over the potato salad with the tomato slices.

6 Sandwich with the remaining bread, press together lightly and then cut the sandwich in half diagonally.

## VARIATIONS

- For a super-speedy sandwich, simply replace the home-made potato salad with 115g/4oz/2 cups ready-made store-bought potato salad.
- Replace the frankfurters with leftover sausages.



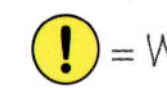 = Watch out! Sharp or electrical tool in use. = Watch out! Heat is involved.

# Ciabatta sandwich

If you can find a ciabatta flavoured with sun-dried tomatoes, it makes the sandwich even tastier. Prosciutto is the Italian name for Parma ham.

*makes* 3

## ingredients

- **mayonnaise**, 60ml/4 tbsp
- **pesto**, 30ml/2 tbsp
- **ciabatta loaf**, 1
- **mozzarella cheese**, 115g/4oz, sliced
- **plum tomatoes**, 4, sliced
- **prosciutto**, 75g/3oz, thinly sliced
- **fresh basil leaves**, 6–8, torn

## tools

- Small bowl
- Wooden spoon
- Chopping board
- Large serrated knife
- Butter knife
- Medium sharp knife

1 Stir together the mayonnaise and pesto in a small bowl with a wooden spoon, until they are thoroughly mixed.

2 On a chopping board, carefully cut the ciabatta in half horizontally with a serrated knife. Adult supervision is required.

3 Spread the cut side of both halves with the pesto mayonnaise.

4 Slice the cheese and tomatoes. Adult supervision is required. Lay the cheese on half of the ciabatta. Cut or tear the prosciutto into strips and arrange over the top.

5 Cover the prosciutto strips with the sliced tomatoes and plenty of torn basil leaves.

6 Top with the other half loaf and press down firmly. With adult supervision, carefully cut into three pieces with the serrated knife and serve.

## VARIATIONS

- For an intense tomatoey flavour, replace the fresh tomatoes with sunblush or sun-dried ones.
- Replace the green pesto with wholegrain or smooth Dijon mustard, if you like.
- This sandwich is also delicious warm. Wrap in foil and place on a baking sheet. Cook in an oven preheated to 180°C/350°F/Gas 4 for 10–15 minutes, until the cheese has melted completely.

# Toasted bacon sandwich

Everyone's favourite, bacon sandwiches are the ultimate in after-school comfort food. It is worth using good-quality bacon to make the snack, and it is a good idea to remove the rind once the bacon is cooked as this makes it easier to eat.

*each serves* 2

## ingredients

- **vegetable oil**, 15ml/1 tbsp
- **smoked** or **unsmoked lean back bacon**, 4 rashers (strips), or **streaky (fatty) bacon**, 8 rashers
- **brown (whole-wheat)** or **white bread**, 4 slices
- **butter**, for spreading
- **mayonnaise**, 30ml/2 tbsp
- **tomato ketchup**, to serve (optional)

## tools

- **Large non-stick frying pan**
- **Fish slice or metal spatula**
- **Bread board**
- **Butter knife**
- **Small sharp knife (optional)**
- **Large serrated knife**

1 With adult supervision, heat the oil in a large frying pan until sizzling.

2 Add the bacon and cook for 2–3 minutes, depending on how crispy you like it, then turn over and cook for a further 2 minutes. Transfer to kitchen paper to drain. Adult supervision is required.

3 Toast the bread on both sides, either in a toaster or under a pre-heated grill (broiler), until golden. Adult supervision is required.

4 Spread half the toast with butter, and the other half with mayonnaise. If you are using tomato ketchup, spread this on top of the butter.

5 Using your fingers or a small sharp knife, pull or cut away the bacon rind from the drained, slightly cooled bacon, if you like.

6 Place two rashers of back bacon or four rashers of streaky bacon on each of the pieces of toast spread with butter. Add tomato ketchup on top of the bacon, if you like.

7 Top with the pieces of bread spread with mayonnaise and press down firmly to secure. With adult supervision, carefully cut in half with a serrated knife and serve.

## VARIATION

• Everyone likes bacon sandwiches done in a particular way. Additions may include sliced tomatoes and lettuce, to make a toasted BLT, mustard or spicy tomato relish.

lettuce

= Watch out! Sharp or electrical tool in use. = Watch out! Heat is involved.

# Cheesy treats

Croque monsieur is a French snack that literally means 'crunch gentleman', and makes a tasty alternative to normal ham and cheese sandwiches. Welsh rarebit is a special recipe of cheese served on toast with mustard and a dash of paprika or cayenne pepper.

Cheddar cheese

*each serves* 2

## ingredients

### for the croque monsieur

- **Gruyère** or **Cheddar cheese**, 75g/3oz
- **butter**, for spreading
- **country-style bread**, 4 slices
- **lean honey roast ham**, 2 slices
- **ground black pepper**
- **flat leaf parsley**, to garnish (optional)

### for the Welsh rarebit

- **bread**, 2 thick slices
- **butter**, for spreading
- **spicy** or **mild mustard**, 10ml/2 tsp
- **Cheddar cheese**, 100g/3¾oz, sliced
- **paprika** or **cayenne pepper**, a pinch
- **ground black pepper**

## tools

- ✱ Chopping board
- ✱ Medium knife
- ✱ Butter knife
- ✱ Oven gloves

1 To make the **croque monsieur**, ask an adult to preheat a grill (broiler) or a sandwich toaster to high.

2 With adult supervision, slice the cheese on a chopping board. Butter the bread. Place the cheese and ham on two slices. Top with the other slices of bread and press together.

3 Cook under the grill or in a sandwich toaster until browned on both sides. Adult supervision is required. Serve garnished with parsley, if using.

4 To make the **Welsh rarebit**, preheat the grill and toast the bread on both sides. Adult supervision is required.

5 Spread the toast with butter and a thin layer of mustard, then top with the cheese. Cook under the grill until the cheese melts and starts to brown. Adult supervision is required.

6 Sprinkle a little paprika or cayenne pepper on the cheese. Season with pepper and serve.

## COOK'S TIP

▶ Bread can quickly become too brown or even burn when cooked under a grill, so it is very important that you ask an adult for help and keep a close watch on the bread while it is cooking.

★★ give it a try | time to cook: **15–20 minutes** | preparation: **15 minutes**

# Cheese toasties

Melted cheese on toast makes a yummy, after-school snack to keep you going until supper time, and these tasty variations are sure to please your stomach.

## VARIATIONS

• Cut the bread into funny shapes with novelty cookie cutters. Small children might enjoy animal shapes or people (to make families) or simple circles, squares or triangles. You could theme the cheese toasts for special occasions, such as Halloween, Valentine's Day or Easter. Or, why not try increasing the quantities and stamping out names (one slice of bread per letter) or messages, such as 'happy birthday' or 'happy anniversary'.

• To make edible noughts and crosses (tic, tac, toe games), use square pieces of bread and top with cheese as in the recipe. Using thin strips of red (bell) pepper, divide the toasts into a grid. Use strips of spring onion (scallion) to make crosses and slices of pepperoni or sliced pitted black olives to make noughts.

*red pepper and spring onions*

*each serves* **4**

## ingredients

- **Cheddar cheese**, 175–225g/6–8oz/1½–2 cups
- **eggs**, 2
- **wholegrain mustard**, 5–10ml/1–2 tsp
- **butter**, 50g/2oz, softened
- **bread**, 4 slices
- **tomatoes**, 2–4, halved (optional)
- **ground black pepper**
- **watercress** or **fresh parsley**, to serve (optional)

### stripy toasts

- **butter**, 50g/2oz, softened
- **bread**, 4 slices
- **white Cheddar cheese**, 100g/4oz, sliced
- **Red Leicester cheese or other red hard cheese**, 100g/4oz, sliced

## tools

- Grater
- Mixing bowl
- Whisk
- Wooden spoon
- Shallow ovenproof dish
- Butter knife
- Non-stick baking sheet
- Oven gloves
- Palette knife or metal spatula

1 Preheat the oven to 230°C/450°F/Gas 8. Grate the Cheddar cheese. Place the eggs in a mixing bowl and whisk lightly. Stir in the grated cheese, wholegrain mustard and black pepper.

2 Grease the inside of an ovenproof dish with some of the butter.

3 Spread the remaining butter on the bread. Lay it, buttered side-down in the ovenproof dish.

4 Divide the cheese and egg mixture among the slices of bread, spreading it out evenly on each slice.

5 Bake in the oven for 10–15 minutes, or until well risen and golden brown.

6 Meanwhile, place the tomatoes (if using) on a non-stick baking sheet. Put the tomatoes in the oven for the last 5 minutes of the toasts' cooking time, until soft and turning golden. Adult supervision is required.

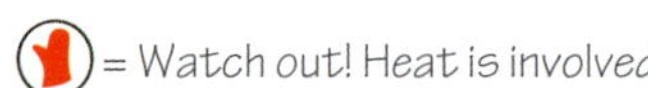

7 Ask an adult to remove the dish from the oven. Lift the cheese toasts out of the dish with a palette knife or metal spatula and serve with the tomatoes. Garnish with sprigs of watercress or parsley (if using).

8 **To make the stripy toast**, grease the inside of an ovenproof dish with some of the butter. Spread the remaining butter on the bread. Lay the bread, buttered side down, in the dish.

9 Arrange alternate slices of Cheddar and Red Leicester cheese on each of the pieces of bread, to make stripes. Bake for 10–15 minutes, or until well risen and golden brown.

!

# Sweet toast toppers

These tasty bites will make a lovely weekend snack or after-school energy booster. They are also lovely as part of a special breakfast in bed for Mum and Dad!

each serves 2–4

## ingredients

### jammy toast

- **butter**, 75g/3oz/6 tbsp, at room temperature
- **vanilla extract**, a few drops
- **bread**, 4 slices
- **jam**, 20ml/4 tsp

### cinnamon toast

- **butter**, 75g/3oz/6 tbsp, at room temperature
- **ground cinnamon**, 10ml/2 tsp
- **caster (superfine) sugar**, 30ml/2 tbsp
- **bread**, 4 slices
- **fresh fruit**, (optional)

## tools

- **Small bowl**
- **Wooden spoon**
- **Butter knife**

raspberry jam

bread

1 **To make the jammy toast**, mix the butter with the vanilla extract in the small bowl with the wooden spoon, until smooth.

2 Toast both sides of the bread in a toaster or under a preheated grill (broiler). Adult supervision is required.

3 Spread the toast thickly on one side with the flavoured butter and the jam. Serve immediately.

4 **To make the cinnamon toast**, mix the butter with the cinnamon and half the sugar in the small bowl with the wooden spoon, until soft and smooth.

5 Toast the bread on both sides, either in a toaster or under a preheated grill. Adult supervision is required. Spread the toast with the cinnamon butter.

6 Sprinkle with the remaining sugar. Serve at once, with pieces of fresh fruit, if you like.

## VARIATION

• To make different-flavoured butters, try adding 10ml/2 tsp orange or lemon juice and a little finely grated orange or lemon rind, almond or coffee extract, mixed spice or honey to the butter.

orange rind

 = Watch out! Sharp or electrical tool in use. = Watch out! Heat is involved.

# Eggtastic

These two classic egg recipes are very simple, but really worth knowing as they can be eaten for breakfast, lunch or as a healthy snack at any time of the day.

each serves 1

## ingredients

### boiled egg with toast soldiers (sticks)

- **egg**, 1
- **bread**, 4 thin slices
- **butter**, a little, for spreading
- **salt**, to taste

### poached egg on toast

- **eggs**, 2
- **lemon juice** or **vinegar**, 5ml/1 tsp
- **bread**, 2 thin slices
- **butter**, for spreading
- **salt** and **ground black pepper**

## tools

- Small pan
- Draining spoon
- Bread board
- Large serrated knife
- Butter knife
- Large, deep frying pan
- Egg poaching rings (optional)
- Knife
- Draining spoon

1 **To make the boiled egg with toast soldiers**, place the egg in a pan and ask an adult to pour in hot water to cover. Bring up to the boil and cook for 3 minutes for a very soft egg or 4 minutes for a soft yolk and firm white.

2 Remove with a slotted spoon and place in an egg cup. Ask an adult for help.

3 Meanwhile, make the soldiers. Toast the bread, spread with butter, then cut it into fingers. Serve the boiled egg with the toast fingers and salt on the side to sprinkle over.

4 **For the poached eggs on toast**, ask an adult to three-quarters fill a frying pan with hot water.

5 Heat gently until just simmering. If you have egg poaching rings, then add them to the pan.

6 Carefully crack open the eggs, and place into the pan or rings. Cook for 2–3 minutes, until the eggs have turned white and set. Adult supervision is required.

7 Meanwhile, lightly toast the bread and spread with butter.

8 Carefully remove the poached eggs from the pan with a slotted spoon, being careful not to break the yolks. Adult supervision is required. Arrange on the toast, season to taste and serve.

# Egg-stuffed tomatoes

You will enjoy slotting the slices of hard-boiled egg into the tomatoes when you make this tasty lunch, but not as much as you will enjoy eating them!

serves 4

## ingredients

- **eggs**, 4
- **mayonnaise**, 175ml/6fl oz/¾ cup
- **chopped fresh chives**, 30ml/2 tbsp
- **chopped fresh basil**, 30ml/2 tbsp
- **chopped fresh parsley**, 30ml/2 tbsp
- **ripe tomatoes**, 4
- **ground black pepper**
- **salad leaves**, to serve

eggs

## tools

- ✱ **Medium pan**
- ✱ **Slotted spoon**
- ✱ **Small bowl**
- ✱ **Spoon**
- ✱ **Egg slicer or sharp knife**
- ✱ **Medium sharp knife**
- ✱ **Chopping board**

1 Ask an adult to fill a pan with hot water and bring up to the boil. Carefully place the eggs on to a slotted spoon and lower into the water. Boil for 8 minutes.

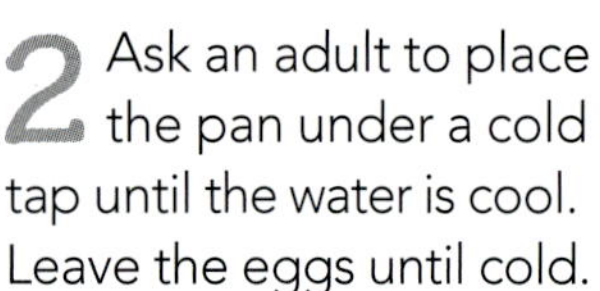

2 Ask an adult to place the pan under a cold tap until the water is cool. Leave the eggs until cold.

3 Mix together the mayonnaise and herbs in a small bowl with a spoon. Set aside.

4 With an egg slicer or sharp knife, cut the peeled hard-boiled eggs into slices, taking care to keep the slices intact. Adult supervision is required.

5 Using a sharp knife, make deep cuts in the tomatoes to 1cm/½in from the base of each tomato. Do not cut right through the bottom. Adult supervision is required. There should be the same number of cuts in each tomato as there are slices of each hard-boiled egg.

6 Gently fan open the tomatoes and sprinkle with black pepper.

7 Carefully place an egg slice into each slit. Place each stuffed tomato on a plate with a few salad leaves and serve immediately with the herb mayonnaise.

 = Watch out! Sharp or electrical tool in use.

 = Watch out! Heat is involved.

# Ham and tomato scramble

Scrambled egg isn't just for breakfast – it makes a delicious and easy lunch or snack. Watch the timings or you could end up with over-cooked, rubbery eggs.

*serves* 2

## ingredients

- **ham**, 2 slices
- **tomato**, 1
- **red (bell) pepper**, ¼, seeded
- **eggs**, 2
- **milk**, 15ml/1 tbsp
- **butter**, 45ml/3 tbsp
- **bread**, 2 slices

## tools

- **Medium sharp knife**
- **Chopping board**
- **Mixing bowl**
- **Fork**
- **Non-stick frying pan**
- **Wooden spatula**
- **Butter knife**
- **Small, novelty-shaped cookie cutters (optional)**

1 Finely chop the ham on a chopping board. Halve the tomato, scoop out and discard the seeds, then chop finely. Finely chop the pieces of pepper. Adult supervision is required.

2 Put the eggs and milk in a bowl and whisk lightly with a fork.

3 Heat a small knob (pat) of butter in a frying pan over medium heat, until foaming. Add the egg mixture with the ham, tomato and pepper and cook gently, stirring all the time, over low heat for about 3 minutes. Remove from the heat. Adult supervision is required.

4 Lightly toast the bread, then spread with the remaining butter. Cut the toast into shapes with small novelty shaped (see Cook's Tips) cookie cutters, if you like. Arrange the toast on serving plates, spoon over the ham and tomato scrambles and serve immediately.

## COOK'S TIPS

- This is a good snack for themed days, such as Halloween or Valentine's Day, using appropriate cutters for the toast. If you don't have special cutters, cut the toast into shapes with a knife. Adult supervision is required.
- Add any of your favourite vegetables, such as corn or peas, to the scramble.

# Dunkin' dippers

This dish is great for a party and all your friends will love dunking their favourite crisps (chips) and vegetables into the rich and creamy dips. Watch out for dunkin' grown-ups, who are bound to want to join in all the fun!

*red, green, yellow and orange peppers*

*serves* 8–10

## ingredients

### for the cheese dip

- **full-fat soft cheese**, 225g/8oz carton
- **milk**, 60ml/4 tbsp
- **fresh chives**, small bunch
- **small carrot**, 1, peeled

### for the saucy tomato dip

- **shallot**, 1
- **garlic**, 2 cloves
- **fresh basil leaves**, a handful, plus a few extra, torn, to garnish
- **ripe tomatoes**, 500g/1¼ lb, cut in half
- **olive oil**, 30ml/2 tbsp
- **salt** and **ground black pepper**
- **green chillies**, 2 (optional)

### for the guacamole

- **red chillies**, 2 (optional)
- **ripe avocados**, 2
- **garlic**, 1 clove, peeled and chopped
- **shallot**, 1, peeled and chopped
- **olive oil**, 30 ml/2 tbsp, plus extra to serve
- **lemon**, juice of 1
- **salt**
- **flat-leaf parsley leaves**, a handful, to garnish

### for dunking

- **cucumber**, 1
- **baby corn**, 4
- **red**, **orange** and **yellow (bell) peppers**, ½ of each, seeded
- **cherry tomatoes**, 8–10
- **tortilla chips** or **crisps**

## tools

- ✱ Mixing bowl
- ✱ Wooden spoon
- ✱ Chopping board
- ✱ Small sharp knife
- ✱ 3 serving bowls
- ✱ Grater
- ✱ Blender or food processor
- ✱ Teaspoon
- ✱ Fork

*tortilla chips*

*baby corn*

1 To make the cheese dip, spoon the full-fat soft cheese into a mixing bowl and beat it with a wooden spoon until soft and creamy.

2 Add the milk to the cheese, a little at a time. Beat the mixture well each time you pour more milk in.

3 Beat the mixture for 2 minutes. If necessary, add more milk to make it runnier. Chop the chives on a board. Adult supervision is required. Reserve some, then add the rest to the dip.

4 Finely grate the carrot. Reserve some and stir the rest into the dip.

5 Spoon into a small serving bowl and sprinkle over the remaining chives and carrot. Cover and set aside.

6 To make the saucy tomato dip, peel and halve the shallot and garlic cloves. Place in a blender with the basil leaves. Adult supervision is required.

7 Blend until finely chopped. Add the tomatoes and blend in short bursts until the tomatoes are finely chopped but not puréed.

8 With the motor running, pour in the olive oil. Adult supervision is required. Season. Spoon into a bowl.



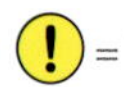 = Watch out! Sharp or electrical tool in use.  = Watch out! Heat is involved.

9 With adult supervision, cut the chillies in half lengthways, if using. Cut out their seeds and membranes, or scrape out with a teaspoon. Slice the chilli halves across their width into strips and stir into the tomato mixture. Wash your hands. Garnish with a few basil leaves.

10 To make the **guacamole**, prepare the chillies as in Step 9, if using, then chop them.

11 Cut the avocados in half lengthways. Adult supervision is required. Remove the stones (pit) and scoop out the flesh into a bowl. Mash with a fork.

12 Stir the garlic and shallot into the avocado with the oil and lemon juice. Add salt to taste. Spoon into a serving bowl. Drizzle with oil and scatter over parsley leaves.

13 To make the **dunks**, cut the cucumber, baby corn and peppers into 7.5cm/3in lengths. Adult supervision is required.

14 Serve the prepared dips with the dunks, tomatoes and tortilla chips or crisps.

# Skinny dips

Baked potatoes in disguise, these delectable bites are served with a spicy dip. Although they aren't quick to make, they are very easy and extremely delicious.

*serves* 4

## ingredients

- **baking potatoes**, 8, scrubbed
- **oil**, 30–45ml/2–3 tbsp
- **salt**, a generous pinch
- **mayonnaise**, 90ml/6 tbsp
- **natural (plain) yogurt**, 30ml/2 tbsp
- **curry paste**, 5ml/1 tsp
- **fresh coriander (cilantro)**, 30ml/2 tbsp, roughly chopped

coriander

## tools

* Fork
* Large, shallow roasting pan
* Oven gloves
* Medium knife
* Chopping board
* Spoon
* Pastry brush
* Small bowl
* Wooden spoon

1 Preheat the oven to 190°C/375°F/Gas 5.

2 Prick the potatoes all over with a fork, then arrange in the roasting pan. Ask an adult to put in the oven. Bake for 45 minutes, or until tender. Ask an adult to remove from the oven. Leave until cool enough to handle.

3 With adult supervision, carefully cut each potato into quarters lengthways, holding it with a clean dish towel if it's hot.

4 Scoop out some of the centre with a knife or spoon and put the skins back in the tin. Adult supervision is required. Save the cooked potato for use in another dish.

5 Brush the potato skins with oil and sprinkle with salt before putting them back in the oven. Cook for 30–40 minutes more, until they are crisp and brown.

6 Meanwhile, put the mayonnaise, yogurt, curry paste and 15ml/1 tbsp coriander in a small bowl.

7 Mix together well with a wooden spoon. Cover with clear film (plastic wrap) and leave the flavours to develop while the skins are cooking.

8 Put the dip in a serving bowl and arrange the skins around the edge. Serve hot, sprinkled with the remaining coriander.

 = Watch out! Sharp or electrical tool in use. (!) = Watch out! Heat is involved.

# Chilli cheese nachos

Crispy tortilla chips smothered in melted cheese served with an avocado dip make the most delicious snack. You could leave out the chillies if you prefer.

serves 4

## ingredients

- **Cheddar cheese**, 50g/2oz
- **Red Leicester cheese**, 50g/2oz
- **pickled green jalapeño chillies**, 50g/2oz (optional)
- **chilli tortilla chips**, 115g/4oz bag

for the dip

- **ripe avocado**, 1
- **beefsteak tomato**, 1
- **lemon juice**, 30ml/2 tbsp
- **salt** and **ground black pepper**

## tools

- Grater
- 2 mixing bowls
- Sieve (strainer)
- Chopping board
- Medium sharp knife
- Teaspoon
- Heatproof plate or shallow dish
- Oven gloves

1 Grate both cheeses and put in a mixing bowl. Drain the chillies, if using, and slice on a chopping board. Wash your hands. Adult supervision is required.

2 **To make the dip**, cut the avocado in half down its length. Remove the stone with a teaspoon. Adult supervision is required.

3 Peel away the skin, then roughly chop the avocado flesh. Roughly chop the beefsteak tomato. Adult supervision is required.

4 Mix together the avocado and tomato in a mixing bowl. Add the lemon juice and season to taste. Mix well to combine everything, then set aside.

5 Ask an adult to preheat a grill (broiler) to medium-hot. Arrange the tortilla chips in a layer on a heatproof plate or dish, overlapping some slightly.

6 Sprinkle over both types of grated cheese and then add jalapeño chillies, or not, depending on your preference.

### COOK'S TIP

► If the chips are burning before the cheese has melted, cover with foil and continue grilling. Adult supervision is required.

7 Ask an adult to put under the grill and toast until the cheese has melted and browned. Ask an adult to remove from the grill. Serve with the dip.

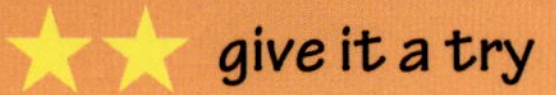
give it a try | time to cook: **5 minutes** | preparation: **5 minutes**

# Cheese and basil tortillas

Tortilla flip-overs are a great easy-cook invention. You'll want to experiment with different fillings and leftovers will never go to waste again.

*serves* 2

## ingredients

- **olive oil**, 15ml/1 tbsp
- **soft flour tortillas**, 2
- **Gruyère cheese**, 115g/4oz, thinly sliced
- **fresh basil leaves**, a handful
- **salt** and **ground black pepper**

*basil leaves*

## tools

- **Medium frying pan**
- **Metal spatula**
- **Chopping board**
- **Large sharp knife**

1 With adult supervision, heat the oil in a frying pan over a low heat. Add one of the tortillas, and heat for 1 minute. Take care not to overcook them.

2 Arrange the Gruyère cheese slices and basil leaves on top of the tortilla and season. Adult supervision is required.

3 Place the remaining tortilla on top of the cheese and basil layer to make a sandwich.

4 Press down lightly on the tortilla to secure, then cook for 1 minute, so the cheese can melt slightly. Carefully flip over with the metal spatula. Adult supervision is required.

5 Cook for a few minutes, until the underneath is golden and crisp.

6 Slide the tortilla on to a chopping board or plate and cut into small wedges with a knife. Adult supervision is required. Serve immediately, as the tortilla will become tough as it cools.

## VARIATION

• These crisp tortillas make excellent snacks to share with friends. If you have a few slices of ham or salami in the refrigerator, add these to the tortillas. They would also be tasty with a handful of pitted olives.

*ham*

(!) = Watch out! Sharp or electrical tool in use. (oven glove) = Watch out! Heat is involved.

# Chicken pitta pockets

These scrummy pittas are packed with succulent chicken and zesty, crunchy salad, and make a perfect substantial snack or weekend lunch.

pitta bread

*makes* 6

## ingredients

- **small cucumber**, 1
- **spring onions (scallions)**, 2, chopped
- **tomatoes**, 3
- **olive oil**, 30ml/2 tbsp
- **parsley**, a small bunch, finely chopped
- **mint**, a small bunch, finely chopped
- **preserved lemon**, ½, rinsed well and finely chopped
- **tahini**, 45–60ml/3–4 tbsp
- **lemon**, juice of 1
- **garlic**, 2 cloves, crushed
- **salt** and **ground black pepper**
- **pitta breads**, 6
- **roast chicken breast fillets**, 2, flesh removed from the bone and cut into strips

## tools

- **Vegetable peeler**
- **Chopping board**
- **Sieve (strainer)**
- **Medium sharp knife**
- **Large mixing bowl**
- **Small bowl**
- **Spoon and fork**

1 Peel the cucumber, then chop into small chunks. Chop the spring onions. Adult supervision is required.

2 Place the tomatoes in a heatproof bowl and ask an adult to pour over boiling water. Leave for 5 minutes, until the skins split. With adult supervision, rinse under cold water.

3 Peel away the skin, cut the tomatoes into quarters and scoop out the seeds with a teaspoon. Chop the flesh into chunks and put in a large mixing bowl. Adult supervision is required.

4 Add the cucumber and the spring onions. Stir in the oil, parsley, mint and preserved lemon. Season.

5 In a second small bowl, mix the tahini with the lemon juice, then thin down the mixture by stirring in a little water, until it has the consistency of thick double (heavy) cream.

6 Beat in the garlic with a fork and season to taste. Ask an adult to preheat the grill (broiler) to hot.

7 Lightly toast the pitta breads well away from the heat until they puff up. Adult supervision is required.

8 Open the breads and stuff them liberally with the chicken and salad. Drizzle a generous amount of tahini sauce into each one and serve with any extra salad.

# Chunky veggie salad

This crunchy snack is packed with vitamins and will give you loads of energy – ideal for after school to get you through your homework! Serve on slices of crusty bread.

*serves* 4

## ingredients

- **small white cabbage**, ¼
- **small red cabbage**, ¼
- **baby carrots**, 8
- **small mushrooms**, 50g/2oz
- **cauliflower**, 115g/4oz
- **small courgette (zucchini)**, 1
- **cucumber**, 10cm/4in piece
- **tomatoes**, 2
- **cheese**, 50g/2oz
- **sprouted seeds**, 50g/2oz (*see* Fact File)
- **peanuts**, 50g/2oz/½ cup (optional)
- **sunflower oil**, 30ml/2 tbsp, plus extra for serving
- **lemon juice**, 15ml/1 tbsp, plus extra for serving
- **salt** and **ground black pepper**

## tools

- ✱ Chopping board
- ✱ Medium sharp knife
- ✱ Vegetable peeler
- ✱ Grater
- ✱ Mixing bowl
- ✱ Wooden spoon

1 On a chopping board, finely chop the white and red cabbage. Peel the carrots with a vegetable peeler, then slice into thin rounds or sticks. Adult supervision is required.

2 Gently wipe the mushrooms clean, then cut into quarters.

3 With adult supervision, cut the cauliflower into small, even-size 'florets'.

4 Grate the courgette with a coarse grater. Cut the cucumber into cubes and chop the tomatoes into similar-size pieces. Grate the cheese coarsely. Adult supervision is required.

5 Put all the prepared vegetables and sprouted seeds in a bowl and mix together well.

6 Stir in the peanuts, if using. Drizzle over the oil and lemon juice. Season well and leave to stand for 30 minutes to allow the flavours to develop.

## FACT FILE

**SPROUTED SEEDS**

These are the sprouts that start to grow when seeds are given the right conditions. They taste great and are full of goodness.

7 Sprinkle grated cheese over just before serving with slices of crusty bread.

 = Watch out! Sharp or electrical tool in use. (!) = Watch out! Heat is involved.

# Chicken and tomato salad

Warm salads are lovely for eating all year round but especially in winter when you fancy a salad but need warm food. This one is delicious and nutritious.

serves 2

## ingredients

- **baby spinach leaves**, 225g/8oz, rinsed
- **cherry tomatoes**, 250g/9oz
- **spring onions (scallions)**, 1 bunch
- **skinless chicken breast fillets**, 2
- **salt** and **ground black pepper**

### for the dressing

- **olive oil**, 45ml/3 tbsp
- **hazelnut oil**, 30ml/2 tbsp (see Variation)
- **white wine vinegar**, 5ml/1 tbsp
- **garlic**, 1 clove, peeled and crushed
- **chopped fresh mixed herbs**, 15ml/1 tbsp

## tools

- ✱ Small bowl or measuring jug (cup)
- ✱ Whisk or fork
- ✱ Chopping board
- ✱ Medium sharp knife
- ✱ Large non-stick frying pan
- ✱ Wooden spatula

## VARIATION

• You can replace the hazelnut oil with more olive oil. Alternatively, you could experiment with other flavoured oils, such as delicious avocado oil.

1 **To make the dressing**, place 30ml/2 tbsp of the olive oil and the hazelnut oil in a small bowl or jug. Whisk together, then slowly add the vinegar, whisking well between each addition. Add the crushed garlic and chopped mixed herbs and whisk well to combine everything thoroughly.

2 Trim any long stalks from the spinach leaves, then place in a large serving bowl.

3 Cut the tomatoes in half. Trim the spring onions, then slice. Adult supervision is required. Add to the bowl with the spinach and toss together.

4 Cut the chicken into thin strips. Heat the remaining olive oil in a frying pan and stir-fry the chicken over a high heat for 7–10 minutes, until it is cooked and brown. Adult supervision is required.

5 Arrange the cooked chicken over the salad.

6 Whisk the dressing to blend, then drizzle it over the salad. Season to taste, toss lightly and serve immediately.

# Country pasta salad

Salads are a brilliant way of using up leftovers, including pasta. You can throw this together quickly and easily for a tasty, filling light lunch or snack.

serves 6

## ingredients

- **dried fusilli**, 300g/11oz/2¾ cups
- **green beans**, 150g/5oz
- **potato**, 1, about 150g/5oz
- **baby tomatoes**, 200g/7oz
- **spring onions (scallions)**, 2
- **black olives**, 6–8, pitted
- **Parmesan cheese**, 90g/3½oz
- **capers in vinegar**, 15–30ml/1–2 tbsp

### for the dressing

- **extra virgin olive oil**, 90ml/6 tbsp
- **balsamic vinegar**, 15ml/1 tbsp
- **chopped fresh flat leaf parsley**, 15ml/1 tbsp
- **salt** and **ground black pepper**

### tools

- Large pan
- Colander
- Chopping board
- Vegetable peeler
- Large mixing bowl
- Small mixing bowl
- Whisk
- Wooden spoon

1 Two-thirds fill a large pan with water and a pinch of salt. Bring up to the boil. Add the pasta and bring back to the boil. Cook for 8–10 minutes, or according to packet instructions, until just tender (*al dente*). Drain in a colander, rinse under cold water. Drain. Adult supervision is required.

2 Meanwhile, trim the ends from the beans with a knife, then cut into 5cm/2in lengths. Peel the potato and cut into cubes. Adult supervision is required.

3 Place the beans and potato in the pan. Cover with water. Bring up to the boil, reduce the heat and simmer for 5–6 minutes or until tender. Drain and cool. Adult supervision is required.

4 Meanwhile, cut the tomatoes in half. Trim the spring onions and slice. Slice the olives. Adult supervision is required.

5 With adult supervision, make shavings from the Parmesan with a vegetable peeler.

6 Put the tomatoes, spring onions, Parmesan, olive rings and drained capers in a large bowl, then add the cold pasta, beans and potato.

7 To make the dressing, put all the ingredients in a small bowl and season to taste. Whisk well to mix.

8 Pour the dressing over the salad and toss well to mix. Cover with clear film (plastic wrap) and leave to stand for 30 minutes. Serve or chill until required.



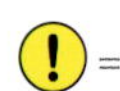 = Watch out! Sharp or electrical tool in use.  = Watch out! Heat is involved.

# Tuna pasta salad

This is ideal for making when you are in a rush and need a sustaining snack or lunch, as most of the ingredients are store cupboard (pantry) items.

serves 6–8

## ingredients

- **short pasta**, such as **ruote**, **macaroni** or **farfalle**, 450g/1lb
- **olive oil**, 60ml/4 tbsp
- **tuna**, 2 x 200 g/7oz cans, drained
- **cannellini or borlotti beans**, 2 x 400g/14oz cans, rinsed and drained
- **small red onion**, 1
- **celery**, 2 sticks
- **lemon**, juice of 1
- **chopped fresh parsley**, 30ml/2 tbsp
- **salt** and **ground black pepper**

## tools

- Large pan
- Colander
- Large mixing bowl
- 2 small mixing bowls
- Fork
- Chopping board
- Medium sharp knife
- Wooden spoon

1 Two-thirds fill a large pan with water and a pinch of salt. Bring up to the boil. Add the pasta and bring back to the boil. Cook for 8–10 minutes, or according to packet instructions, until just tender (*al dente*). Drain in a colander and rinse under cold water. Adult supervision is required.

2 Leave to drain, shaking the colander from time to time. Toss with the olive oil in the large mixing bowl, and set aside until cold.

3 Put the tuna in a small mixing bowl and separate into flakes with the fork. Add to the pasta with the beans.

4 Peel the onion, then slice. Trim the celery and slice. Adult supervision is required. Add to the pasta.

5 In a small bowl, mix the lemon juice with the parsley. Mix into the other ingredients. Season. Allow the salad to stand for at least 1 hour before serving.

## COOK'S TIP

▶ It is important to run the pasta under cold water as soon as you have drained it as this will stop it from cooking any further. For most dishes this is not a problem, but for pasta salads you want the pasta to stay soft with a bit of bite (*al dente*).

# Quick and easy suppers

Being able to create a healthy, tasty meal in a short amount of time is a very useful skill to have and will really impress your parents. This collection of easy recipes ranges from warming soups and quick egg dishes to pasta, rice, pizza and a mouth-watering selection of fish, meat and chicken dishes.

# Chilled tomato soup

Although cold soup may sound a bit odd, it tastes fantastic. The fresh vegetable flavours of this tomato soup are brought out by the tasty pesto, which is ideal for a special supper.

*serves 4*

## ingredients

- **ripe tomatoes**, 800g/1¾lb
- **shallots**, 2
- **sun-dried tomato purée (paste)**, 25ml/1½ tbsp
- **vegetable stock**, 600ml/1 pint/2½ cups
- **salt** and **ground black pepper**
- **ice cubes**, to serve

### for the rocket pesto

- **rocket (arugula) leaves**, 15g/½oz
- **olive oil**, 75ml/5 tbsp
- **pine nuts**, 15g/½oz/2 tbsp
- **garlic**, 1 clove
- **freshly grated Parmesan cheese**, 25g/1oz/⅓ cup

## tools

- ✷ Chopping board
- ✷ Medium sharp knife
- ✷ Food processor or blender
- ✷ Sieve (strainer)
- ✷ Metal spoon
- ✷ Large pan
- ✷ Plastic or rubber spatula
- ✷ Large bowl
- ✷ Mortar and pestle
- ✷ Ladle

1 On a chopping board chop the tomatoes. Peel and chop the shallots. Adult supervision is required.

2 Place the tomatoes and shallots in a food processor or blender. Add the tomato purée and blend until smooth. Adult supervision is required.

3 Push the mixture through a sieve into a large pan, scraping all the mixture out with the plastic or rubber spatula.

4 Add the stock and heat gently for 4–5 minutes. Adult supervision is required. Season, pour into a bowl and cool. Chill for at least 4 hours.

5 **To make the rocket pesto**, put the rocket leaves, olive oil, pine nuts and garlic in a clean food processor or blender and blend to form a paste. Adult supervision is required. Alternatively, use a mortar and pestle. Stir in the Parmesan cheese using the pestle or a spoon.

6 Ladle the soup into serving bowls and add a few ice cubes to each. Spoon some of the rocket pesto into the centre of each portion and serve.

### COOK'S TIP

► A mortar is a bowl in which you grind food with a pestle, a baseball bat-shaped baton.

= Watch out! Sharp or electrical tool in use.

= Watch out! Heat is involved.

# Chilled avocado soup

This unusual no-cook recipe comes from Spain, where avocados grow really well. It is mild and creamy and perfect for a quick supper on a summer's day with a hunk of French bread.

serves 4

## ingredients

- **ripe avocados**, 3
- **ground cumin**, 1.5ml/¼ tsp
- **paprika**, 1.5ml/¼ tsp
- **spring onions (scallions)**, 1 bunch, white parts only, trimmed and chopped
- **garlic**, 2 cloves, chopped
- **lemon**, juice of 1
- **chicken** or **vegetable stock**, 450ml/¾ pint/scant 2 cups
- **iced water**, 300ml/½ pint/1¼ cups
- salt and **ground black pepper**
- **fresh flat leaf parsley**, to serve

avocado

## tools

- Chopping board
- Medium sharp knife
- Teaspoon
- Food processor or blender
- Wooden spoon

1 On a chopping board using a sharp knife, cut the avocados in half lengthways. Twist each half in opposite directions and pull apart so you get two halves. Adult supervision is required. Using a teaspoon, carefully dig out the stone (pit) from each avocado and discard.

2 Using the teaspoon, scoop out the flesh from each half. Place in a food processor or blender.

3 Repeat with the remaining avocados. Add the cumin, paprika, spring onions, garlic and lemon juice. Blend. Adult supervision is required.

4 With the motor of the food processor or blender running, gradually add the stock until it is combined with the avocado. Adult supervision is required. Stir in the iced water, season and garnish with parsley.

5 Serve immediately so it doesn't get warm.

## COOK'S TIP

► If you can't serve the soup at once, put it in the refrigerator before you add the iced water, seasoning and garnish, and when you are ready take it out of the refrigerator and stir these in.

# Broccoli soup

They call broccoli a 'super food' because it is packed with goodness. This soup is also full of flavour. Instead of serving it with the garlic toasts you may prefer it with plain bread.

serves 6

## ingredients

- **broccoli spears**, 675g/1½lb
- **chicken stock**, 1.75 litre/3 pints/7½ cups
- **salt** and **ground black pepper**
- **fresh lemon juice**, 30ml/1 tbsp

to serve

- **white bread**, 6 slices
- **garlic**, 1 large clove, cut in half
- **freshly grated Parmesan cheese**

## tools

* **Vegetable peeler**
* **Chopping board**
* **Small sharp knife**
* **Large pan**
* **Blender or food processor**
* **Wooden spoon**
* **Ladle**

1 Using a vegetable peeler, peel the broccoli stems, starting from the base of the stalks and pulling up towards the florets. Chop the broccoli into small chunks. Adult supervision is required.

2 Pour the stock into a large pan and bring to the boil. Add the broccoli.

3 Simmer for 20 minutes, or until soft. Remove from the heat and cool. Adult supervision is required.

4 Carefully pour half into a blender and blend until smooth. Stir into the mixture in the pan. Season and add lemon juice. Adult supervision is required.

5 Toast the bread on both sides until crisp and golden, then rub with the garlic (see Cook's Tip).

6 Break each into several pieces and place in the bottom of each bowl. Reheat the soup until hot and ladle over the toast. Serve at once, with Parmesan cheese.

## COOK'S TIP

▶ When you rub garlic over toast the rough surface catches the garlic, giving the toast a strong garlicky flavour. If you prefer a milder garlic flavour, just rub lightly over the toast once or twice, or alternatively don't use the garlic.

garlic

 = Watch out! Sharp or electrical tool in use.  = Watch out! Heat is involved.

# Chinese soup

You may have had this delicious meal-in-a-bowl soup in a restaurant before, and this home-made version, with a side of prawn (shrimp) crackers, will taste even better.

*serves* 4–6

## ingredients

- **chicken breast fillets**, 225g/8oz
- **sesame oil**, 15ml/1 tbsp
- **spring onions (scallions)**, 4, chopped
- **chicken stock**, 1.2 litres/2 pints/5 cups
- **soy sauce**, 15ml/1 tbsp
- **frozen corn kernels**, 115g/4oz/1 cup
- **medium egg noodles**, 115g/4oz
- **salt** and **ground black pepper**
- **carrot**, 1, thinly sliced
- **prawn crackers**, to serve (optional)

## tools

- **Chopping board**
- **Medium sharp knife**
- **Large pan**
- **Wooden spoon**

*egg noodles*

*soy sauce*

1 Remove the skin from the chicken, then trim any fat off the chicken. Cut into small cubes. Adult supervision is required.

2 With adult supervision, heat the oil in a pan. Add the chicken and spring onions. Cook, stirring, until the meat has browned all over.

3 Add the stock and the soy sauce and bring the soup up to the boil.

4 Stir in the corn, then add the egg noodles, breaking them up roughly with your fingers. Taste the soup and season, if needed. Adult supervision is required when using heat.

5 Simmer, uncovered, for 1–2 minutes until the noodles and corn are beginning to soften.

6 Add the carrots and simmer for 5 minutes.

7 Serve immediately in bowls with prawn crackers, if you like.

## COOK'S TIP

► For a special fun touch that is often used in Chinese restaurants, you can make carrot decorations. After peeling the carrots, cut into thin slices along the length, with adult supervision. Using a small novelty cutter, such as a flower, stamp out carrot shapes to add to the soup.

# Potato and pepper frittata

Packed with flavour, this tasty omelette contains potatoes and cannellini beans, making it a really satisfying supper dish that is best served with a salad.

serves 6

## ingredients

- **potatoes**, 225g/8oz, peeled and diced
- **olive oil**, 30ml/2 tbsp
- **onion**, 1, chopped
- **red (bell) pepper**, 1, chopped
- **celery sticks**, 2, chopped
- **cannellini beans**, 400g/14oz can, drained
- **eggs**, 8
- **salt** and **ground black pepper**
- **oregano sprigs**, to garnish
- **green salad** and **olives**, to serve

## tools

- Large pan
- Colander
- Large non-stick frying pan
- Wooden spoon
- Small mixing bowl
- Fork
- Wooden spatula
- Oven gloves

1 Cook the potatoes in a pan of boiling water for 8–10 minutes, until tender. Ask an adult to drain.

2 With adult supervision, heat the oil in a frying pan. Add the onion, red pepper and celery. Cook for 3–5 minutes, stirring often, until soft but not coloured.

3 Add the potatoes and beans and cook, stirring with a wooden spoon, for several minutes to heat through. Adult supervision is required when using heat.

4 In a small bowl, beat the eggs with a fork, then season well with salt and ground black pepper.

5 Pour the egg mixture over the vegetables in the frying pan and stir gently.

6 Push the mixture towards the centre of the pan using a spatula, allowing the liquid egg to run on to the base and cook. Preheat the grill (broiler). Adult supervision is required.

### VARIATION

- Try using other vegetables, such as corn, peas, asparagus, drained artichokes or (bell) peppers in oil.

7 When it is set, place under the grill for 2–3 minutes, until the top is golden brown. Ask an adult to remove from under the grill and cut into wedges. Adult supervision is required. Garnish with oregano and serve with salad and olives.



(!) = Watch out! Sharp or electrical tool in use. (glove) = Watch out! Heat is involved.

# Tomato omelette envelopes

Nothing beats an omelette when you're in a hurry and want something tasty. This one is filled with a colourful tomato and melted cheese mixture.

*serves* 2

## ingredients

- **small onion**, 1
- **tomatoes**, 4
- **vegetable oil**, 30ml/2 tbsp
- **eggs**, 4
- **chopped fresh chives**, 30ml/2 tbsp
- **salt** and **ground black pepper**
- **Camembert cheese**, 115g/4oz, rind removed and cut into cubes
- **lettuce leaves** and **Granary (whole-wheat) bread**, to serve (optional)

*lettuce*

## tools

- ✱ Chopping board
- ✱ Medium sharp knife
- ✱ Large frying pan
- ✱ Wooden spoon
- ✱ Whisk or fork
- ✱ Non-stick omelette pan or small frying pan
- ✱ Non-stick baking sheet

1 Preheat the oven to 170°C/340°F/Gas Mark 3.

2 Cut the onion into thin wedges. Cut the tomatoes into wedges of similar size. Heat 15ml/1 tbsp of the oil in a frying pan. Add the onion and cook, stirring, for 2 minutes. Adult supervision is required.

3 Increase the heat, add the tomatoes and cook for a further 2 minutes, then remove from the heat. Adult supervision is required.

4 Using a whisk or fork, beat the eggs with the chives in a bowl and season to taste. Heat the remaining oil in the omelette pan.

5 Add half the egg mixture and tilt the pan to spread thinly. Cook for 1 minute. Flip the omelette over and cook for 1 minute more. Remove to a baking sheet and keep hot in the oven. Make a second omelette with the remaining egg mixture as before. Adult supervision is required.

6 Return the tomato mixture to a high heat. Add the cheese and toss over the heat for 1 minute.

7 Divide the mixture between the omelettes and fold them over. Serve immediately with crisp lettuce leaves and chunks of Granary bread, if you like.

# Fiorentina pizza

If you like eggs, then you'll love this pizza. The egg is gently cooked as the pizza bakes to give a soft set that combines wonderfully with the spinach and cheese.

serves 2–3

## ingredients

- **fresh spinach**, 175g/6oz
- **olive oil**, 45ml/3 tbsp
- **small red onion**, 1, thinly sliced
- **pizza base (crust)**, 1, about 25–30cm/10–12in in diameter
- **pizza sauce**, 1 small jar
- **nutmeg**, freshly grated
- **mozzarella cheese**, 150g/5oz
- **egg**, 1
- **Gruyère cheese**, 25g/1oz/¼ cup, grated

*egg*

## tools

- ✱ Frying pan
- ✱ Wooden spoon
- ✱ Non-stick baking sheet
- ✱ Pastry brush
- ✱ Small metal spoon
- ✱ Small sharp knife
- ✱ Chopping board
- ✱ Oven gloves
- ✱ Grater

1 Remove the stalks from the spinach.

2 Heat 15ml/1 tbsp of the oil in a frying pan. Add the onion and fry for 5 minutes, until soft. Add the spinach and fry until wilted. Drain off any excess liquid. Adult supervision is required.

3 Preheat the oven to 220°C/425°F/Gas 7. Place the pizza base on a baking sheet. Brush with half the remaining olive oil. Spread the pizza sauce evenly over the base using the back of a metal spoon, leaving a small border all around the edge.

4 Top with the spinach mixture. Sprinkle over a little freshly grated nutmeg.

5 With adult supervision, slice the mozzarella and arrange over the spinach. Drizzle over the remaining oil. Bake for 10 minutes, then remove from the oven.

6 Make a small hole in the centre of the topping and break the egg into the hole. Sprinkle the grated Gruyère on top. Return to the oven for a further 5–10 minutes, until crisp and golden. Ask an adult to remove from the oven and serve immediately.

 = Watch out! Sharp or electrical tool in use.  = Watch out! Heat is involved.

★★ give it a try | time to cook: 30 minutes | preparation: 20 minutes

# Ham and pineapple pizza

Easy to assemble and loved by all – you can really go to town experimenting with different toppings for this French bread pizza.

*serves* 4

## ingredients

- **small baguettes**, 2
- **sliced cooked ham**, 75g/3oz
- **canned pineapple**, 4 rings, drained well
- **small green (bell) pepper**, ½, seeded
- **mature (sharp) Cheddar cheese**, 75g/3oz

### for the tomato sauce

- **olive oil**, 15ml/1 tsp
- **onion**, 1, finely chopped
- **garlic**, 2 cloves, finely chopped
- **chopped tomatoes**, 400g/14oz can
- **tomato purée (paste)**, 15ml/1 tbsp
- **fresh chopped mixed herbs** (such as oregano, parsley, thyme and basil), 15ml/1 tbsp
- **sugar**, pinch of
- **salt** and **ground black pepper**

## tools

- Large pan
- Wooden spoon
- Large serrated knife
- Chopping board
- Non-stick baking sheet
- Oven gloves
- Medium sharp knife
- Grater

1 To make the tomato sauce, heat the oil in a pan with adult supervision. Add the onion and garlic and fry for 5 minutes, until softened.

2 Add the tomatoes, tomato purée, herbs, sugar and seasoning. Stir. Adult supervision is required.

3 Bring the mixture up to the boil. Reduce the heat slightly and simmer, uncovered, stirring often, for 10 minutes or until the tomatoes have reduced to a thick pulp. Remove from the heat and set aside. Adult supervision is required.

4 Preheat the oven to 180°C/350°F/Gas 4. With adult supervision, cut the baguettes in half lengthways with a serrated knife. Place on a baking sheet. Bake in the oven for 5 minutes until they are just beginning to crisp.

5 Ask an adult to remove the oven and spread the cooled tomato sauce over the baguettes.

6 With adult supervision, slice the ham into strips, chop the pineapple into chunks and cut the pepper into strips.

7 Arrange the ham, pineapple and pepper on the baguettes.

8 Grate the Cheddar and sprinkle on top. Bake for 10 minutes, until crisp and golden. Ask an adult to remove from the oven. Serve immediately.

# Mexican tomato rice

This dish is a delicious mixture of rice, tomatoes, peas and spices. If you don't like too much heat, reduce the number of chillies you use.

serves 4

## ingredients

- **chopped tomatoes**, 400g/14oz can
- **olive oil**, 30ml/2 tbsp
- **onion**, ½, roughly chopped
- **garlic**, 2 cloves, roughly chopped
- **long grain rice**, 500g/1¼lb/2½ cups
- **vegetable stock**, 750ml/1¼ pints/3 cups
- **salt**, 2.5ml/½ tsp
- **fresh mild chillies**, 1–2 (see Cook's Tip)
- **frozen peas**, 150g/5oz/1 cup
- **ground black pepper**

## tools

- Blender or food processor
- Large heavy pan with a tight-fitting lid
- Wooden spoon
- Fork

1 Pour the tomatoes and their juice into a blender or food processor and blend until smooth. Adult supervision is required.

2 With adult supervision, heat the oil in a pan. Add the onion and garlic and cook over a medium heat, stirring, for 2 minutes, until softened.

3 Stir in the rice and fry for 1–2 minutes. Add the tomatoes and cook, stirring, for 3–4 minutes until the liquid has evaporated.

4 Stir in the stock, salt, chillies and peas. Bring to a boil. Cover and simmer for 6 minutes, until the rice is tender. Adult supervision is required when using heat.

5 Remove the pan from the heat, cover it with the lid and leave it to stand for 5 minutes, so the flavours are absorbed.

6 Remove the chillies, fluff up the rice with a fork, and serve sprinkled with black pepper. The chillies can be used as a garnish, if you like.

## COOK'S TIP

► Remember that the general rule is that the smaller the chilli the hotter it will be. This is because the smaller chillies tend to have more membranes and seeds (the part where most of the heat is). So, if you like a lot of spice, use small, hot chillies and for a milder flavour use the larger variety and remove the seeds.



! = Watch out! Sharp or electrical tool in use. = Watch out! Heat is involved.

# Quick and easy risotto

A traditional Italian risotto is made by very gradually stirring stock into rice as it cooks. This recipe is a cheat's dish because it all goes in the pan at the same time.

serves 3–4

## ingredients

- **mozzarella cheese**, 115g/4oz/1 cup
- **cooked ham**, 75g/3oz slice
- **fresh parsley**, 30ml/2 tbsp
- **chicken stock**, 1 litre/1¾ pints/4 cups
- **risotto rice**, 275g/10oz/1½ cups
- **freshly grated Parmesan cheese**, 30ml/2 tbsp, plus extra, to serve
- **salt** and **ground black pepper**

## tools

- **Chopping board**
- **Medium sharp knife**
- **Large heavy pan with a tight-fitting lid**
- **Wooden spoon**

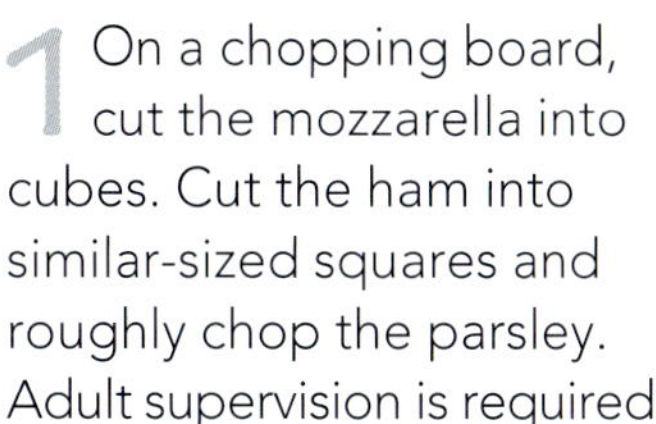

1 On a chopping board, cut the mozzarella into cubes. Cut the ham into similar-sized squares and roughly chop the parsley. Adult supervision is required.

2 With adult supervision, put the stock in a large pan and bring to the boil. Reduce the heat and bring to simmering point.

3 Add the rice. Bring back up to the boil. Cover and simmer, stirring regularly, for 18–20 minutes until the rice is tender. Adult supervision is required.

4 Ask an adult to remove from the heat and quickly stir in the mozzarella, Parmesan, ham and parsley. Season to taste.

5 Cover the pan and leave to stand for 2–3 minutes to allow the cheese to melt, then stir again to combine everything thoroughly.

6 Spoon into warmed serving bowls and serve immediately, with extra Parmesan cheese sprinkled over the top.

## VARIATIONS

- This is a really easy recipe and the ingredients can be altered to suit your taste. For example, you could replace ham with leftover, cooked chicken and add a handful of frozen corn or peas, or you could add sliced, cooked sausages and fresh broccoli florets.
- You can use Cheddar cheese instead of Parmesan, if you like.

# Presto pasta sauces

From fresh and tangy to rich and creamy, here are four classic pasta sauces to use for any occasion. Simply serve with your favourite cooked pasta.

spaghetti

*all serve* 4

## ingredients

*for the basic tomato sauce*

- **olive oil**, 15ml/1tbsp
- **butter**, 15g/½ oz/1 tbsp
- **garlic**, 1 clove, peeled and finely chopped
- **small onion**, 1, peeled and finely chopped
- **celery**, 1 stick, finely chopped
- **chopped tomatoes**, 400g/14oz can
- **fresh basil leaves**, a handful, torn
- **salt** and **ground black pepper**

*for the roasted vegetable sauce*

- **red** or **orange (bell) peppers**, 2
- **small onion,** 1
- **small aubergine (eggplant)**, 1
- **tomatoes**, 2
- **garlic**, 2 cloves, unpeeled
- **olive oil**, 30–45ml/2–3 tbsp
- **lemon juice**, 15ml/1 tbsp

*for the pesto sauce*

- **basil leaves**, 50g/2oz/1 cup
- **garlic**, 2 cloves, peeled and finely chopped
- **pine nuts**, 30ml/2 tbsp
- **salt** and **ground black pepper**
- **olive oil**, 120ml/4 fl oz/½ cup
- **freshly grated Parmesan cheese**, 40g/1½ oz/½ cup

*for the cream and Parmesan sauce*

- **butter**, 50g/2oz/¼ cup
- **double (heavy) cream**, 120ml/4fl oz/½ cup
- **freshly grated Parmesan cheese**, 50g/2oz/⅔ cup

## tools

- **Chopping board**
- **Medium sharp knife**
- **Large heavy pan**
- **Wooden spoon**
- **Non-stick baking sheet**
- **Oven gloves**
- **Metal spoon**
- **Blender or food processor**
- **Sieve (strainer, optional)**
- **Small pan**
- **Medium heavy pan**

1 **To make the basic tomato sauce**, heat the oil and butter in a heavy pan. Add the garlic, onion and celery. Cook over a low heat, stirring occasionally, for 15–20 minutes, until the onion softens and begins to colour. Adult supervision is required.

2 Stir in the tomatoes and bring up to the boil. Reduce the heat, cover and simmer for 10–15 minutes, stirring occasionally, until the mixture is thick. Adult supervision is required.

3 Add the basil leaves, season and stir. Serve hot with cooked pasta.

4 **To make the roasted vegetable sauce**, cut the peppers, onion and aubergine and tomatoes in half. Remove any seeds and membranes. Adult supervision is required.

5 Ask an adult to preheat the grill (broiler). Place the vegetables on a baking sheet with the garlic.

6 Place under the grill and cook until the skins are blackened and charred, and the flesh is tender. Adult supervision is required.

7 Ask an adult to remove from the heat and leave until cool.

8 Peel the skins from the peppers, onions and tomatoes. Scoop the flesh from the aubergines and squeeze the flesh from the garlic.



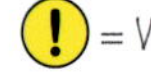 = Watch out! Sharp or electrical tool in use.  = Watch out! Heat is involved.

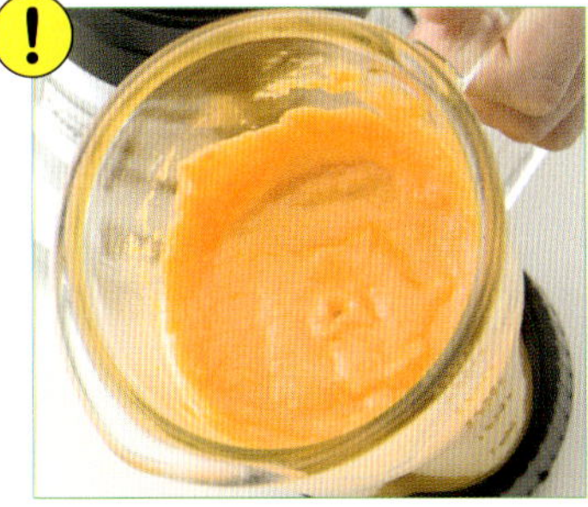

9 Place in a blender or food processor and blend to a smooth purée. Adult supervision is required.

10 Taste and add oil and lemon juice if necessary. If you prefer a smooth sauce, rub the purée through a fine sieve.

11 **To make the pesto sauce**, place the basil, garlic, pine nuts and seasoning in a blender or food processor. Blend until smooth. With the motor running, add the oil in a thin stream. Add the cheese and blend well. Adult supervision is required.

12 Heat the sauce gently in a small pan. Serve hot with cooked pasta.

13 **To make the cream and Parmesan sauce**, gently heat the butter, cream and Parmesan in a pan until melted. Adult supervision is required.

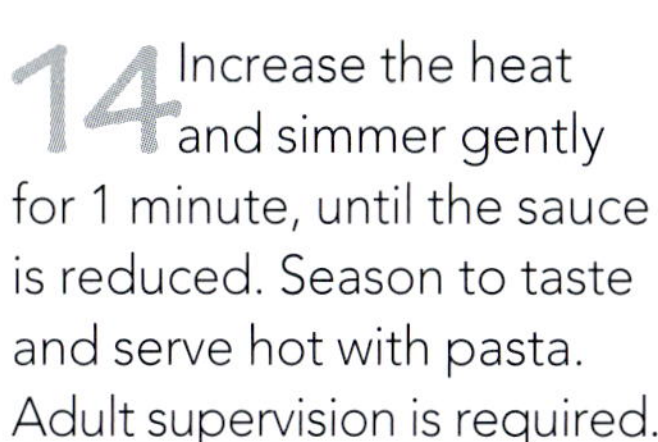

14 Increase the heat and simmer gently for 1 minute, until the sauce is reduced. Season to taste and serve hot with pasta. Adult supervision is required.

# Baked macaroni cheese

It is definitely worth knowing how to make this all-time favourite dish. Once you've made the sauce for this you'll be able to make white sauces for all kinds of recipes.

macaroni

serves 6

## ingredients

- **milk**, 500ml/16fl oz/2 cups
- **bay leaf**, 1
- **butter**, 50g/2oz/4 tbsp
- **plain (all-purpose) flour**, 35g/1¼oz/⅓ cup
- **salt** and **ground black pepper**
- **grated nutmeg**, a pinch (optional)
- **freshly grated Parmesan** or **Cheddar cheese**, or a **combination of both**, 175g/6oz/1½ cups
- **fresh white breadcrumbs**, 40g/1¾oz/⅓ cup
- **macaroni**, 450g/1lb

## tools

- **Small heavy pan**
- **Sieve (strainer)**
- **Measuring jug (cup)**
- **Medium pan**
- **Whisk**
- **Wooden spoon**
- **Heatproof bowl**
- **Large pan**
- **Ovenproof dish**
- **Colander**
- **Oven gloves**

1 Put the milk in a small pan with the bay leaf. Heat gently, remove from the heat and strain into a jug. Adult supervision is requried.

2 Melt the butter in a medium pan. Add the flour and whisk. Cook, whisking, for 2–3 minutes, then remove from the heat.

3 Gradually mix the milk into the butter and flour mixture. Return to the heat and bring up to the boil, beating, until thickened. Adult supervision is required.

4 Remove the pan from the heat and season with salt and pepper, adding the nutmeg, if using.

5 Add all but 30ml/2 tbsp of the cheese and stir until melted. Transfer to a heatproof bowl. Cover with a layer of clear film (plastic wrap). Set aside.

6 Fill a large pan with water and bring up to the boil. Preheat the oven to 200°C/400°F/Gas 6.

7 Grease an ovenproof dish and sprinkle with some breadcrumbs.

8 Add the macaroni to the pan of boiling water, and cook according to the packet instructions until it is just tender (al dente). Adult supervision is required.

9 Ask an adult to drain the macaroni in a colander. Combine it with the sauce. Pour it into the dish. Sprinkle the top with the remaining breadcrumbs and cheese and bake for 20 minutes, until melted and golden.

 = Watch out! Sharp or electrical tool in use.  = Watch out! Heat is involved.

# Farfalle with tuna

This is a fantastic recipe that needs only six ingredients that you will find in most kitchen cupboards. It's tasty and filling and good for you – perfect!

serves 4

## ingredients

- **salt**, a pinch
- **dried farfalle pasta**, 400g/14oz/3½ cups
- **olive oil**, 5ml/1 tsp
- **passata (bottled strained tomatoes)**, 600ml/1 pint/2½ cups (see Cook's Tips)
- **pitted black olives**, 8–10, cut into rings (see Cook's Tips)
- **tuna in olive oil**, 175g/6oz can

black olives

canned tuna

## tools

- ✱ **Large pan**
- ✱ **Small pan**
- ✱ **Wooden spoon**
- ✱ **Colander**
- ✱ **Fork**
- ✱ **Large heatproof bowl**

1 Two-thirds fill a large pan with water and add the oil and a pinch of salt. Bring up to the boil. Add the dried pasta and bring back to the boil. Cook for 8–10 minutes, or according to packet instructions, until just tender (al dente). Adult supervision is required.

2 With adult supervision, place the passata in a small pan with the black olives and heat through gently over a medium heat. Stir occasionally with a spoon to prevent it sticking and burning, until the sauce is bubbling slightly.

3 Drain the canned tuna in the colander and flake it with a fork.

4 Add the tuna to the tomato sauce with about 60ml/4 tbsp of the hot water used for cooking the pasta, with adult help. Taste the sauce and adjust the seasoning as necessary.

5 Ask an adult to drain the cooked pasta in a colander and tip it into a large heatproof bowl.

6 Pour the tuna and tomato sauce over the top of the pasta and toss lightly to mix. Serve immediately in warmed serving bowls.

## COOK'S TIPS

- ▶ Ready-sliced pitted black olives are available in cans and jars from most large supermarkets.
- ▶ Passata is Italian puréed, strained tomatoes, available in jars from delis and supermarkets.

# Tortellini with ham

There's a huge variety of fresh pasta available and it works well served with simple ingredients, such as the ham and creamy tomato sauce.

*serves* 4

## ingredients

- **large onion**, ¼
- **pancetta**, 115g/4oz piece, cut into cubes
- **tortellini alla carne** (meat-filled tortellini), 250g/9oz packet
- **olive oil**, 30ml/2 tbsp
- **strained crushed Italian plum tomatoes**, 150ml/¼ pint/⅔ cup
- **salt** and **ground black pepper**
- **double (heavy) cream**, 100ml/3½fl oz/ scant ½ cup
- **freshly grated Parmesan cheese**, about 90g/31⁄2oz/generous 1 cup
- **salt** and **ground black pepper**

## tools

- ✱ **Chopping board**
- ✱ **Medium sharp knife**
- ✱ **2 large pans**
- ✱ **Wooden spoon**
- ✱ **Measuring jug (pitcher)**
- ✱ **Colander**

1 Peel and finely chop the onion. Adult supervision is required.

2 Two-thirds fill a large pan with water and add a pinch of salt. Bring up to the boil. Add the pasta and bring back to the boil. Cook for 8–10 minutes, according to packet instructions, until just tender (al dente). Adult supervision is required.

3 Meanwhile, with adult supervision, heat the oil in another large pan. Add the onion. Cook over a low heat, stirring often, for 5 minutes, until softened.

4 Add the cubed pancetta and cook for 5 minutes, until it is golden. Add the tomatoes with 150ml/¼pt/ ⅔ cup water. Adult supervision is required.

5 Stir well, then season to taste.

6 Bring up to the boil, then lower the heat and simmer for 3–4 minutes, stirring, until the sauce has reduced slightly. Adult supervision is required.

7 Stir in the cream. Ask an adult to drain the pasta and add it to the pan.

8 Add a handful of grated Parmesan to the pan and stir gently with a wooden spoon to combine, taking care not to break up the fragile cooked pasta.

9 Transfer the pasta to warmed serving bowls, top with the remaining Parmesan and serve immediately.

 = Watch out! Sharp or electrical tool in use. = Watch out! Heat is involved.

# Spaghetti carbonara

This rich and creamy dish is really tasty and easy to make. The bacon adds a lovely flavour, but you could leave it out if you prefer.

serves 4

## ingredients

- **small onion**, 1
- **garlic**, 1 large clove
- **rindless smoked bacon** or **pancetta**, 175g/6oz
- **olive oil**, 30ml/2 tbsp
- **fresh** or **dried spaghetti**, 350g/12oz
- **eggs**, 4
- **crème fraîche**, 90–120ml/6–8 tbsp
- **freshly grated Parmesan cheese**, 60ml/4 tbsp, plus extra to serve
- **salt** and **ground black pepper**

## tools

- **Chopping board**
- **Medium sharp knife**
- **2 large pans**
- **Wooden spoon**
- **Mixing bowl**
- **Whisk or fork**
- **Colander**
- **Tongs**

1 Peel and chop the onion and garlic. Cut the bacon or pancetta into pieces. Adult supervision is required.

2 Heat the oil in a large pan. Add the onion and garlic and fry, stirring, for about 5 minutes, until softened. Add the bacon or pancetta and cook for 10 minutes, stirring frequently. Adult supervision is required.

3 Two-thirds fill a large pan with water and add a pinch of salt. Bring up to the boil. Add the pasta and cook for 8–10 minutes, or according to packet instructions, until just tender. Adult supervision is required.

4 Put the eggs, crème fraîche, Parmesan and black pepper in a bowl. Beat with a whisk or fork.

5 Ask an adult to drain the pasta thoroughly in a colander. Tip the pasta into the pan with the onion and pancetta or bacon and toss well to mix.

6 Turn off the heat, then immediately add the egg mixture to the pan and toss thoroughly so that it cooks and coats the pasta. Adult supervision is required.

7 Season to taste, then divide the pasta among four warmed bowls and sprinkle with ground black pepper. Top with extra grated Parmesan and serve immediately.

### VARIATION

- You can replace the crème fraîche with double (heavy) cream, single (light) cream or sour cream if you like.

# Bubble and squeak

Whether you use leftovers or cook this cabbage and potato recipe from fresh, be sure to give it a really good 'squeak' (fry) in the pan so it turns a rich honey brown.

*serves* 4

## ingredients

- **potatoes**, 500g/1lb 2oz, peeled and roughly chopped
- **vegetable oil**, 60ml/4 tbsp
- **onion**, 1, finely chopped
- **cooked cabbage** or **Brussels sprouts**, 225g/8oz, finely chopped
- **salt** and **ground black pepper**
- **pork chops**, cooked, to serve (optional)

*potatoes*

## tools

- ✱ Vegetable peeler
- ✱ Sharp knife
- ✱ Chopping board
- ✱ Large pan
- ✱ Colander
- ✱ Large, heavy frying pan
- ✱ Large mixing bowl
- ✱ Wooden spoon
- ✱ Fish slice or metal spatula
- ✱ Large flat plate

1 Place the potatoes in a pan and cover with water. Bring up to the boil and cook for 10 minutes, or until tender. Ask an adult to drain in a colander and return to the pan. Mash. Set aside.

2 With an adult, heat 30ml/2 tbsp of the oil in a frying pan. Add the onion. Cook for 5 minutes, stirring, until soft.

3 Squeeze the cabbage or sprouts to remove excess water. Place in a bowl with the potatoes and season to taste. Mix well.

4 Add the vegetables to the pan with the cooked onions, stir well, then press the mixture into a large, even cake shape. Adult supervision is required.

5 Cook over a medium heat for 5 minutes, until browned underneath. Check this by lifting up with the fish slice or spatula. Adult supervision is required.

6 Ask an adult to place a plate over the pan, and, holding it tightly against the pan, turn them both over together.

7 Return the empty frying pan to the heat and add the remaining oil. When hot, slide the cake back into the pan, browned-side uppermost.

8 Cook over a medium heat for 10 minutes, or until the underside is brown. Serve hot, in wedges with pork chops, if you like.

 = Watch out! Sharp or electrical tool in use. = Watch out! Heat is involved.

# Bean and tomato chilli

Packed with flavour, this makes a great alternative to a meat chilli. The coriander adds a flavoursome touch, but you can use parsley instead, if you like.

serves 4

## ingredients

- **fresh red chilli**, 1
- **tomato and herb sauce**, 400g/14oz jar
- **mixed beans**, 2 x 400g/14oz cans
- **salt** and **ground black pepper**
- **fresh coriander (cilantro)**, a handful
- **sour cream**, 120ml/4fl oz/½ cup

## tools

- **Chopping board**
- **Medium sharp knife**
- **Medium pan with a lid**
- **Colander**
- **Wooden spoon**
- **Ladle**

1 On a chopping board, cut the chilli in half and carefully cut out and discard the seeds and membranes. Thinly slice the chilli into slivers. Adult supervision is required. Wash your hands.

2 Put the sliced chilli in a medium pan with the tomato sauce.

3 Drain the canned beans in a colander and rinse well under cold running water.

4 Add the beans to the tomato sauce and beans and season well with salt and black pepper.

5 With adult supervision, chop the coriander.

6 Set some coriander aside for the garnish and add the remainder to the pan. Stir to mix.

7 Bring the mixture up to the boil, then reduce the heat, cover and simmer gently for 10 minutes, stirring occasionally. Add a little water if it starts to dry out. Adult supervision is required.

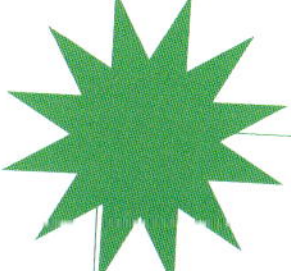

## COOK'S TIP

▶ Take care when chopping chillies and always wash your hands in soapy water after touching them. They contain a chemical called capsaicin, which is a powerful irritant and will cause eyes to sting if it comes into contact with them.

8 Ask an adult to remove from the heat and carefully ladle the chilli into warmed individual bowls and top with sour cream. Sprinkle with the reserved coriander and serve.

# Tuna and corn fish cakes

This simple recipe is a lovely way to use up leftover mashed potatoes. If you like, try making fish- or star-shaped cakes using cookie cutters.

serves 4

## ingredients

- **potatoes**, 350g/12oz
- **tuna fish**, 200g/7oz can, drained
- **canned** or **frozen corn**, 115g/4oz/¾ cup
- **chopped fresh parsley**, 30ml/2 tbsp
- **salt** and **ground black pepper**
- **fresh breadcrumbs**, 50g/2oz/1 cup
- **vegetable oil**, 30ml/2 tbsp
- **baby plum tomatoes**, grilled (broiled), **salad** and **lemon wedges**, to serve

## tools

- Vegetable peeler
- Chopping board
- Medium sharp knife
- Large pan
- Potato masher
- Large mixing bowl
- Wooden spoon
- Large flat plate
- Frying pan

1 Peel the potatoes and roughly chop them with a knife. Put in a large pan and cover with cold water. Bring up to the boil and boil for 10 minutes or until tender. Adult supervision is required.

2 Ask an adult to drain, then return to the pan. Mash with a masher until smooth. Set aside to cool.

3 Place the mashed potatoes in a large mixing bowl and stir in the tuna fish, corn and chopped fresh parsley. Season to taste with salt and black pepper and combine thoroughly.

4 Mix together, then divide the mixture into eight. Form into patty shapes with your hands.

5 Spread out the breadcrumbs on a plate. Press the fish cakes into the breadcrumbs and coat evenly on both sides.

6 Heat the oil in a frying pan, add the cakes and cook for 2 minutes on each side, until golden brown. Adult supervision is required. Serve with grilled tomatoes, salad and lemon wedges.

## COOK'S TIP

► When you shape fish cakes, patties or meatballs of any kind it really helps if you dip your hands in water before you start and whenever the mixture starts to stick to your hands. It is better to make smaller rather than larger ones because they cook better.

 = Watch out! Sharp or electrical tool in use. = Watch out! Heat is involved.

# Fast fishes

What a catch you'll make with these tasty home-made fish fingers. They are called 'fast' because as well as being good swimmers, they cook in just 10 minutes!

serves 2

## ingredients

- **hoki** or **cod fillets**, 2, each 115g/4oz
- **salt**
- **carrot**, 1, peeled
- **egg**, 1, beaten
- **fresh breadcrumbs**, 115ml/4oz/2 cups
- **sesame seeds**, 20ml/4 tsp
- **vegetable oil**, 20ml/4 tsp
- **frozen peas**, 30ml/2 tbsp
- **frozen corn kernels**, 4
- **new potatoes**, boiled, to serve

## tools

- 2 chopping boards
- Long, thin sharp knife
- Small shallow dish
- Whisk or fork
- Large flat plate
- Large frying pan
- Fish slice or metal spatula
- Small pan

1 Place the fish fillet on a chopping board, skin-side down. Dip the fingers of one hand in salt. Hold on to the fish with this hand.

2 Using a knife, carefully cut under the fish flesh along the skin. Adult supervision is required. Discard the skin. Rinse the fish and pat dry on kitchen paper. Cut into four pieces.

3 Cut the carrot into long thin slices, then cut out fin and tail shapes and tiny triangles for fish mouths. Adult supervision is required.

4 Put the egg in a small dish and whisk. Mix the breadcrumbs and sesame seeds on a plate. Dip pieces of fish in egg first, then in the breadcrumbs to coat on both sides.

5 Heat the oil in a frying pan. Add the fish and fry over a medium-high heat for 4–5 minutes, turning with the fish slice or metal spatula, until golden brown. Adult supervision is required.

6 Meanwhile, bring a pan of water to the boil. Add the peas and corn and cook for 3–4 minutes until tender. Ask an adult to drain.

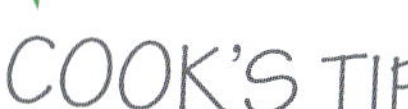

### COOK'S TIP

▶ You can freeze the uncooked breaded fish portions on a tray, then transfer to sealed containers. Thaw at room temperature and cook as Step 5.

7 Arrange the fish on two plates. Position the carrot pieces, and use the corn as eyes and peas as bubbles. Serve with boiled new potatoes.

# Colourful chicken kebabs

You'll have a great time making your own kebabs. They're wonderful cooked under the grill or on the barbecue in the summer.

serves 2–4

## ingredients

- **easy-cook long grain rice**, 100g/4oz
- **ground turmeric**, 5ml/1 tsp
- **green (bell) pepper**, ½
- **orange (bell) pepper**, ½
- **button (white) mushrooms**, 4
- **baby corn**, 4
- **cherry tomatoes**, 4
- **chicken breast fillet**, 100g/4oz, cut into thin strips
- **salad dressing**, 60ml/4 tbsp (see Cook's Tip)

## tools

- **4 wooden skewers**
- **Shallow dish**
- **Large pan**
- **Sieve (strainer)**
- **Chopping board**
- **Medium sharp knife**
- **Teaspoon**
- **Oven gloves**

1 Put the wooden skewers in a dish of cold water. Leave them to soak for about 30 minutes. This will stop them burning.

2 Put the rice and turmeric in a large pan. Cover with boiling water, and bring to a boil. Reduce the heat slightly and simmer for 15 minutes, until tender. Adult supervision is required.

3 Ask an adult to preheat the grill (broiler), then to drain the rice in a sieve. Return to the pan and cover.

4 Place the peppers on a chopping board and cut in half. Cut out the seeds and membranes. Cut them into chunks. Cut the mushrooms and baby corn into similar-sized pieces. Adult supervision is required.

5 Thread a tomato on to each of the skewers, then a piece of chicken, then some pepper, mushroom and corn. Continue until the skewers are full.

6 Spoon over a little dressing. Grill (Broil) for 5 minutes, then turn over and grill for another 5 minutes, until the chicken is cooked. Adult supervision is required.

### COOK'S TIP

► To make the salad dressing, put 60ml/4 tbsp sunflower oil, 30ml/2 tbsp vinegar, 15ml/1 tbsp clear honey, and a dash of pepper in a jar with a tight-fitting lid, then shake it well to combine everything.

7 Divide the rice between the serving plates and arrange the kebabs on top.

 = Watch out! Sharp or electrical tool in use.  = Watch out! Heat is involved.

# Sticky chicken

These delicious bites are perfect for a tasty supper. The sticky, sweet marinade makes a fabulous coating – just don't forget to serve it with a fingerbowl!

serves 2–4

## ingredients

- **chicken drumsticks**, 4
- **vegetable oil**, 10ml/2 tsp
- **soy sauce**, 5ml/1 tsp
- **smooth peanut butter**, 15ml/1 tbsp
- **tomato ketchup**, 15ml/1 tbsp
- **small baked potatoes**, **corn** and **tomato wedges**, to serve

## tools

- **Small sharp knife**
- **Chopping board**
- **Heatproof dish**
- **Medium bowl**
- **Pastry brush**
- **Wooden spoon**
- **Skewer**
- **Oven gloves**

1 Preheat the oven to 200°C/400°F/Gas 6.

2 Rinse the drumsticks under cold water, pat dry on kitchen paper and peel off the skin with your fingers. As you get to the thin end you will need to cut the skin off with a knife. Make three or four slashes and place in a heatproof dish. Adult supervision is required.

3 Put the oil, soy sauce, peanut butter and ketchup in a medium bowl and mix with a wooden spoon. Spread thickly over the top of the chicken.

4 Cook in the oven for 15 minutes. Turn the drumsticks over and baste with the peanut butter mixture and meat juices. Adult supervision is required.

5 Cook for a further 20 minutes or until the juices run clear when the chicken is pierced with a skewer. Ask an adult to remove from the oven.

6 Cool slightly, then wrap a piece of foil around the base of each drumstick. Serve with baked potatoes, corn, and tomato wedges.

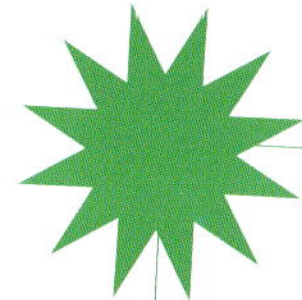

## VARIATIONS

- Use chicken thighs or breasts instead of drumsticks, if you like.
- This recipe also works with sausages or pork ribs (these need part-cooking in the oven before spreading over the marinade and cooking for a further 20 minutes).

sausages

# Honey mustard chicken

This is a tasty variation of Sticky Chicken, using a sweet mustard dressing and succulent chicken thighs. It is perfect for a quick and easy meal.

serves 4

## ingredients

- **chicken thighs**, 8
- **wholegrain mustard**, 60ml/4 tbsp
- **clear honey**, 60ml/4 tbsp
- **salt** and **ground black pepper**
- **tomatoes**, 8
- **red onion**, ½
- **olive oil**, 15ml/1 tbsp

## tools

- Roasting pan
- 2 small glass bowls
- 2 spoons
- Pastry brush
- Small knife
- Chopping board

red onion

## COOK'S TIP

▶ To check the chicken is cooked through, skewer it with a sharp knife or a metal skewer; the juices should run clear.

▶ For a really speedy supper, brush the chicken thighs with the marinade and refrigerate overnight or until needed.

1 Preheat the oven to 190°C/375°F/Gas 5.

2 Put the chicken thighs in a single layer in a roasting pan.

3 Mix together the mustard and honey in a small glass bowl with a spoon.

4 Season with salt and ground black pepper to taste.

5 Brush all over the thighs. Cook for 25–30 minutes, brushing the chicken with the pan juices occasionally, until cooked through (see Cook's Tip). Adult supervision is required.

6 Meanwhile, cut the tomatoes into quarters, chunks or thick slices and place in a small bowl. Adult supervision is required.

7 Finely chop the red onion and add to the tomatoes in the bowl. Add the olive oil and stir to mix.

8 Ask an adult to remove the chicken from the oven. Serve immediately with the tomato salad.



(!) = Watch out! Sharp or electrical tool in use.  = Watch out! Heat is involved.

# Yellow bean chicken

Chinese food is really quick to make and uses some different ingredients that you may not have tried before. These can be found in specialist stores or supermarkets.

serves 4

## ingredients

- **groundnut (peanut) oil**, 30ml/2 tbsp
- **salted cashew nuts**, 75g/3oz/¾ cup
- **spring onions (scallions)**, 4
- **skinless chicken breast fillets**, 450g/1lb
- **yellow bean sauce**, 165g/5½oz jar
- **cooked rice**, to serve

## tools

- **Wok or large, deep frying pan**
- **Wooden spatula**
- **Draining spoon**
- **2 chopping boards**
- **2 medium sharp knives**

cashew nuts

1 Heat 15ml/1 tbsp of the oil in a wok or frying pan, add the nuts and cook over a low heat, stirring frequently, for 2 minutes, until browned. You need to keep an eye on the nuts to prevent them from burning. Remove with a draining spoon. Set aside. Adult supervision is required.

2 Chop the spring onions. On a separate board, cut the chicken into strips, using a clean knife. Adult supervision is required.

3 Heat the remaining oil in the wok or pan and cook the spring onions and chicken for 5–8 minutes, until the meat is cooked.

4 Return the nuts to the wok or frying pan. Add the sauce. Stir to combine and cook for 1–2 minutes, until heated through. Adult supervision is required when using heat.

5 Serve immediately with a bowl of cooked rice.

## VARIATION

- If you like fish, you could make this dish with monkfish fillet or prawns (shrimp) instead of chicken. Cook diced monkfish in the same way as the chicken. For raw prawns, cook them in Step 3 until they change colour. Or you could use thin strips of pork fillet (tenderloin) or rump (round) steak.

prawns

# Turkey patties

These delicious fresh-tasting pasties (burgers) are a great midweek supper served in buns with potato wedges and salad. Choose a tasty relish to serve with them.

*serves* 4

## ingredients

- **small red onion**, 1
- **minced (ground) turkey**, 675g/1½lb
- **fresh thyme leaves**, small handful
- **lime-flavoured olive oil**, 30ml/2 tbsp
- **salt** and **ground black pepper**
- **burger buns**, 4, lightly toasted, to serve
- **relish** or **tomato ketchup**, to serve

## tools

- ✱ Chopping board
- ✱ Medium sharp knife
- ✱ Mixing bowl
- ✱ Griddle (grill) pan
- ✱ Pastry brush
- ✱ Fish slice or metal spatula

*burger buns*

1 Peel and finely chop the onion. Put it in a mixing bowl with the turkey. Adult supervision is required.

2 Add the thyme and 15ml/1 tbsp of the oil and season well with salt and ground black pepper. Cover and chill for up to 4 hours.

3 Divide the mixture into six equal portions and shape into round patties using damp hands. If the mixture starts to stick, dampen your hands again.

4 With adult supervision, preheat a griddle pan. Brush the patties with half of the remaining oil.

5 Place the patties on the griddle pan and cook for 10–12 minutes. Adult supervision is required.

6 Turn the patties over, brush with more oil, and cook for 10–12 minutes on the second side, or until cooked right through. Adult supervision is required.

## COOK'S TIP

► If you find it difficult to find lime-flavoured oil, simply add some finely grated lime zest to the turkey mince and cook the patties in ordinary olive oil.

*lime*

7 Ask an adult to lift the patties from the pan. Serve in warmed buns, with relish or tomato ketchup.

 = Watch out! Sharp or electrical tool in use. (!) = Watch out! Heat is involved.

★★ give it a try | time to cook: 10 minutes | preparation: 15 minutes

# Pittas with lamb koftas

These slightly spicy koftas can be made in advance and stored in an airtight container for three days, ready for you to grill or barbecue at a moment's notice.

serves 4

## ingredients

- **minced (ground) lamb**, 450g/1lb/2 cups
- **salt** and **ground black pepper**
- **small onion**, 1
- **harissa paste**, 10ml/2 tsp (see Cook's Tip)
- **fresh mint**, a small handful
- **natural (plain) yogurt**, 150ml/¼pt
- **pitta breads**, 8
- **cucumber** and **tomato slices**, to serve

*pitta breads*

## tools

- 8 wooden bamboo skewers
- Large mixing bowl
- Chopping board
- Medium sharp knife
- Small mixing bowl
- Spoon
- Oven gloves

1 Ask an adult to prepare a barbecue or preheat the grill (broiler). Soak eight wooden skewers in cold water for 1 hour to prevent them burning.

2 Meanwhile, place the lamb in a large bowl and season generously with salt and black pepper.

3 Peel and finely chop the onion and add to the bowl of mince with the harissa paste. Mix to combine. Adult supervision is required.

4 Divide the mixture into eight equal pieces and, using wet hands, press the meat on to the skewers in a sausage shape.

5 Cook for 10 minutes over the hot coals or under the grill, turning occasionally, until cooked. Adult supervision is required.

6 Chop the mint and mix it with the yogurt. Season to taste and set aside. Warm the pitta breads on the barbecue or under the grill for a few seconds, then split in half. Adult supervision is required.

7 Place a kofta in each pitta and remove the skewer. Add some cucumber and tomato slices. Drizzle with the yogurt sauce.

## COOK'S TIP

► Harissa is a North African paste made from chillies and garlic. If you can't find it, try chopping one small chilli and adding to the lamb with a clove of crushed garlic and 5ml/1 tsp ground cumin and 5ml/1 tsp ground coriander instead.

# Mexican tacos

Piling salad, cheese and mince into taco shells is a fun way to eat. This recipe is ideal for easy party food that everyone will enjoy tucking into.

taco shells

minced beef

serves 4

## ingredients

- **small iceberg lettuce**, ½
- **small onion**, 1, peeled
- **tomatoes**, 2
- **avocado**, 1
- **olive oil**, 15ml/1 tbsp
- **lean minced (ground) beef** or **turkey**, 250g/9oz
- **salt** and **ground black pepper**
- **garlic**, 2 cloves, crushed
- **ground cumin**, 5ml/1 tsp
- **mild chilli powder**, 5–10ml/1–2 tsp
- **ready-made taco shells**, 8
- **sour cream**, 60ml/4 tbsp
- **Cheddar cheese**, 125g/4oz/1 cup

## tools

- ✱ **Chopping board**
- ✱ **Medium sharp knife**
- ✱ **Teaspoon**
- ✱ **Large, deep frying pan**
- ✱ **Wooden spoon**
- ✱ **Oven gloves**

1 With adult supervision, shred the lettuce. Chop the onion and tomatoes.

2 Cut the avocado in half lengthways. Using a teaspoon, remove and discard the stone (pit). Cut the halves in half, pull off the skin and slice the flesh. Adult supervision is required.

3 Heat the oil in a frying pan. Add the meat and brown over a medium heat, stirring frequently to break up any large lumps. Adult supervision is required.

4 Season to taste, add the garlic and spices and cook for 10 minutes more, until cooked.

5 Meanwhile, warm the taco shells according to the packet instructions. Don't let them get too crisp.

6 Spoon the lettuce, onion, tomatoes and avocado into the taco shells. Top with the sour cream followed by the minced beef or turkey mixture.

### COOK'S TIP

▶ Tacos are eaten with the fingers and there's usually a certain amount of 'fall out', so make sure you have plenty of paper napkins handy.

7 With adult supervision, grate the cheese, then sprinkle into the tacos. Serve immediately, as the cheese melts from the heat of the cooked meat.

 = Watch out! Sharp or electrical tool in use.

 = Watch out! Heat is involved.

★★ give it a try | time to cook: **30 minutes** | preparation: **15 minutes**

# Meatballs in tomato sauce

These tasty and easy meatballs are very easy to make. Use beef or pork mince, whichever you prefer. The sausages will add some subtle spice to their flavour.

*serves* 4

## ingredients

- **minced (ground) beef**, 225g/8oz
- **salt** and **ground black pepper**
- **Sicilian-style sausages**, 4
- **pomodorino tomatoes**, 2 x 400g/14oz cans
- **cooked pasta or rice**, to serve
- **Parmesan cheese shavings**, to serve

## tools

- **Mixing bowl**
- **Medium sharp knife**
- **Fork**
- **Large, shallow baking dish**
- **Food processor or blender**

1 Put the minced beef in a bowl and season with salt and pepper. Slit the sausages and squeeze out the meat. Add to the bowl. Mash everything with a fork.

2 Shape into balls about the size of walnuts and arrange in a single layer in a baking dish.

3 Cover the dish and chill for 30 minutes. Preheat the oven to 180C/350F/Gas Mark 4.

4 Place the tomatoes in a food processor or blender and blend until just smooth. Adult supervision is required. Season with salt and pepper to taste.

5 Pour the tomato sauce over the meatballs in the baking dish, making sure they are all covered.

6 Cover with foil and bake for 30 minutes. Ask an adult to remove the foil after 15 minutes and stir occasionally during cooking, until cooked through.

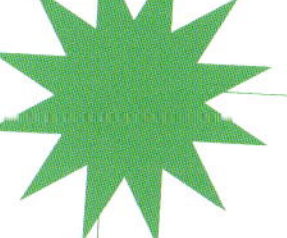

## COOK'S TIP

▶ Pomodorino tomatoes are another name for cherry tomatoes that are vine ripened. You can use cans of cherry tomatoes instead if you like, and these are widely available.

tomatoes

7 Serve the meatballs hot with cooked pasta or rice, sprinkled with Parmesan shavings.

# Pork satay

These tasty kebabs are perfect for cooking under the grill or on the barbecue. Serve with natural yogurt for dipping for a super-duper supper.

macadamia nuts

makes 8–12

## ingredients

- **pork fillet (tenderloin)**, 450g/1lb
- **light muscovado (brown) sugar**, 15ml/1 tbsp
- **shrimp paste**, 1cm/½in cube
- **lemon grass stalks**, 1–2
- **coriander seeds**, 30ml/2 tbsp
- **macadamia nuts** or **blanched almonds**, 6
- **onions**, 2, peeled and chopped
- **fresh red chilli**, 1, seeded and chopped (wash your hands after touching chilli)
- **ground turmeric**, 2.5ml/½ tsp
- **canned coconut milk**, 300ml/½ pint/1¼ cups
- **sunflower oil**, 30ml/2 tbsp

## tools

- **2 chopping boards**
- **2 medium sharp knives**
- **Non-metallic dish**
- **Foil**
- **Non-stick frying pan**
- **Blender or food processor**
- **8–12 wooden skewers, soaked in water for 1 hour**
- **Oven gloves**

1 Cut the pork into chunks. Adult supervision is required. Spread out in a layer in a dish. Sprinkle with sugar, cover and set aside.

2 Wrap the shrimp paste in foil. Heat a frying pan, then add the parcel. Heat for a few minutes, then remove from heat.

3 Using a clean board and knife, cut off the lower 5cm/2in of the lemon grass and chop finely.

4 Dry-fry the coriander seeds in the non-stick pan for 2 minutes. Put in a blender or food processor and blend to a powder. Adult supervision is required.

5 Remove the foil from the shrimp paste. Add the nuts and lemon grass to the blender and blend briefly, then add the onions, chilli, shrimp paste and turmeric. Blend to a paste. Adult supervision is required.

6 Pour in the coconut milk and oil and blend briefly to combine.

7 Pour the mixture over the pork and leave to marinate for 1–2 hours at room temperature or overnight in the refrigerator. Ask an adult to preheat the grill (broiler) to hot.

8 Thread three or four pieces of pork on to each skewer (reserving any leftover marinade) and put on a foil-lined grill (broiler) pan.

9 Cook for 8–10 minutes, until tender, basting frequently with the remaining marinade. Adult supervision is required. Serve immediately.

 = Watch out! Sharp or electrical tool in use.

= Watch out! Heat is involved.

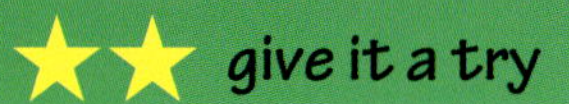 give it a try | time to cook: **25 minutes** | preparation: **15 minutes**

# Honey chops

These tasty, sticky chops are very easy to prepare and grill, but they would be just as good cooked on a barbecue. Serve with herby mash potatoes.

*serves* 4

## ingredients

- **carrots**, 450g/1lb
- **butter**, 15ml/1 tbsp
- **soft brown sugar**, 15ml/1 tbsp
- **sesame seeds**, 15ml/1 tbsp
- **herby mash**, to serve

### for the chops

- **pork loin (tenderloin) chops**, 4
- **butter**, 50g/2 oz/¼ cup
- **clear honey**, 30ml/2 tbsp
- **tomato purée (paste)**, 15ml/1 tbsp

## tools

- **Chopping board**
- **Medium sharp knife**
- **Small heavy pan**
- **Foil**
- **Small mixing bowl**
- **Wooden spoon**
- **Oven gloves**

1 With adult supervision, cut the carrots into matchsticks. Put in a small pan and just cover with water.

2 Add the butter and sugar and bring to a boil. Reduce the heat and simmer for 15 minutes, until most of the liquid has boiled away. Adult supervision is required.

3 Meanwhile, line a grill (broiler) pan with foil and arrange the pork chops on the rack.

4 In a bowl, beat together the butter and honey with a wooden spoon. Beat in the tomato purée, to make a paste. Ask an adult to preheat the grill (broiler) to high.

5 Spread half the honey paste over the chops and grill them for about 5 minutes, until browned. Ask an adult to remove the pan from under the grill.

6 Turn the chops over, spread them with the remaining paste. Ask an adult to return to the grill.

### COOK'S TIP

► This paste could also be used to coat sausages before cooking them, or drizzled over vegetables for roasting, such as courgettes (zucchini) and (bell) peppers.

7 Grill the chops for a further 5 minutes, until cooked. Transfer to plates. Sprinkle the sesame seeds over the carrots and serve with the chops and mash.

# Main meals

The main meal of the day is very important, and needs to be yummy, healthy and satisfying. This chapter contains a great range of family favourites, from colourful vegetable treats to meaty mouthfuls, all of which are bound to be popular. All you have to do is choose a dish, put on your apron and get cooking!

# Corn and potato chowder

This creamy, chunky soup is rich with the sweet taste of corn. It's yummy served with crusty bread and topped with some melted cheese for a warming dinner.

celery

serves 4

## ingredients

- **onion**, 1, peeled
- **medium baking potato**, 1, peeled
- **celery sticks**, 2
- **garlic**, 1 clove
- **small green (bell) pepper**, 1
- **sunflower oil**, 30ml/2 tbsp
- **butter**, 25g/1oz/2 tbsp
- **stock** or **water**, 600ml/1 pint/2½ cups
- **salt** and **ground black pepper**
- **milk**, 300ml/½ pint/1¼ cups
- **cannellini beans**, 200g/7oz can
- **corn kernels**, 300g/11oz can
- **dried sage**, good pinch
- **Cheddar cheese**, 50g/2oz grated, to serve

## tools

- Chopping board
- Large sharp knife
- Garlic crusher
- Large pan
- Wooden spoon
- Grater

1 On a chopping board, chop the onion, potato and celery into small pieces. Crush the garlic clove using a garlic crusher. Adult supervision is required.

2 Cut the pepper in half, then remove and discard the membrane and seeds. Chop the rest into small pieces.

3 Put the onion, garlic, potato, celery and pepper into a large heavy pan with the oil and butter.

4 Heat until sizzling, then reduce the heat to low. Cover and cook for about 10 minutes, stirring occasionally. Adult supervision is required when using heat.

5 Pour in the stock or water, season to taste and bring to the boil. Reduce the heat, cover and simmer for 15 minutes, until the vegetables are tender.

6 Add the milk, beans and corn – with their liquids – and the sage. Simmer, uncovered, for 5 minutes. Sprinkle with cheese and serve.

## COOK'S TIP

► If you prefer soup without chunks, leave the soup to cool slightly, then put the soup in a blender or food processor (adult supervision is required) and blend. Return to the pan and reheat. Adult supervision is required.



(!) = Watch out! Sharp or electrical tool in use. (oven glove) = Watch out! Heat is involved.

# Carrot soup

Carrots are said to improve your eyesight so this delicious soup might help you see in the dark. Serve with toast or chunks of bread for a light meal.

carrots

serves 4

## ingredients

- **carrots**, 450g/1lb
- **onion**, 1
- **sunflower oil**, 15ml/1 tbsp
- **split red lentils**, 75g/3oz/scant ½ cup
- **vegetable** or **chicken stock**, 1.2 litres/2 pints/5 cups
- **ground coriander**, 5ml/1 tsp
- **chopped fresh parsley**, 45ml/3 tbsp
- **salt** and **ground black pepper**
- **fresh coriander (cilantro) leaves** and **natural (plain) yogurt**, to serve

## tools

- Peeler
- Chopping board
- Medium sharp knife
- Large pan
- Wooden spoon
- Small bowl
- Sieve (strainer)
- Blender or food processor

1 Peel the carrots, then trim off the ends and slice into rounds. Peel the onion and cut in half. Lay the halves flat and slice into half moon crescents. Adult supervision is required.

2 Heat the oil in a pan, add the onion and cook, stirring, for 5 minutes. Adult supervision is required.

3 Add the carrots and cook gently, stirring, for about 4–5 minutes, until they start to soften.

4 Meanwhile, put the lentils in a small bowl and cover with cold water. Pour off any bits that float on the surface. Tip into a sieve and rinse under cold running water.

5 With adult supervision, add the lentils, stock and ground coriander to the pan. Bring up to the boil. Lower the heat, cover and simmer for 30 minutes, or until the lentils are tender.

6 Add the parsley, season and cook for 5 minutes. Set the pan aside to cool slightly.

7 Pour the soup into a blender or food processor and blend until smooth. (You may have to do this in two batches.) Adult supervision is required.

8 Return the soup to the pan and reheat until piping hot. Ladle into bowls and garnish with coriander and a spoonful of yogurt.

# Super duper soup

This fantastic vegetable soup is healthy, tasty and extremely easy to make. You can vary the vegetables, using whichever ones you like best.

serves 4–6

## ingredients

- **onion**, 1
- **carrots**, 2
- **potatoes**, 675g/1½lb
- **broccoli**, 115g/4oz
- **courgette (zucchini)**, 1
- **mushrooms**, 115g/4oz
- **vegetable oil**, 15ml/1 tbsp
- **vegetable stock**, 1.2 litres/2 pints/5 cups
- **chopped tomatoes**, 450g/1lb can
- **medium-hot curry powder**, 7.5ml/1½ tsp (optional)
- **dried mixed herbs**, 5ml/1 tsp
- **salt** and **ground black pepper**

## tools

* **Vegetable peeler**
* **Chopping board**
* **Medium sharp knife**
* **Large pan**
* **Metal spoon**

1 Peel the onion, carrots and potatoes. On a chopping board, slice the onion and carrots. Adult supervision is required.

2 Cut the potatoes into large chunks. Cut the broccoli into stalks (florets). Slice the courgette and the mushrooms. Set aside.

3 Heat the vegetable oil in a pan. Add the onion and carrots and fry gently for about 5 minutes, stirring occasionally, until they start to soften. Adult supervision is required.

4 Add the potatoes and fry gently for 2 minutes more, stirring frequently.

5 Add the stock, tomatoes, broccoli, courgette and mushrooms.

6 Add the curry powder (if using) and herbs. Season and bring up to the boil. Cover and simmer for 30–40 minutes, or until the vegetables are tender. Serve immediately.

## COOK'S TIP

► You can also add dried pasta to the soup 8–10 minutes before the end of cooking. Look out for special small pasta shapes in large supermarkets and delicatessens. Allow about 25g/1oz per person and add a little extra water to the soup.

 = Watch out! Sharp or electrical tool in use.  = Watch out! Heat is involved.

# Tomato and bread soup

This simple tomato and basil soup is thickened with stale bread, and makes a delicious, filling meal.

*serves* 4

## ingredients

- **stale bread**, 175g/6oz
- **medium onion**, 1
- **garlic**, 2 cloves
- **olive oil**, 90ml/6 tbsp
- **dried chilli**, small piece, crumbled (optional)
- **ripe tomatoes**, 675g/1½lb, peeled and chopped, or **peeled plum tomatoes**, 2 x 400g/14oz cans, chopped
- **chopped fresh basil**, 45ml/3 tbsp
- **salt** and **ground black pepper**
- **meat** or **vegetable stock** or **water**, or **a combination**, 1.5 litres/2½ pints/6¼ cups
- **extra virgin olive oil**, to serve (optional)

## tools

- Chopping board
- Large serrated knife
- Medium sharp knife
- Large pan
- Slotted spoon
- Wooden spoon
- Medium pan
- Fork

1 On a chopping board, cut away the crusts from the bread using a large serrated knife. Cut into cubes. Adult supervision is required.

2 Peel the onion. Cut in half lengthways, then lay flat on the board and chop into small pieces. Peel and finely chop the garlic cloves.

3 Heat 60ml/4 tbsp of the oil in a large pan. Add the chilli if using, and stir over high heat for 1–2 minutes. Add the bread cubes and cook until golden, stirring. Adult supervision is required.

4 Remove with a slotted spoon and transfer to a plate lined with kitchen paper. Set aside.

5 With adult supervision, add the remaining oil, the onion and garlic, and cook, stirring occasionally until the onion softens.

6 Stir in the tomatoes, bread cubes and basil. Season to taste. Cook over moderate heat, stirring occasionally, for 15 minutes. Adult supervision is required.

7 Meanwhile, place the stock or water in a pan and bring to a boil. Add to the pan containing the tomato mixture and mix well. Bring to a boil, lower the heat slightly and simmer for 20 minutes. Adult supervision is required.

8 Remove the soup from the heat. Use a fork to mash the tomatoes and the bread together. Season to taste.

9 Allow to stand for 10 minutes. Just before serving, swirl in a little extra virgin olive oil, if you like.

# Boston baked beans

This tasty speciality from Boston may take a long time to cook but it is very easy to prepare and is ideal for a cold day, as it fills the kitchen with its wonderful aroma.

serves 8

## ingredients

- **dried haricot beans**, 450g/1lb/2½ cups
- **bay leaf**, 1
- **cloves**, 4
- **onions**, 2, peeled
- **treacle (molasses)**, 185g/6½oz/½ cup
- **soft dark brown sugar**, 150g/5oz/¾ cup
- **Dijon-style mustard**, 15ml/1 tbsp
- **salt**, 5ml/1 tsp
- **pepper**, 5ml/1 tsp
- **boiling water**, 250ml/8fl oz/1 cup
- **salt pork**, 225g/8oz piece

## tools

- Colander
- Large mixing bowl
- 2 large pans
- Large ovenproof dish or heavy pan with a lid
- Small mixing bowl
- Chopping board
- Small sharp knife
- Oven gloves

1 Rinse the beans in a colander under running water. Drain and place in a bowl. Cover with water and leave to soak overnight. Drain and rinse again.

2 Put in a pan with the bay leaf and cover with fresh cold water. Bring to the boil, cover and simmer until tender, 1½–2 hours.

3 Preheat the oven to 140°C/275°F/Gas 1. Ask an adult to drain the beans, then put in an ovenproof dish or heavy pan. Stick two cloves in each of the onions and add them to the dish.

4 In a bowl, combine the treacle, sugar and mustard. Season. Ask an adult to add the boiling water.

5 Pour this mixture over the beans. Add more water if necessary so the beans are almost covered with liquid.

6 Fill the unused pan with water. Add the salt pork and bring to a boil. Boil for 3 minutes. Ask an adult to drain the pork in a colander. Leave to cool.

7 Score the rind with 1cm/½in cuts, using a sharp knife. Add to the casserole and push down below the surface, skin-side up. Adult supervision is required.

8 Cover and bake for 4½–5 hours. Uncover for the last 30 minutes. Ask an adult to remove from the oven and serve.

 = Watch out! Sharp or electrical tool in use. = Watch out! Heat is involved.

# Courgette and potato bake

This delicious dish is great served with warm crusty bread and a crisp green salad. It is easy to make, satisfying and looks good when brought to the table.

serves 6

## ingredients

- **courgettes (zucchini)**, 675g/1½lb
- **potatoes**, 450g/1lb
- **onion**, 1
- **garlic**, 3 cloves
- **large red (bell) pepper**, 1
- **chopped tomatoes**, 400g/14oz can
- **olive oil**, 150ml/¼ pint/⅔ cup
- **hot water**, 150ml/¼ pint/⅔ cup
- **dried oregano**, 5ml/1 tsp
- **salt** and **ground black pepper**
- **fresh flat leaf parsley**, 45ml/3 tbsp, chopped, plus a few extra sprigs, to garnish (optional)

## tools

- ✱ Chopping board
- ✱ Medium sharp knife
- ✱ Large baking dish
- ✱ Vegetable peeler
- ✱ Wooden spoon
- ✱ Oven gloves

1 Preheat the oven to 190°C/375°F/Gas 5. Slice the courgettes into rounds and put in a baking dish. Peel the potatoes and cut them into chunks. Adult supervision is required.

2 With adult supervision, peel and chop the onion and garlic and deseed and chop the pepper.

3 Add the onion, garlic, red pepper and tomatoes to the dish and mix well, then stir in the olive oil, hot water and dried oregano.

4 Spread the mixture evenly in the dish, then season to taste with salt and pepper. Bake for 30 minutes.

5 Ask an adult to remove from the oven. Stir in the parsley and a little more water.

6 Ask an adult to return the dish to the oven and cook for 1 hour, increasing the temperature to 200°C/400°F/Gas 6 for the final 10–15 minutes, so that the potatoes brown.

### COOK'S TIP

► You can prepare this dish a day in advance. Simply make up to the end of Step 3, cover and chill. The next day, continue from Step 4.

7 Ask an adult to remove the dish from the oven and allow to cool for 5 minutes before serving garnished with flat leaf parsley, if you like.

# Creamy coconut noodles

When everyday vegetables such as carrots and cabbage are given the Thai treatment, the result is a delectable creamy dish that everyone will enjoy. If you like your food spicy, you could add a little more red curry paste.

*serves* 4

## ingredients

- **vegetable oil**, 30ml/2 tbsp
- **lemon grass stalk**, 1, finely chopped
- **Thai red curry paste**, 15ml/1 tbsp
- **onion**, 1, halved and sliced
- **courgettes (zucchini)**, 3, sliced into rounds
- **Savoy cabbage**, 115g/4oz, shredded
- **carrots**, 2, sliced into rounds
- **broccoli**, 150g/5oz, cut into florets
- **coconut milk**, 2 x 400ml/14fl oz cans
- **vegetable stock**, 475ml/16fl oz/2 cups
- **dried egg noodles**, 150g/5oz
- **coriander (cilantro)**, 60ml/4 tbsp
- **Thai fish sauce**, 15ml/1 tbsp
- **soy sauce**, 30ml/2 tbsp

*lemon grass*

## tools

* **Large pan or wok**
* **2 wooden spoons**
* **Chopping board**
* **Large sharp knife**

1 Heat the oil in a large pan or wok until just smoking. Add the lemon grass and red curry paste and stir-fry for 2–3 seconds, keeping it moving all the time. Adult supervision is required when using heat.

2 Add the onion and reduce the heat to medium. Cook, stirring occasionally with a wooden spoon, for about 5–10 minutes, until the onion has softened but not browned.

3 Add the courgettes, cabbage, carrots and broccoli florets to the pan. Using two spoons, toss the vegetables to combine everything well. Reduce the heat to low.

4 Cook the mixture, stirring often, for a further 5 minutes. Increase the heat to medium, then stir in the coconut milk, stock and noodles and bring up to the boil.

5 With adult supervision, chop the coriander. Add to the pan with the fish sauce and soy sauce. Stir and cook for 1 minute. Transfer to bowls and serve immediately.



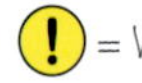 = Watch out! Sharp or electrical tool in use.

 = Watch out! Heat is involved.

# Crunchy summer rolls

These rolls are crunchy, pretty and tasty to eat – perfect for a quick light meal in the summer. There are lots of dipping sauces available in Asian stores, but you could just use soy sauce, if you like.

*serves* 4

## ingredients

- **round rice papers**, 12
- **small cucumber**, 1
- **carrots**, 2–3
- **spring onions (scallions)**, 3
- **lettuce**, 1, leaves separated and ribs removed
- **mung beansprouts**, 225g/8oz
- **fresh mint leaves**, 1 bunch
- **coriander (cilantro) leaves**, 1 bunch
- **Asian dipping sauce**, such as **nuoc cham**, **tuk tre** or **soy sauce**, to serve

## tools

- **Shallow dish**
- **Vegetable peeler**
- **Spoon**
- **Chopping board**
- **Medium sharp knife**

1 Pour some lukewarm water into a shallow dish. Soak the rice papers, 2–3 at a time, for 5 minutes until they are soft. Place on a clean dish towel and cover to keep them moist.

2 Peel the cucumber, carefully cut it in half lengthways, then remove the seeds with a spoon. Cut the remaining flesh into short matchsticks. Adult supervision is required.

3 Peel the carrots and cut them in half widthways, then lengthways. Slice into matchsticks. Trim the spring onions, cut into short pieces, then cut into matchsticks. Adult supervision is required.

4 Work with one paper at a time. Place a lettuce leaf towards the edge nearest to you, leaving about 2.5cm/1in to fold over. Place a mixture of the vegetables on top, followed by some mint and coriander.

5 Fold the edge nearest to you over the filling, tuck in the sides, and roll tightly to the edge on the far side. Repeat with the other papers and vegetables. Serve with dipping sauce.

# Chinese omelette parcels

A filled omelette makes a nourishing dinner. If you are not keen on stir-fries, you can use any other filling instead. Wash your hands after touching chillies.

*serves* 4

## ingredients

- **broccoli**, 130g/4½oz, cut into florets
- **groundnut (peanut) oil**, 30ml/2 tbsp
- **fresh root ginger**, 1cm/½in piece, peeled and finely grated
- **garlic**, 1 large clove, finely chopped
- **red chilli**, 1, seeded and sliced
- **spring onions (scallions)**, 4, sliced
- **pak choi (bok choy)**, 175g/6oz/3 cups, trimmed and shredded
- **fresh coriander (cilantro) leaves**, 50g/2oz/2 cups, plus extra to garnish
- **beansprouts**, 115g/4oz/½ cup
- **courgette (zucchini)**, 1, cut into strips
- **black bean sauce**, 45ml/3 tbsp
- **eggs**, 4
- **salt** and **ground black pepper**
- **soy sauce**, to serve

## tools

- Medium pan
- Slotted spoon
- Wok or large, deep frying pan
- Wooden spoon
- Chopping board
- Medium sharp knife
- Small bowl
- Fork
- Omelette pan
- Palette knife or metal spatula

## FACT FILE

### CORIANDER

There are two types of coriander: the fresh leafy herb used in this recipe (known as cilantro in America) and coriander seeds, which are usually dry-fried before being ground up and used to add a distinctive taste to a range of spiced dishes. The fragrant, bright green leaves of the fresh type add a wonderful flavour, colour and aroma to many dishes, especially Asian ones, and can be bought from most supermarkets or in specialist Asian stores.

*fresh coriander*

**1** Bring a pan of water up to the boil, add the broccoli and cook for 2 minutes. Lift out with a slotted spoon and rinse under cold water. Adult supervision is required.

**2** Meanwhile, heat 15ml/1 tbsp oil in a wok or frying pan. Add the ginger, garlic and half the chilli and stir-fry for 1 minute. Adult supervision is required when using heat.

**3** Add the spring onions, broccoli and pak choi and stir-fry for 2 minutes.

**4** With adult supervision, chop three-quarters of the coriander.

**5** Add the coriander, beansprouts and courgette strips to the wok or frying pan and stir-fry for 1 minute. Add the black bean sauce, stir to combine and heat for 1 minute more.

 = Watch out! Sharp or electrical tool in use. = Watch out! Heat is involved.

6 Beat the eggs in a small bowl with a fork and season with salt and pepper. Heat a little of the remaining oil in an omelette pan and add a quarter of the egg.

7 Swirl the egg until it covers the base of the pan in a thin layer, then scatter over a quarter of the coriander leaves. Cook until set, turning over with a palette knife or spatula.

8 Turn out on to a plate and keep warm while you make three more omelettes, adding a little oil each time.

9 Spoon the cooked vegetables on to one side of each omelette and roll up. Cut in half and serve garnished with coriander and chilli, if you like, and some soy sauce.

# Raving ravioli

Making your own pasta is great fun and very impressive. If you have a pasta machine, follow the manufacturer's instructions, otherwise just use a rolling pin.

*serves* 4

## ingredients

- **fresh spinach**, 75g/3oz
- **strong white bread flour**, 275g/10oz/2½ cups
- **eggs**, 3, beaten
- **vegetable oil**, 15ml/1 tbsp
- **salt** and **ground black pepper**
- **double (heavy) cream**, 300ml/½ pint/1¼ cups
- **fresh coriander (cilantro)**, 15ml/1 tbsp, chopped
- **freshly grated Parmesan cheese**, 30ml/2 tbsp, plus extra to serve

### for the filling

- **trout fillet**, 115g/4oz
- **ricotta cheese**, 50g/2oz/⅓ cup
- **lemon**, 1, grated rind
- **fresh chopped coriander (cilantro)**, 30ml/2 tbsp

## FACT FILE

### PARMESAN CHEESE

Used in many different dishes, Parmesan cheese is a strongly flavoured hard cheese from Italy. Because it has a powerful flavour, you only need to use a small amount.

Parmesan cheese

## tools

- ✱ Medium pan
- ✱ Blender or food processor
- ✱ Large deep frying pan
- ✱ Colander
- ✱ Small mixing bowl
- ✱ Large rolling pin
- ✱ Medium sharp knife or pastry wheel
- ✱ Teaspoon
- ✱ Small pan

1 Remove the stalks from the spinach and tear up the leaves. Place in a medium pan with 15ml/1 tbsp water and heat gently, covered, until the spinach has wilted. Adult supervision is required.

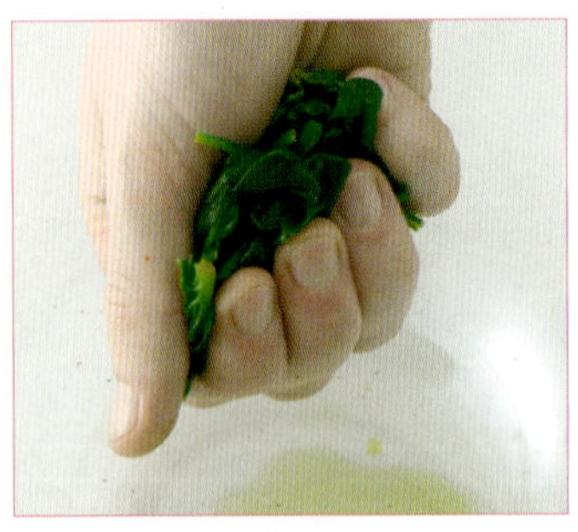

2 Cool, then squeeze out as much water as you can. Put the leaves into a blender or food processor, with the flour, eggs and oil.

3 Season to taste and blend until it forms a smooth dough. Adult supervision is required.

4 Transfer the dough to a lightly floured surface and knead it for about 5 minutes, until it is smooth. Wrap it well with clear film (plastic wrap) and chill in the refrigerator for at least 30 minutes.

5 **To make the filling,** place the trout fillet in a frying pan. Cover with water and bring up to the boil. Reduce the heat and simmer gently for 3–4 minutes, until tender and flaking easily. Adult supervision is required.

6 Ask an adult to drain in a colander. Leave to cool. Remove the skin and flake the flesh into a bowl.

7 Sprinkle a work surface lightly with flour. Roll out the dough to make a 50 x 46cm/20 x 18in rectangle, the thickness of thin card. Leave to dry out for about 15 minutes.

8 Use a sharp knife or pastry wheel to trim the edges, then cut the dough in half. Adult supervision is required.

 = Watch out! Sharp or electrical tool in use. (!) = Watch out! Heat is involved.

9 Add the ricotta, lemon rind and coriander to the trout. Season with salt and pepper. Beat together.

10 Put four small spoonfuls of the trout filling across the top of the dough, leaving a small border round the edge of each. Carry on putting the filling mixture in lines, to make eight rows.

11 Lift up the second sheet of pasta on the rolling pin and lay it over the first sheet. Run your finger between the bumps to remove any air and to press the dough together.

12 Using the knife or pastry wheel, cut the ravioli into small parcels and trim round the edge as well, to seal each one.

13 Cook in lightly salted boiling water for 2–3 minutes. Ask an adult to drain. Return to the pan.

14 Put the cream, remaining coriander and the Parmesan in a small pan and heat gently, without boiling, until the cheese has melted. Adult supervision is required. Pour over the ravioli and stir.

15 Transfer to serving dishes and serve immediately, garnished with a sprig of coriander and grated Parmesan

# Spudtastic!

Baked potatoes are really easy to cook and, served with one of these scrumptious toppings, are a real treat. Each topping makes enough to fill four potatoes.

serves 4

## ingredients

- **medium baking potatoes**, 4
- **olive oil**
- **sea salt**
- **a filling of your choice** (see below)

### for the stir-fried veg

- **sunflower oil**, 45ml/3 tbsp
- **leeks**, 2, thinly sliced
- **carrots**, 2, cut into sticks
- **courgette (zucchini)**, 1, thinly sliced
- **baby corn**, 115g/4oz, halved
- **button (white) mushrooms**, 115g/4oz/1½ cups, sliced
- **soy sauce**, 45ml/3 tbsp
- **dry sherry** or **vermouth**, 30ml/2 tbsp
- **sesame oil**, 15ml/1 tbsp
- **sesame seeds**, to garnish

### for the red bean chilli

- **red kidney beans**, 425g/15oz can, drained
- **cream cheese**, 200g/7oz/scant 1 cup
- **mild chilli sauce**, 30ml/2 tbsp
- **ground cumin**, 5ml/1 tsp

### for the cheese and creamy corn

- **creamed corn**, 425g/15oz can
- **grated Cheddar cheese**, 115g/4oz/1 cup
- **mixed dried herbs**, 5ml/1 tsp
- **fresh parsley sprigs**, to garnish

## COOK'S TIP

► Choose potatoes that are the same size and have undamaged skins, and scrub them thoroughly. If they are cooked before you want to serve them, ask an adult to take them out of the oven and wrap them up in a warm cloth until they are needed.

## tools

- Small sharp knife
- Non-stick baking sheet
- Oven gloves
- Chopping board
- Wok or frying pan
- Wooden spoon
- Metal spoon
- Small mixing bowl
- 2 small pans

1 Preheat the oven to 200°C/400°F/Gas 6.

2 With adult supervision, score the potatoes with a cross using a sharp knife. Rub the skins all over with oil. Place on a baking sheet and cook for 45–60 minutes, until a knife inserted into the centre comes out clean.

3 Ask an adult to remove the potatoes from the oven and leave to cool slightly for a few minutes.

4 Place the potatoes on a chopping board and cut them open along the scored lines with a knife. Push up the flesh. Season to taste and fill with your chosen filling.

5 To make the **stir-fried veg**, heat the oil in a wok or large frying pan until really hot. Adult supervision is required.

6 Add the leeks, carrots, courgette and baby corn and stir-fry together for about 2 minutes, then add the mushrooms and stir-fry for a further minute.

7 Mix together the soy sauce, sherry or vermouth and sesame oil in a small bowl.

8 Pour the mixture over the vegetables in the frying pan. Heat through until just bubbling, then scatter over the sesame seeds. Serve immediately with the potatoes.

 = Watch out! Sharp or electrical tool in use. = Watch out! Heat is involved.

9 **To make the red bean chilli**, heat the beans in a small pan for 5 minutes or in a microwave for about 3 minutes, until hot. Adult supervision is required.

10 Stir in the cream cheese, chilli sauce and cumin. Heat for 1 minute. Spoon on to the potatoes and top with more chilli sauce.

11 **To make the cheese and creamy corn filling**, heat the corn in a small pan with the cheese and herbs for about 5 minutes, until hot. Mix well. Adult supervision is required.

12 Spoon the mixture on to the potatoes and garnish with fresh parsley sprigs.

★★ give it a try | time to cook: **35 minutes** | preparation: **15 minutes**

# Vegetable paella

This extremely easy all-in-one-pan meal includes lots of colourful, tasty vegetables and is a sure hit with vegetarians and meat-eaters alike.

*serves* 6

## ingredients

- **leeks**, 2
- **celery**, 3 sticks
- **red (bell) pepper**, 1
- **courgettes (zucchini)**, 2
- **brown cap mushrooms**, 175g/6oz/2½ cups
- **onion**, 1, peeled and chopped
- **garlic**, 2 cloves, peeled and chopped
- **frozen peas**, 175g/6oz/1½ cups
- **long grain brown rice**, 450g/1lb/2 cups
- **vegetable stock**, 900ml/1½ pints/3¾ cups
- **saffron**, a few threads
- **cannellini beans**, 400g/14oz can, drained
- **cherry tomatoes**, 225g/8oz/2 cups
- **fresh mixed herbs**, 45–60ml/3–4 tbsp, chopped

## tools

- **Chopping board**
- **Medium sharp knife**
- **Paella pan or large, deep frying pan**
- **Wooden spoon**

1 Slice the leeks and chop the celery, reserving any leaves. Adult supervision is required when cutting.

2 Cut the pepper in half and remove the seeds and membranes. Slice. Slice the courgettes and the mushrooms.

3 Put the onion, garlic, leeks, celery, pepper, courgettes and mushrooms in a paella pan.

4 Add the peas, brown rice, vegetable stock and saffron threads to the pan and mix well with a wooden spoon to combine.

5 Bring the mixture to the boil, stirring often. Lower the heat and simmer, uncovered, stirring often, for 30 minutes, until almost all the liquid has been absorbed and the rice is tender. Add the beans and cook for 5 minutes more. Adult supervision is required.

6 Meanwhile, cut the cherry tomatoes in half and add to the pan with the chopped herbs. Serve immediately, garnished with the reserved celery leaves.

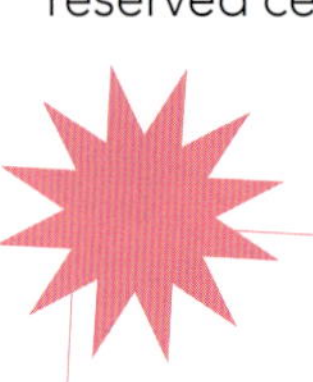

VARIATION

• If preferred, use white long grain rice instead of brown.



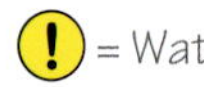

(!) = Watch out! Sharp or electrical tool in use. = Watch out! Heat is involved.

# Fish and rice paella

If you have had paella on holiday in Spain then you'll be keen to give it a try at this recipe. Using a mixture of frozen fish saves doing too much fussy preparation.

*serves* 4

## ingredients

- **red (bell) pepper**, 1
- **oil**, 30ml/2 tbsp
- **onion**, 1, peeled and sliced
- **mushrooms**, 115g/4oz, chopped
- **ground turmeric**, 10ml/2 tsp
- **rice** and **grain mix** (or just rice), 225g/8oz/scant 1½ cups
- **fish**, **chicken** or **vegetable stock**, 750ml/1¼ pints/3 cups
- **salt** and **ground black pepper**
- **frozen premium seafood selection**, 400g/14oz bag, thawed
- **frozen large tiger prawns (jumbo shrimp)**, 115g/4oz, thawed

## tools

- **Chopping board**
- **Medium sharp knife**
- **Paella pan or large, deep frying pan**
- **Wooden spoon**

1 With adult supervision, cut the pepper in half. Seed and chop.

2 Heat the oil in a paella pan. Add the onion and fry for 5 minutes, stirring. Add the pepper and mushrooms and fry for 1 minute. Adult supervision is required.

3 Stir in the turmeric and then the grains. Stir until well mixed, then carefully pour on the stock.

4 Season, cover and leave to simmer gently for 15 minutes. Uncover and stir once or twice during the cooking time.

5 Uncover and add the seafood selection and prawns. Stir and bring the liquid back to the boil.

6 Cover and simmer for 3–5 minutes more, stirring once or twice, until the fish and shellfish are opaque. Serve immediately.

## VARIATION

• You can use whatever mixture of fish you like in this dish, or simply use either prawns or some canned tuna if you prefer to keep it simple.

*canned tuna*

# Plaice with tomato sauce

These crispy fishy morsels beat store-bought fish fingers (sticks) hands down. Instead of reaching for the tomato ketchup, try serving with this tasty tomato sauce.

*serves* 4

## ingredients

- **plain (all-purpose) flour**, 25g/1oz/¼ cup
- **eggs**, 2, beaten
- **dried breadcrumbs**, 75g/3oz/¾ cup
- **small plaice or flounder**, 4, skinned
- **salt** and **ground black pepper**
- **butter**, 25g/1oz/2 tbsp
- **sunflower oil**, 30ml/2 tbsp
- **lemon**, 1, quartered, to serve

### for the tomato sauce

- **red onion**, 1
- **garlic**, 1 clove
- **olive oil**, 30ml/2 tbsp
- **chopped tomatoes**, 400g/14oz can
- **tomato purée (paste)**, 15ml/1 tbsp
- **fresh basil leaves**, 15ml/1 tbsp, torn

## tools

- **Chopping board**
- **Medium sharp knife**
- **Large pan**
- **Wooden spoon**
- **3 large shallow dishes**
- **2 large frying pans**
- **Fish slice or metal spatula**

1 **To make the tomato sauce**, finely chop the red onion and garlic. Adult supervision is required.

2 Heat the oil in a large pan, add the onion and garlic, and cook for 2–3 minutes, stirring occasionally until softened but not brown. Adult supervision is required.

3 Stir in the chopped tomatoes and tomato purée. Bring up to the boil and simmer for 10 minutes.

4 Meanwhile, spread out the flour in one shallow dish, pour the beaten eggs into another and spread out the breadcrumbs in a third.

5 Lightly season the fish pieces on both sides. Dip each in turn first in the flour on both sides, then in egg on both sides and finally in the breadcrumbs. Aim for an even coating of breadcrumbs that is not too thick. Gently shake off any excess breadcrumbs and set the fish aside.

6 Heat the butter and oil in a frying pan until foaming. Add the fish and fry for about 5 minutes on each side, until the outside is brown and the fish is cooked. Adult supervision is required.

7 Ask an adult to remove with a fish slice or spatula and transfer to kitchen paper to drain.

8 Season the tomato sauce to taste, then stir in the basil. Transfer the fish to plates and serve with the sauce. Offer lemon wedges separately for squeezing over the top.

 = Watch out! Sharp or electrical tool in use.  = Watch out! Heat is involved.

# Fish and cheese pies

This creamy mixture of fish, corn and cabbage topped with potato and cheese is easy to make, warming and filling – perfect for a winter's dinner.

serves 2

## ingredients

- **medium potato**, 1, peeled and chopped
- **green cabbage**, 25g/1oz, shredded
- **cod** or **hoki fillets**, 115g/4oz, skinned
- **milk**, 150ml/¼ pint/⅔ cup
- **butter**, 15ml/1 tbsp
- **plain (all-purpose) flour**, 15ml/1 tbsp
- **frozen corn**, 25g/1oz/2 tbsp
- **Red Leicester** or **mild Cheddar cheese**, 25g/1oz/¼ cup, grated
- **sesame seeds**, 5ml/1 tsp
- **cooked carrot sticks** and **mangetouts (snow peas)**, to serve

## tools

- ✱ 2 large pans with lids
- ✱ Colander
- ✱ Table knife
- ✱ Sieve (strainer)
- ✱ Wooden spoon
- ✱ 2 small ovenproof dishes
- ✱ Potato masher
- ✱ Oven gloves

1 Three-quarters fill a large pan with water and bring up to the boil. Add the potato and cook for 10 minutes. Add the cabbage and cook for 5 minutes more, until tender. Adult supervision is required.

2 Ask an adult to drain in a colander. Return to the pan and cover with a lid.

3 Meanwhile, place the skinned fish fillets and all but 10ml/2 tsp of the milk in another large pan. Bring up to the boil, then cover, reduce the heat and simmer very gently for 8–10 minutes, until the fish flakes easily when pressed gently with the tip of a table knife. Adult supervision is required.

4 Ask an adult to strain, reserving the liquid. Wash the pan.

5 With adult supervision, melt the butter in the clean pan. Stir in the flour and cook, stirring, for 1–2 minutes. Remove from heat and stir in the reserved cooking liquid. Return to the heat and bring up to the boil, stirring until thickened.

6 Ask an adult to preheat the grill (broiler) to medium-hot. Add the fish and corn to the sauce with half of the cheese. Spoon into the dishes.

7 Mash the potato and cabbage with the remaining milk. Stir in half the remaining cheese. Spoon over the fish. Sprinkle with the sesame seeds and the remaining cheese.

8 Grill until browned. Adult supervision is required. Serve.

# Tandoori-style chicken

Create an Indian classic at home with this easy recipe, then use the same marinade to tandoori your favourite meats and fish.

serves **6**

## ingredients

- **chicken thighs**, 6 (see Cook's Tips)
- **natural (plain) yogurt**, 150g/5oz
- **paprika**, 6.5ml/1¼ tsp
- **hot curry paste**, 5ml/1 tsp
- **coriander seeds**, 5ml/1 tsp, roughly crushed (see Cook's Tips)
- **cumin seeds**, 2.5ml/½ tsp, roughly crushed
- **ground turmeric**, 2.5ml/½ tsp
- **vegetable oil**, 5ml/2 tsp

to serve

- **fresh mint leaves**, a small handful
- **natural (plain) yogurt**, 150g/5oz
- **cucumber**, ½
- **spring onions (scallions)**, 2
- **cooked basmati rice, mixed salad** and **lemon wedges**, to serve (optional)

turmeric

## COOK'S TIPS

▶ Use chicken drumsticks, if preferred, or chicken breasts on the bone.

▶ Crush spices in either a special spice grinder (sometimes attached to a food processor) or in a mortar and pestle. Otherwise place in a small metal bowl and crush with the end of a rolling pin. Or place spices on a chopping board and roll with a heavy rolling pin to crush.

## tools

- **2 chopping boards**
- **2 medium sharp knives**
- **Non-metallic shallow dish**
- **1 small serving bowl**
- **Spoon**
- **Tongs**
- **Wire rack (to fit over roasting pan)**
- **Medium roasting pan**
- **Kettle or pan**
- **Oven gloves**
- **Skewer**
- **Grater**
- **Fish slice or metal spatula**

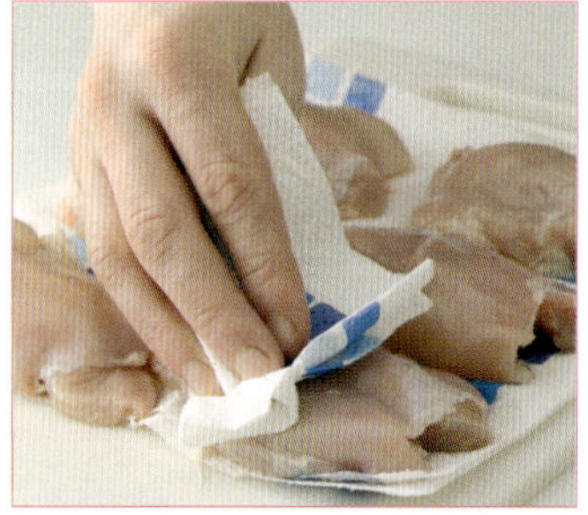

1 On a chopping board, carefully cut away the skin from the chicken thighs with a sharp knife – you will need to pull it off to free it completely. Use the knife to make two or three deep slashes in the meaty parts. Adult supervision is required.

2 Rinse the chicken, then pat dry on kitchen paper. Place in a shallow dish.

3 Place the yogurt, paprika, curry paste, coriander and cumin seeds and turmeric in a small bowl and mix together.

4 Spoon over the chicken thighs and turn over to coat in the paste.

5 Cover with clear film (plastic wrap). Leave the chicken in the refrigerator to marinate for at least 2 hours – longer if possible.

6 Preheat the oven to 200°C/400°F/Gas 6. Arrange the marinated chicken thighs on a wire rack set over a roasting pan, allowing a little room between them. Spread with any leftover marinade and drizzle with a little oil.

 = Watch out! Sharp or electrical tool in use.  = Watch out! Heat is involved.

7 Ask an adult to pour a little boiling water from the kettle into the base of the tin (to create steam). Cook in the preheated oven for 40 minutes or until the juices run clear when the chicken is pierced deeply with a skewer.

8 With adult supervision, chop the spring onions and mint.

9 Put the yogurt in a serving bowl. Grate the cucumber and stir in. Add the spring onions and mint and mix well. Season.

10 Ask an adult to remove the roasting tin from the oven and lift off the chicken with a fish slice or metal spatula.

11 Transfer the chicken to serving dishes and serve with the yogurt mixture, rice, salad and lemon wedges, if using. The cooked chicken is delicious eaten warm, or cold the next day, if you like.

# Chicken fajitas

These fabulous fajitas are perfect for the weekend, and it's lots of fun preparing all the different fillings and bringing them to the table so people can help themselves.

### COOK'S TIP

▶ Soak the wooden skewer for at least 1 hour before using, to prevent them burning when you cook the onions under the grill.

*serves* 6

## ingredients

- **lime**, 2, finely grated rind of 1 and the juice of 2
- **olive oil**, 120ml/4fl oz/½ cup
- **garlic**, 1 clove, peeled and finely chopped
- **dried oregano**, 2.5ml/½ tsp
- **dried red chilli flakes**, a good pinch
- **roasted coriander seeds**, 5ml/1 tsp, crushed
- **salt** and **ground black pepper**
- **boneless chicken breast fillets**, 6
- **Spanish (Bermuda) onions**, 3, peeled and thickly sliced
- **large red**, **yellow** or **orange (bell) peppers**, 2, seeded and cut into strips
- **chopped fresh coriander (cilantro)**, 30ml/2 tbsp

### for the salsa

- **tomatoes**, 450g/1lb, peeled, seeded and chopped
- **garlic**, 2 cloves, peeled and finely chopped
- **small red onion**, 1, peeled and finely chopped
- **green chilli**, 1, seeded and finely chopped (optional)
- **lime**, ½, finely grated rind
- **fresh coriander (coriander)**, 30ml/2 tbsp, chopped
- **caster (superfine) sugar**, a pinch
- **roasted cumin seeds**, 2.5–5ml/½–1 tsp, ground

### to serve

- **soft flour tortillas**, 12–18
- **guacamole**
- **sour cream**, 120ml/4fl oz/½ cup
- **crisp lettuce leaves**
- **fresh coriander (cilantro) sprigs**
- **lime wedges**

## tools

- ✱ Ovenproof dish
- ✱ Grater
- ✱ Juicer
- ✱ 2 small sharp knives
- ✱ 2 chopping boards
- ✱ Medium sharp knife
- ✱ Wooden skewer (see Cook's Tip)
- ✱ Grill (broiler) rack
- ✱ Oven gloves
- ✱ Griddle (grill) pan
- ✱ Large frying pan
- ✱ Wooden spoon

1 In an ovenproof dish, mix the lime rind and juice, 75ml/5 tbsp of the oil, the garlic, oregano, chilli flakes and coriander seeds and season. With adult supervision, slash the skin on the chicken several times. Turn them in the mixture.

2 Cover and set aside to marinate for 2 hours.

3 **To make the salsa**, combine the tomatoes, garlic, onion, chilli (if using), lime rind and coriander. Season with salt, pepper, caster sugar and cumin.

4 Set the salsa aside for 30 minutes, then taste and adjust the seasoning, adding more cumin and sugar, if necessary.

5 Ask an adult to heat the grill (broiler). Thread the onions on to a skewer.

6 Brush the onions with 15ml/1 tbsp of the remaining oil and season. Grill for about 10 minutes, until softened and charred in places. Adult supervision is required. Preheat the oven to 200°C/400°F/Gas 6.

7 Cover the ovenproof dish containing the marinated chicken with foil, then cook in the oven for 20 minutes. Remove from the oven, then cook in a griddle pan for 8–10 minutes, until browned and fully cooked. Adult supervision is required.

 = Watch out! Sharp or electrical tool in use.  = Watch out! Heat is involved.

8 Meanwhile, with adult supervision, heat the remaining oil in a frying pan, add the peppers and cook for about 10 minutes, until softened and browned in places. Add the grilled onions and fry briskly for 2–3 minutes.

9 Add the chicken cooking juices and fry over a high heat, stirring frequently, until the liquid evaporates. Stir in the chopped coriander. Adult supervision is required.

10 Reheat the tortillas following the instructions on the packet.

11 Using a sharp knife, cut the chicken into strips and transfer to a serving dish. Place the pepper mixture and the salsa in separate dishes.

12 Serve the dishes of chicken, onions and peppers and salsa with the tortillas, guacamole, sour cream, lettuce and coriander for people to help themselves. Serve lime wedges on the side so that people can choose whether to squeeze over the lime juice, depending on their personal preference.

# Turkey croquettes

These crunchy potato and turkey bites served with a really tomatoey sauce are so tasty you may want to make double the amount!

serves 4

## ingredients

- **potatoes**, 450g/1lb, peeled and diced
- **eggs**, 3
- **milk**, 30ml/2 tbsp
- **salt** and **ground black pepper**
- **turkey rashers (strips)**, 175g/6oz, chopped
- **spring onions (scallions)**, 2, finely sliced
- **fresh breadcrumbs**, 115g/4oz/2 cups
- **vegetable oil**, for deep-frying

### for the sauce

- **olive oil**, 15ml/1 tbsp
- **onion**, 1, finely chopped
- **chopped tomatoes**, 400g/14oz can
- **tomato purée (paste)**, 30ml/2 tbsp
- **fresh parsley**, 15ml/1 tbsp, chopped

## tools

* 2 medium pans
* Colander
* Potato masher
* Mixing bowl
* Wooden spoon
* 2 small shallow dishes
* Heavy pan or deep-fat fryer
* Draining spoon

1 Put the potatoes in a pan and cover with water. Bring up to the boil and boil for 10–15 minutes, until tender. Adult supervision is required.

2 Ask an adult to drain in a colander. Return to the pan. Heat gently for 1–2 minutes to make sure all the excess water evaporates. Remove from the heat.

3 Mash the potatoes with two eggs and the milk, until smooth. Season well. Stir in the turkey and spring onions. Transfer to a mixing bowl, cover and chill for 1 hour.

4 Meanwhile, **to make the sauce** heat the oil in a medium pan and fry the onion for 5 minutes, stirring occasionally, until softened. Drain and add the tomatoes and tomato purée, stir and bring up to the boil. Simmer for 10 minutes. Stir in the parsley and season to taste. Adult supervision is required.

5 Remove the potato mixture from the refrigerator and divide into eight pieces. Wet your hands and shape each into a sausage shape. Place the remaining egg in a dish and spread the breadcrumbs on another dish. Dip the croquettes into the egg and then breadcrumbs to coat.

6 Ask an adult to heat the oil in a heavy pan or deep-fat fryer to 175°C/330°F and add the croquettes. Cook for 5 minutes, or until golden and crisp. Ask an adult to remove with a draining spoon and drain on kitchen paper. Reheat the sauce gently and serve with the croquettes.

 = Watch out! Sharp or electrical tool in use. = Watch out! Heat is involved.

# Turkey surprise packages

You'll have cooking all wrapped up with this easy supper recipe. Cooking in paper parcels is really healthy because it doesn't require any added oil.

serves 4

## ingredients

- **spring onions (scallions)**, 2
- **fennel**, 50g/2oz
- **carrot**, 1
- **celery**, 1 small stick
- **turkey breast steaks**, 4, weighing 150–175g/5–6oz each
- **parsley**, 30ml/2 tbsp, chopped
- **streaky (fatty) bacon**, 8 rashers (strips)
- **lemon**, 1, grated rind and juice
- **salt** and **ground black pepper**
- **lemon** or **lime wedges**, to serve

*fennel*

## tools

- **2 chopping boards**
- **Medium sharp knife**
- **Pastry brush**
- **Large, shallow roasting tin**
- **Oven gloves**
- **Fish slice or metal spatula**

1 On a chopping board, cut the spring onions, fennel, carrot and celery into thin strips of about the same thickness. Set aside. Adult supervision is required.

2 Lay the turkey breast steaks flat on a separate board and pat chopped parsley over each.

3 Wrap two rashers of bacon around each turkey breast in a cross shape. Preheat the oven to 190°C/375°F/Gas 5.

4 Cut 4 x 30cm/12in circles out of baking parchment, brush lightly with oil and put a turkey breast just off centre on each one.

5 Arrange the vegetable strips on top of the turkey breasts, sprinkle the lemon rind and juice over and season well.

6 Fold the paper over the meat and vegetables and, starting at one side, twist and fold the paper edges together.

7 Work your way around the semi-circle of baking parchment, sealing the edges of the parcels together neatly.

8 Put the parcels in the tin and cook for 35–45 minutes, or until the meat is cooked and tender when tested with the tip of a knife. Ask an adult to remove from the oven and lift out the packages with a fish slice or metal spatula.

9 Serve the packages with the lemon wedges on the side to squeeze over them.

# Pork and pineapple curry

This easy curry is packed with juicy chunks of meat and pineapple in a fragrant, creamy sauce. Serve with plenty of long grain rice to soak up all those delicious juices.

*serves* 4

## ingredients

- **medium pineapple**, ½
- **coconut milk**, 400ml/14fl oz can
- **Thai red curry paste**, 10ml/2 tsp
- **pork loin (tenderloin) steaks**, 400g/14oz, cut into bitesize pieces
- **Thai fish sauce**, 15ml/1 tbsp
- **light muscovado (brown) sugar**, 5ml/1 tsp
- **tamarind paste**, 5ml/1 tsp
- **kaffir lime leaves**, 2
- **fresh red chilli**, 1, thinly sliced (optional)
- **cooked rice**, to serve (optional)

*pineapple*

## tools

- ✱ **Chopping board**
- ✱ **Large sharp knife**
- ✱ **Small sharp knife**
- ✱ **Medium mixing bowl**
- ✱ **Measuring jug (cup)**
- ✱ **Large pan**
- ✱ **Wooden spoon**

1 Ask an adult to help you slice the base and top off the pineapple. Stand upright. Cut away the skin by 'sawing' down. Using the tip of a small, sharp knife, cut out the 'eyes' (dark round pieces). Cut the pineapple in half lengthways, then cut out the core. Chop half into pieces and set aside.

2 Pour the coconut milk into a bowl and let it settle, so that the cream rises to the top. Scoop the cream into a measuring jug. Add some liquid, if needed, so you have 250ml/8fl oz/1cup.

3 Pour the coconut cream into the large pan and bring it to the boil. Adult supervision is required.

4 Cook over a medium heat for 8 minutes, until the cream separates, stirring frequently.

5 Stir in the red curry paste. Cook, stirring occasionally, for about 3 minutes, until the sauce thickens slightly.

6 Add the pork with the fish sauce and sugar. Mix the tamarind paste with 15ml/1 tbsp warm water in the jug, then add to the sauce and stir well. Cook, stirring, for 2–3 minutes, until the sugar has dissolved and the pork is cooked. Adult supervision is required.

7 Add the remaining coconut milk, lime leaves and pineapple chunks to the pan and bring to the boil. Reduce the heat and simmer gently for 3 minutes, or until the pork is fully cooked.

8 Transfer to serving dishes, add the chilli, if using, and serve with rice.

 = Watch out! Sharp or electrical tool in use. (!) = Watch out! Heat is involved.

# Thai pork patties

These zesty patties make a tasty change from the usual burger. Serve with slices of tomato and crunchy lettuce in a warm bread roll for a flavoursome snack.

*serves* 4

## ingredients

- **minced (ground) pork**, 450g/1lb
- **salt** and **ground black pepper**
- **fresh root ginger**, 2.5cm/1inch piece, peeled
- **lemon grass**, 1 stalk
- **sunflower oil**, 30ml/2 tbsp
- **4 bread rolls**, to serve
- **2 tomatoes**, to serve
- **½ lettuce**, to serve

## tools

- **Large mixing bowl**
- **Grater**
- **Chopping board**
- **Medium sharp knife**
- **Wooden spoon**
- **Plate**
- **Non-stick griddle (grill) pan**

1 Place the pork in a large mixing bowl and season well with salt and ground black pepper.

2 Grate the ginger using a fine grater. Remove the tough outer layers from the lemon grass stalk and discard, then chop the centre finely. Adult supervision is required.

3 Add the ginger and lemon grass to the bowl and mix well. Wet your hands slightly and shape the meat into four patties, place on a plate, cover with clear film (plastic wrap) and chill for 20 minutes.

4 Heat the oil in a large, non-stick griddle pan and add the patties.

5 Cook for 3–4 minutes on each side, until golden and cooked through. Adult supervision is required.

6 With adult supervision, cut the bread rolls in half, slice the tomatoes and shred the lettuce. Drain the patties on kitchen paper, then serve in the buns with the tomatoes and lettuce.

### FACT FILE

**LEMON GRASS**

Readily available from most large supermarkets, lemon grass has a lovely fresh, lemony flavour and aroma. If you have some left over, don't throw it away – place into a sealed food bag and freeze it for up to 3 months.

*lemon grass*

# Sausage casserole

This casserole is guaranteed to keep you warm on a chilly winter night, and it's great for serving to guests.

*serves* 4–6

## ingredients

- **large pork, beef, lamb or vegetarian sausages**, 450g/1lb
- **vegetable oil**, 15ml/1 tbsp
- **onion**, 1, peeled and chopped
- **carrots**, 225g/8oz, peeled and chopped
- **plain (all-purpose) flour**, 15ml/1 tbsp
- **beef stock**, 450ml/¾ pint/scant 2 cups
- **tomato purée (paste)**, 15ml/3 tsp
- **soft light brown sugar**, 15ml/3 tsp
- **Worcestershire sauce**, 15ml/1 tbsp
- **Dijon mustard**, 10ml/2 tsp
- **bay leaf**, 1
- **dried chilli**, 1, chopped
- **salt** and **ground black pepper**
- **mixed beans in water**, 400g/14oz can, drained
- **mashed potatoes**, to serve

## tools

- **Small sharp knife**
- **Fork**
- **Large frying pan**
- **Fish slice (spatula) or tongs**
- **Ovenproof casserole dish with lid**
- **Draining spoon**
- **Wooden spoon**
- **Oven gloves**

1 Preheat the oven to 180°C/350°F/Gas 4. Separate the sausages if necessary by cutting the links with the knife, then prick all over with the fork. Adult supervision is required.

2 With adult supevision, heat the oil in a frying pan over a medium-high heat.

3 Add the sausages and cook, turning frequently with the fish slice or tongs, for about 10 minutes, until evenly browned on all sides but not cooked through. Transfer the browned sausages to the casserole dish with the draining spoon. Adult supervision is required.

4 Add the onion and carrots to the pan and fry for about 5 minutes until softened and lightly browned. Add the flour and stir well.

5 Stir in 150ml/¼ pint/ ⅔ cup beef stock, 5ml/1 tsp tomato purée and 5ml/1 tsp sugar.

6 Add the Worcestershire sauce, remaining beef stock, tomato purée, sugar, mustard, bay leaf and chilli to the pan. Season, bring up to the boil, then pour into the casserole dish. Cover and cook for 30 minutes. Add the beans and cook for 5 minutes more. Serve immediately with mashed potatoes.

 = Watch out! Sharp or electrical tool in use.

 = Watch out! Heat is involved.

# Mini toads-in-the-hole

The 'toads' in this dish are little sausages, while the holes are made in a batter.

*serves* 2

## ingredients

- **plain (all-purpose) flour**, 60ml/4 tbsp
- **salt**, a pinch
- **egg**, 1
- **milk**, 60ml/4 tbsp
- **chipolata sausages**, 3
- **vegetable oil**, 5ml/1 tsp
- **baked beans** and **steamed green beans**, to serve

## tools

- **Sieve (strainer)**
- **Large mixing bowl**
- **Whisk**
- **Measuring jug (cup)**
- **2 small sharp knives**
- **2 x 10cm/4in tartlet tins (pans)**
- **Pastry brush**
- **Oven gloves**

1 Sift the flour into a large bowl. Add a pinch of salt. Make a well (hole) in the centre. Whisk the egg and add to the well. Gradually whisk in the milk, beating until a smooth batter is formed. Pour into a jug.

2 Preheat the oven to 220°C/425°F/Gas 7.

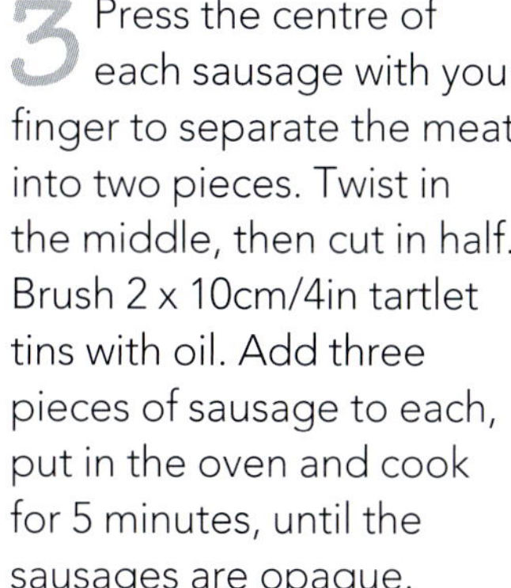

3 Press the centre of each sausage with your finger to separate the meat into two pieces. Twist in the middle, then cut in half. Brush 2 x 10cm/4in tartlet tins with oil. Add three pieces of sausage to each, put in the oven and cook for 5 minutes, until the sausages are opaque.

4 Ask an adult to remove the tins from the oven and immediately pour in the batter. Return to the oven and bake for 15 minutes, until risen and golden.

5 Ask an adult to remove from the oven. Loosen the edges. Serve with baked beans and green beans.

## COOK'S TIP

▶ To make sure you get light, well-risen batter it is important that the batter is added to a very hot tin and then returned to the oven as quickly and carefully as possible. It is also necessary to avoid opening the oven during the cooking time.

# Lamb and potato pies

These easy-to-make pies are made with chunks of lamb, potato, onion and shortcrust pastry. They taste truly great and look very impressive.

*serves* **4**

## ingredients

**for the pastry**

- **plain (all-purpose) flour**, 500g/1¼lb/5 cups
- **butter**, 250g/9oz/generous 1 cup, cubed
- **chilled water**, 120ml/4fl oz/½ cup

- **boneless lamb** or **mutton**, 450g/1lb
- **onion**, 1, finely chopped
- **carrots**, 2, finely chopped
- **potato**, 1, finely chopped
- **celery**, 2 sticks, finely chopped
- **salt** and **ground black pepper**
- **egg**, 1, beaten

## tools

- Large bowl
- Table knife
- Baking parchment
- Small sharp knife
- Chopping board
- Spoon
- Rolling pin
- Serving plate
- Pastry brush
- 2 baking sheets
- Oven gloves

1 **To make the pastry**, put the flour into a large bowl and add the butter. Rub the butter into the flour with your fingertips until the mixture resembles coarse breadcrumbs.

2 Add the chilled water. Mix with a knife until the mixture clings together.

3 Turn on to a floured worktop and knead once or twice until smooth. Wrap in baking parchment and chill for 20 minutes before using.

4 Trim any fat or gristle from the meat and cut it up into very small pieces. Place in a large bowl and add the chopped onion, carrots, potato and celery. Mix well and season to taste.

5 Preheat the oven to 180°C/350°F/Gas 4. Cut a third off the pastry ball and reserve to make the lids. Roll out the rest.

6 Cut out six circles by placing a plate on the pastry and cutting round it.

7 Divide the meat mixture between the circles, piling it in the middle.

8 Roll out the reserved pastry. Cut out six circles, about 10cm/4in across.

9 Lay the lids on top of the meat. Dampen the edges of the bases, bring the pastry up and pinch the edges together.

10 Make a hole in the top of each pie, brush with egg and slide on to baking sheets. Bake for an hour. Serve hot or cold.

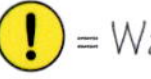 = Watch out! Sharp or electrical tool in use.  = Watch out! Heat is involved.

# Shepherd's pie

You can't go wrong with a shepherd's pie – especially in the cold winter months. Double or triple the quantities, depending on how many you want to serve.

serves 2

## ingredients

- **small onion**, ½, peeled
- **lean minced (ground) beef**, 175g/6oz
- **plain (all-purpose) flour**, 10ml/2 tsp
- **tomato ketchup**, 30ml/2 tbsp
- **beef stock**, 150ml/¼ pint/⅔ cup
- **dried mixed herbs**, a pinch of
- **salt** and **ground black pepper**
- **swede (rutabaga)**, 50g/2oz, peeled
- **parsnip**, ½, about 50g/2oz, peeled
- **potato**, 1, about 115g/4oz, peeled
- **milk**, 10ml/2 tsp
- **butter**, 15g/½oz/1 tbsp
- **cooked carrots** and **peas**, to serve

## tools

- Chopping board
- Medium sharp knife
- Large non-stick frying pan
- Wooden spoon
- Large pan
- Colander
- Potato masher
- 2 ovenproof dishes
- Fork
- Oven gloves

1 Preheat the oven to 190°C/375°F/Gas 5. Finely chop the onion. Adult supervision is required. Place in a large frying pan with the mince.

2 With adult supervision, dry-fry (fry without oil) over a low heat, stirring, until evenly browned.

3 Add the flour, stirring, then add the ketchup, stock and herbs. Season. Bring up to the boil, reduce the heat, cover and simmer for 30 minutes, stirring often. Adult supervision is required.

4 With adult supervision, chop the swede, parsnip and potato.

5 Place the vegetables in a pan, cover with water and bring up to the boil. Reduce the heat. Simmer for 20 minutes, until tender. Ask an adult to drain in a colander. Return to the pan.

6 Mash the vegetables with the milk and half of the butter.

7 Spoon the meat into two ovenproof dishes. Place the vegetables on top and fluff up with a fork. Dot with the remaining butter.

8 Place on a baking sheet and cook for 25–30 minutes, until browned on top. Serve with cooked carrots and peas.

# Guard of honour

This cut of meat, also called a crown roast, is just lamb chops that are still joined together. Here, two racks are interlocked, creating a cavity to stuff with fruity rice.

serves 4

## ingredients

- **racks of lamb**, 2, with at least four chops in each piece
- **butter**, 25g/1oz/2 tbsp
- **spring onions (scallions)**, 4, roughly chopped
- **basmati rice**, 115g/4oz/⅔ cup
- **stock**, 300ml/½ pint/1¼ cups
- **large ripe mango**, 1, peeled and roughly chopped
- **salt** and **ground black pepper**
- **boiled new potatoes** and **minted peas**, to serve

## tools

- ✱ Small sharp knife
- ✱ Chopping board
- ✱ Large non-stick pan
- ✱ Wooden spoon
- ✱ Roasting pan
- ✱ Spoon
- ✱ Fine string
- ✱ Oven gloves

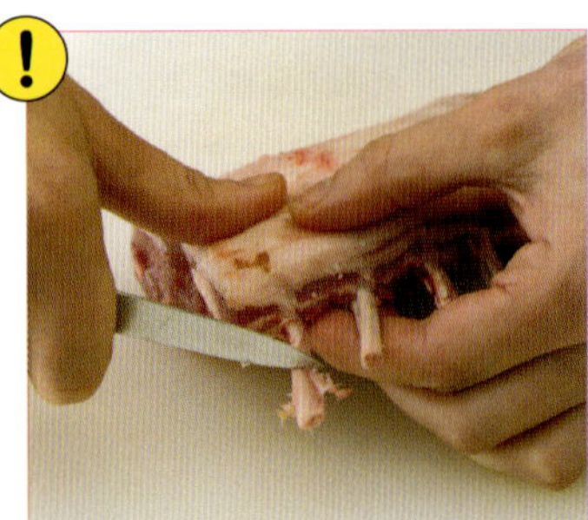

1 Use a sharp knife to cut the meat off the ends of the bones. Discard the skin. Scrape the bones clean. Chop the trimmings into pieces. (The butcher can do all this, if you prefer.) Adult supervision is required.

2 With adult supervision, melt the butter in a pan, add the spring onions and trimmings and fry until the meat has browned.

3 Add the rice, stir well and pour in the stock. Bring to the boil, lower the heat, put a lid on the pan and leave to simmer for 8–10 minutes, until the rice is tender. Adult supervision is required.

4 Ask an adult to remove the pan from the heat. Stir in the mango. Check the seasoning. Preheat the oven to 190°C/375°F/Gas 5.

5 Place the two racks of lamb next to each other and spoon the stuffing in between them. Interlock the bones and tie together with a piece of string. Stand in a roasting pan.

6 Wrap the ends of the bones in a strip of foil. Cook for 1½–2 hours, until the lamb is cooked (see Cook's Tip). Serve with new potatoes and minted peas.

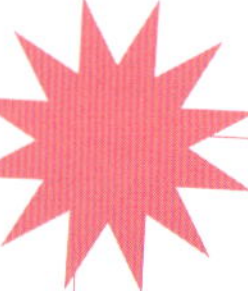

### COOK'S TIP

▶ To test if the lamb is done, insert a skewer deep into the thickest part of the meat. For slightly pink lamb the juices that run from the hole should be just tinged with pink. For well-done lamb, the meat juices should be clear.

(!) = Watch out! Sharp or electrical tool in use. (oven glove) = Watch out! Heat is involved.

# Lamb stew

Tender cubes of lamb and vegetables smothered in a rich gravy are the perfect partner to hot, creamy mashed potato or crusty bread… mmmm!

serves 2

## ingredients

- **lamb fillet**, 115g/4oz
- **small onion**, ¼
- **small carrot**, 1, about 50g/2oz
- **small parsnip**, ½, about 50g/2oz
- **small potato**, 1
- **oil**, 5ml/1 tsp
- **lamb stock**, 150ml/¼ pint/⅔ cup
- **dried rosemary**, a pinch of
- salt and **ground black pepper**
- **crusty bread**, to serve

## tools

- 2 medium sharp knives
- 2 chopping boards
- Vegetable peeler
- Large non-stick pan with a lid
- Wooden spoon

1 Rinse the lamb under cold running water, then pat dry on kitchen paper. Cut away any fat or gristle and cut into small cubes. Adult supervision is required.

2 Using a separate, clean knife and chopping board, peel and chop the onion, carrot and parsnip. Peel the potato and cut into larger pieces. Adult supervision is required.

3 Heat the oil in a pan. Add the lamb and onion, and fry gently for about 10 minutes, stirring occasionally, until the meat is browned. Adult supervision is required when using heat.

4 Add the carrot, parsnip and potato and fry for 3 minutes more, stirring occasionally, until they have softened slightly.

5 Add the lamb stock, dried rosemary and a little salt and pepper to the pan and stir to mix. Bring up to the boil, cover, reduce the heat slightly and simmer for 35–40 minutes, or until the meat and vegetables are tender.

6 Spoon the stew into shallow bowls and serve immediately with crusty bread.

## VARIATION

- This stew works just as well with stewing beef and beef stock, or pork fillet (tenderloin) and pork stock. For vgetarians, omit the meat and add 115g/4oz extra root vegetables, such as carrots or parsnips.

carrots

★★ give it a try | time to cook: 10–15 minutes | preparation: 15 minutes

# Steak with tomato salsa

Nothing beats a nice juicy steak, and since they require very little cooking they are both quick and easy to rustle up. Serve with a lovely tangy tomato salsa.

*serves* 2

## ingredients

- **large plum tomatoes**, 3
- **steaks**, 2, about 2cm/¾in thick (see Cook's Tip)
- **salt** and **ground black pepper**
- **spring onions (scallions)**, 2, thinly sliced
- **balsamic vinegar**, 30ml/2 tbsp

## tools

- ✱ **Small sharp knife**
- ✱ **Large heatproof bowl**
- ✱ **Chopping board**
- ✱ **Teaspoon**
- ✱ **Large non-stick frying pan**
- ✱ **Tongs**
- ✱ **Wooden spoon**

### COOK'S TIP

► Choose rump (round), sirloin or fillet steak (beef tenderloin). If you prefer to grill (broil) the steak, the timing is the same as in the recipe, but take into account the thickness of the meat – thick pieces take longer.

1 Preheat the oven to 160°C/330°F/Gas 2. Score a cross in the top of the tomatoes. Place in a heatproof bowl, then ask an adult to pour over boiling water to cover. Leave for 5 minutes. When the skins split, ask an adult to drain. Rinse under cold water. Peel away the skin.

2 With adult supervision, cut the tomatoes in half. Scoop out the seeds with a teaspoon and discard. Chop the flesh into small pieces. Set aside.

3 Trim any excess fat from the steaks, then season on both sides. Adult supervision is required.

4 Heat the frying pan and cook the steaks for about 3 minutes on each side for medium rare. Cook for a little longer if you like your steak well cooked. Remove from the pan with tongs and transfer to plates. Adult supervision is required. Keep warm while you prepare the salsa.

5 Add the spring onions to the frying pan with the tomatoes, balsamic vinegar, 30ml/2 tbsp water and a little seasoning. Stir briefly until warm, scraping up any meat residue. Spoon the salsa over the steaks and serve.

 = Watch out! Sharp or electrical tool in use. = Watch out! Heat is involved.

# Cheesy burgers

These look the same as ordinary burgers, but contain a hidden heart of soft, melted cheese. Serve with your favourite accompaniments, such as salad and salsa.

serves 4

## ingredients

- **lean minced (ground) beef**, 450g/1lb
- **bread**, 2 slices, crusts removed
- **egg**, 1
- **spring onions (scallions)**, 4, chopped
- **garlic**, 1 clove, peeled and chopped
- **salt** and **ground black pepper**
- **mango chutney**, 15ml/1 tbsp
- **dried mixed herbs**, 10ml/2 tsp
- **mozzarella cheese**, 50g/2oz (see Variation)
- **burger buns**, 4, to serve
- **salad leaves**, to serve (optional)

## tools

* Blender or food processor
* Chopping board
* Small sharp knife
* Fish slice or metal spatula
* Oven gloves

1 Put the minced beef, bread, egg, chopped spring onions and chopped garlic in a blender or food processor. Season, then blend in short bursts until well combined. Adult supervision is required.

2 Add the chutney and herbs and blend again.

3 Divide the mixture into four equal portions. Wet your hands (to stop sticking) and shape each portion into a burger.

4 With adult supervision, cut the cheese into four pieces. Push one in to the centre of each burger and shape the meat around it.

5 Cover with clear film (plastic wrap) and chill for 30 minutes. Ask an adult to preheat the grill (broiler) to medium-hot.

6 Put the burgers on a foil-lined grill (broiler) pan. Cook under the grill for 10–18 minutes, turning once with a fish slice or spatula, until cooked through and brown. Adult supervision is required.

7 Split the buns in half, put some greens, if using, on the bottom, and place the burger on top. Sandwich with the other half of the bun.

## VARIATION

• You can use any cheese instead of the mozzarella, if you like. Good ones that melt well and have a strong flavour include Cheddar cheese, red Leicester, Gruyère, Emmental, Monterey Jack or Danish blue.

Danish blue

# Desserts and drinks

Always the best part of a meal, desserts are well worth making yourself. This great selection contains the works – from sticky chocolatey treats and fruity crumbles to creamy mousses, ice creams and an impressive cheesecake. There is also a choice of super cool drinks, including fabulous fruit slushes and juices as well as thick smoothies and milkshakes.

# Magic chocolate pudding

Abracadabra…this divine, gooey chocolate pud, with a secret layer of sauce under a moist sponge topping, really is a magical dessert to have up your sleeve.

serves 4

## ingredients

- **butter**, 50g/2oz/4 tbsp, plus extra for greasing
- **self-raising (self-rising) flour**, 90g/3½oz/scant 1 cup
- **ground cinnamon**, 5ml/1 tsp
- **unsweetened cocoa powder**, 75ml/5 tbsp
- **light muscovado (brown)** or **demerara (raw) sugar**, 200g/7oz/generous 1 cup
- **milk**, 475ml/16fl oz/2 cups
- **crème fraîche**, **Greek (US strained plain) yogurt** or **vanilla ice cream**, to serve

## tools

- 1.5 litre/2½pt/6¼cup ovenproof dish
- Baking sheet
- Sieve (strainer)
- 2 mixing bowls
- Medium pan
- Wooden spoon

1 Preheat the oven to 180°C/350°F/Gas 4. Lightly grease an ovenproof dish, place on a baking sheet and set aside.

2 Sift the flour and ground cinnamon into a mixing bowl. Sift over 15ml/1 tbsp of the cocoa and mix well.

3 Place the remaining butter in a pan. Add 115g/4oz/½ cup of the sugar and 150ml/¼ pint/⅔ cup of the milk. Heat gently without boiling, stirring occasionally, until the butter has melted and all the sugar has dissolved. Remove from the heat. Adult supervision is required.

4 Stir the flour mixture into the pan. Pour the mixture into the prepared dish and level the surface.

5 Mix the remaining sugar and cocoa in a bowl, then sprinkle over the pudding mixture. Pour the remaining milk evenly over the pudding.

## FACT FILE

**MUSCOVADO SUGAR**

This type of brown sugar is unrefined, which means it has not been processed.

muscovado sugar

6 Bake for 45–50 minutes or until the sponge has risen to the top and is firm to the touch. Serve hot, with the crème fraîche, yogurt or ice cream.



(!) = Watch out! Sharp or electrical tool in use. (oven glove) = Watch out! Heat is involved.

# Rice pudding

A firm family favourite, rice pudding is delicious, easy to make and perfect for a cold winter day. Stir in clear honey or warm jam for an extra-special treat.

pudding rice

serves 4

## ingredients

- **raisins**, 75g/3oz/½ cup
- **water**, 75ml/5 tbsp
- **short grain rice**, 90g/3½ oz/½ cup
- **pared lemon peel**, 3 or 4 strips
- **water**, 250ml/8fl oz/1 cup
- **milk**, 475ml/16fl oz/2 cups
- **cinnamon stick**, 1, about 7.5cm/3in in length
- **sugar**, 225g/8oz/1 cup
- **salt**, a pinch
- **butter**, 15g/½ oz/1 tbsp, diced
- **toasted flaked (sliced) almonds** (see Cook's Tip), to decorate (optional)
- **chilled orange segments**, to serve

## tools

- ✱ Small pan
- ✱ Wooden spoon
- ✱ Large heavy pan
- ✱ Fork
- ✱ Sieve (strainer)

1 Put the raisins and water in a pan. Heat until warm, then remove from the heat. Adult supervision is required.

2 Mix the rice, lemon peel and water in a pan and bring to the boil. Lower the heat, cover and simmer for 20 minutes, stirring occasionally. Remove the lemon peel.

3 Add the milk and the cinnamon to the pan, then stir. Continue to cook over a gentle heat until the rice has absorbed the milk.

4 Stir in the sugar and salt. Add the butter and stir constantly until the butter has melted. Adult supervision is required.

5 Drain the raisins in a sieve and stir into the rice mixture. Cook for 2–3 minutes, stirring to prevent it sticking.

6 Transfer to serving bowls, top with the toasted flaked almonds and serve with the orange segments.

## COOK'S TIP

▶ To toast flaked almonds, either add to a heated small non-stick frying pan (with no oil) and heat gently, stirring often, until golden. Or, spread on a foil-lined baking sheet and toast under a medium grill (broil) for 1–2 minutes, until golden. Adult supervision is required.

# Lazy pastry pudding

You don't need to be neat to make this pudding, as it looks best when it's really craggy and rough. It is scrummy served hot or cold with cream or custard.

*serves* 6

## ingredients

- **plain (all-purpose) flour**, 225g/8oz/2 cups
- **caster (superfine) sugar**, 15ml/1 tbsp
- **mixed (apple pie) spice**, 15ml/1 tbsp
- **butter** or **margarine**, 150g/5oz/⅔ cup
- **egg**, 1, separated
- **cooking apples**, 450g/1lb
- **lemon juice**, 30ml/2 tbsp
- **raisins**, 115g/4oz/⅔ cup
- **demerara (raw) sugar**, 75g/3oz/½ cup
- **hazelnuts**, 25g/1oz/¼ cup, toasted and chopped (optional)

## tools

- **Mixing bowl**
- **Wooden spoon**
- **Rolling pin**
- **Non-stick baking sheet**
- **Vegetable peeler**
- **Small sharp knife**
- **Chopping board**
- **Pastry brush**
- **Oven gloves**

1 Preheat the oven to 200°C/400°F/Gas 6. Put the flour, sugar and spice in a bowl. Add the butter or margarine and rub it into the flour with your fingertips, until it resembles breadcrumbs.

2 Add the egg yolk and use your hands to pull the mixture together. (You may need to add a little water.)

3 Turn the dough on to a lightly floured surface and knead gently until smooth. Roll out the pastry with a rolling pin to make a rough circle about 30cm/12in across. Use the rolling pin to carefully lift the pastry on to a baking sheet. The pastry may hang over the edges slightly – this doesn't matter.

4 Peel the apples and cut them into quarters, then cut out the core. Discard the core and slice the apples on the chopping board. Adult supervision is required. Toss them in the lemon juice, to stop them from turning brown.

5 Scatter some of the apples over the middle of the pastry, leaving a 10cm/4in border all around. Scatter some of the raisins over the top. Reserve 30ml/2 tbsp of the demerara sugar. Scatter some of the remaining sugar on top. Keep making layers of apple, raisins and sugar until you have used them up.

6 Preheat the oven to 200°C/400°F/Gas 6. Fold up the pastry edges to cover the fruit, overlapping it where necessary. Brush the pastry with the egg white and sprinkle over the reserved sugar. Scatter over the nuts (if using). Cover the central hole with foil. Cook for 30–35 minutes, until the pastry is browned.

 = Watch out! Sharp or electrical tool in use. (!) = Watch out! Heat is involved.

# Plum crumble

If you like to get your hands dirty when you cook, then you'll love rubbing a crumble mixture together. Custard, cream or ice cream are the perfect partners.

plums

serves 4–6

## ingredients

- **ripe red plums**, 900g/2lb
- **caster (superfine) sugar**, 50g/2oz/¼ cup

for the topping

- **plain (all-purpose) flour**, 225g/8oz/1 cup
- **butter**, 115g/4oz/½ cup, cut into pieces
- **caster (superfine) sugar**, 50g/2oz/¼ cup
- **marzipan**, 175g/6oz
- **rolled oats**, 60ml/4 tbsp
- **flaked (sliced) almonds**, 60ml/4 tbsp
- **custard**, to serve

## tools

* Chopping board
* Knife
* Medium pan
* Large ovenproof dish
* Large mixing bowl
* Wooden spoon
* Grater
* Baking sheet
* Oven gloves

1 Preheat the oven to 190°C/375°F/Gas 5. Cut the plums into quarters. Remove and discard the stones (pits). Adult supervision is required.

2 Place the plums in a pan with the sugar and 30ml/2 tbsp water. Cover and simmer for 10 minutes, until the plums have softened. Adult supervision is required.

3 Spoon the plums into a large ovenproof dish.

4 **To make the topping,** place the flour in a large mixing bowl. Add the pieces of butter and, using your fingertips, rub the butter into the flour until the mixture looks like breadcrumbs. Stir in the caster sugar.

5 Grate the marzipan on the largest holes of the grater. Adult supervision is required. Stir into the mixture with the oats and almonds. Spoon over the plums.

6 Place on a baking sheet and cook for 20–25 minutes, until golden brown. Leave to cool slightly before serving with custard.

## VARIATIONS

- You can vary the fruits, according to what is in season. Try cooking apples, peaches or pears.
- If the plums are very tart, you may need to add extra sugar.
- You can also use hazelnuts, pecans or pine nuts.

# Lemon surprise pudding

The surprise comes when you come to serve this heavenly pudding and find that beneath the layer of fluffy sponge lies a smooth tangy lemon sauce.

serves 4

## ingredients

- **butter**, 50g/2oz/¼ cup, plus extra for greasing
- **lemons**, 2, grated rind and juice
- **caster (superfine) sugar**, 115g/4oz/½ cup
- **eggs**, 2, separated
- **self-raising (self-rising) flour**, 50g/2oz/½ cup
- **milk**, 300ml/½ pint/1¼ cups
- **icing (confectioners') sugar**, for dusting

## tools

- **1.2 litre/2 pint/5 cup ovenproof dish**
- **Wooden spoon or electric mixer**
- **2 mixing bowls**
- **Whisk**
- **Large metal spoon**
- **Foil**
- **Roasting pan**
- **Oven gloves**
- **Sieve (strainer)**

1 Preheat the oven to 190°C/375°F/Gas 5. Lightly grease a 1.2 litre/2 pint/5 cup ovenproof dish.

2 Using a wooden spoon or an electric mixer, beat the remaining butter, lemon rind and sugar in a bowl until creamy and pale. Add the egg yolks and flour and beat together. Adult supervision is required.

3 Gradually beat in the lemon juice and milk in several batches (the mixture may curdle horribly, but don't worry!). Be careful not to splash it everywhere.

4 In a large clean bowl, using a clean whisk, whisk the egg whites until they form stiff, dry peaks when the whisk is lifted out of the mixture.

5 Using a large metal spoon, fold the egg whites gently into the lemon mixture, then pour into the prepared dish.

6 Place a large piece of double-folded foil in a large roasting pan and position the dish on top, so the sides of the foil come about 5cm/2in above the rim of the dish.

7 Ask an adult to put the roasting pan in the oven and pour in hot water from the kettle to come halfway up the sides of the dish. Cook for 45 minutes until golden brown.

8 Ask an adult to remove from oven and take the dish out of the roasting tin. Serve dusted with sifted icing sugar.

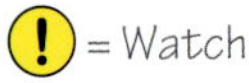

(!) = Watch out! Sharp or electrical tool in use. = Watch out! Heat is involved.

# Baked bananas

They may look slightly unappealing, but soft, cooked bananas served in their skins are simply delicious, especially with ice cream and a hot hazelnut sauce.

hazelnuts

serves 4

## ingredients

- **large bananas**, 4
- **lemon juice**, 15ml/1 tbsp
- **vanilla ice cream**, 8 scoops

for the sauce

- **unsalted butter**, 25g/1oz/2 tbsp
- **hazelnuts**, 50g/2oz/½ cup, toasted and coarsely chopped
- **golden (light corn) syrup**, 45ml/3 tbsp
- **lemon juice**, 30ml/2 tbsp

## tools

- Non-stick baking sheet
- Pastry brush
- Small heavy pan
- Wooden spoon
- Oven gloves
- Small sharp knife

1 Preheat the oven to 180°C/350°F/Gas 4. Place the unpeeled bananas on a baking sheet and generously brush the skins with lemon juice using a pastry brush.

2 Bake in the oven for about 20 minutes, until the skins are turning black and the bananas feel soft when gently squeezed.

3 Meanwhile, **make the sauce**. Melt the butter in a small, heavy pan. Add the hazelnuts and cook over a low heat, stirring frequently, for 1 minute. Adult supervision is required.

4 Add the golden syrup and lemon juice and heat gently, stirring constantly with a wooden spoon, for 1 minute more.

5 To serve, ask an adult to remove the bananas from the oven. With adult supervision, slit each banana open along its length with a small sharp knife and open out the skins.

6 Transfer to serving plates and serve with generous scoops of vanilla ice cream. Pour over the hazelnut sauce.

## VARIATION

- To make a chocolate sauce, place 150ml/¼ pint/⅔ cup double (heavy) cream in a pan with 75g/3oz milk chocolate, broken into squares, and 15g/½oz/1 tbsp butter. With adult supervision, heat gently, stirring occasionally, until the chocolate melts and the ingredients combine to make a sauce. Pour over the bananas.

# Banana and toffee ice cream

serves **4–6**

A combination of bananas, creamy toffees, condensed milk and cream are used to make this indulgent ice cream.

## ingredients

- **ripe bananas**, 3
- **lemon**, 1, juice of
- **sweetened condensed milk**, 370g/12½oz can
- **whipping cream**, 150ml/¼ pint/⅔ cup
- **toffees**, 150g/5oz, plus extra to decorate

## tools

- **Blender or food processor**
- **Plastic or rubber spatula**
- **Freezerproof container**
- **Metal spoon**
- **Kitchen scissors or hammer and chopping board (optional)**
- **Fork**

bananas

whipping cream

sweetened condensed milk

**1** Peel the bananas and put them in a blender or food processor. Blend until smooth, then add the lemon juice and blend to mix. Adult supervision is required. Scrape into a freezerproof container.

**2** Pour in the condensed milk into the container, stirring with a metal spoon, then stir in the cream.

**3** Mix well to combine, cover and freeze for about 4 hours, or until semi-frozen and mushy.

**4** Meanwhile, cut the toffees into small pieces with scissors. Alternatively, put the toffees in the refrigerator until cold and hard, then transfer to a chopping board and bash with a small hammer.

**5** Beat the semi-frozen ice cream with a fork to break up the ice crystals, then stir in the toffees.

**6** Return to the freezer for 3–5 hours, or until firm. Remove from the freezer and allow to soften slightly, then scoop into bowls or glasses and decorate with chopped toffees. Serve immediately.

## COOK'S TIP

► If you have an ice cream machine, mix the banana purée with the condensed milk and cream in a bowl, then transfer to the machine and churn, according to the manufacturer's instructions, until thick. Transfer to a freezerproof container, stir in the chunks of toffee, then freeze for 3–5 hours and serve as in the recipe.

 = Watch out! Sharp or electrical tool in use.  = Watch out! Heat is involved.

# Pineapple sorbet on sticks

Make sure you choose a ripe pineapple so that you get maximum sweetness.

*makes about* 12

## ingredients

- **medium pineapple**, 1, about 1.2kg/2½lb
- **caster (superfine) sugar**, 115g/4oz/½ cup
- **lime juice**, 30ml/2 tbsp

## tools

- Chopping board
- Medium and small sharp knives
- Blender or food processor
- Plastic sieve (strainer)
- Mixing bowl
- Small heavy pan
- Wooden spoon
- Freezerproof container
- Electric mixer
- 12 lolly (popsicle) moulds and sticks

1 Ask an adult to help you slice the base and top off the pineapple. Stand it upright on a board. Cut away the skin by cutting down with a sawing action. Use a small knife to cut out the 'eyes' (small, dark, rough pieces).

2 Cut the pineapple in half lengthways and cut away the core in the middle.

3 Pulp the pineapple in a blender or food processor. Adult supervision is required. Press through a sieve placed over a bowl to extract as much juice as you can.

4 Ask an adult to help you heat the sugar and 300ml/½ pint/1¼ cups water in a pan, stirring, until the sugar dissolves. Boil for 3 minutes, without stirring.

5 Remove from the heat and leave to cool. Stir the lime and pineapple juice into the syrup, then chill until cold. Pour into a non-metallic freezerproof container and freeze for 3–4 hours.

6 Twice during the first 2 hours, beat with an electric mixer until smooth, then return to the freezer. Adult supervision is required.

### COOK'S TIP

► If you haven't got lolly moulds, you could use washed yogurt containers.

7 Spoon the mixture into 12 ice lolly moulds. Press a wooden lolly stick into the centre of each. Freeze overnight until firm.

8 To serve, dip the moulds in hot water for 1–2 seconds, then pull each lolly from its mould.

# Strawberry mousse

Creamy and fruity, this long-standing favourite is easy to make and tastes great.

serves 4

## ingredients

- **strawberries**, 250g/9oz, hulled
- **caster (superfine) sugar**, 90g/3¾ oz/½ cup
- **cold water**, 150ml/¼ pint/⅔ cup
- **powdered gelatine**, 15ml/1 tbsp, or **leaf gelatine**, 8 sheets
- **boiling water**, 60ml/4 tbsp
- **double (heavy) cream**, 300ml/½ pint/ 1¼ cups
- **fresh mint leaves**, to decorate

strawberries

## tools

- ✱ **Small sharp knife**
- ✱ **Chopping board**
- ✱ **Food processor or blender**
- ✱ **Measuring jug (cup)**
- ✱ **Large heatproof bowl**
- ✱ **Metal spoon**
- ✱ **Large mixing bowl**
- ✱ **Whisk**

1 With adult supervision, chop most of the strawberries, reserving a few whole ones for decoration.

2 Transfer to a food processor or blender, add the sugar and 75ml/ 2½fl oz/⅓ cup water, and blend to a smooth purée. Adult supervision is required.

3 Put the remaining cold water in a large bowl and sprinkle over the gelatine (or immerse the leaf gelatine, if using).

4 Leave the gelatine to soak for 5 minutes, then ask an adult to add the boiling water. Leave for 2–3 minutes, until the gelatine has dissolved completely.

5 Add the strawberry and sugar mixture to the bowl of gelatine and mix to combine. Chill for about 30 minutes in the refrigerator, until the mixture has thickened.

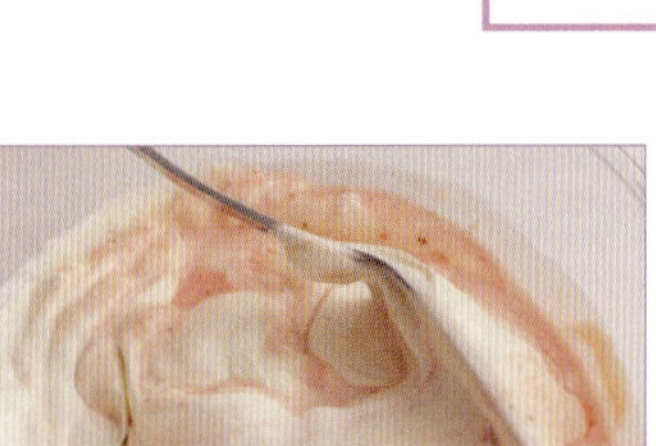

6 Lightly whip the cream in a large bowl, until soft peaks form, then fold into the strawberry mixture.

7 Spoon the mousse into serving glasses and chill overnight. Just before serving, garnish with a whole strawberry and some mint leaves.

## VARIATION

• You could use other soft summer berries, such as raspberries or redcurrants, or ripe peaches and nectarines to make this mousse instead of strawberries. Taste and add more sugar if necessary.

(!) = Watch out! Sharp or electrical tool in use. = Watch out! Heat is involved.

# Eton mess

Perfect for summer when strawberries are at their best, this 'mess' consists of a mixture of whipped cream, crushed meringue and sliced strawberries.

*serves* 4

## ingredients

- **ripe strawberries**, 450g/1lb
- **elderflower cordial** or **fruit juice** (such as orange, apple or pomegranate), 45ml/3 tbsp
- **double (heavy) cream**, 300ml/½ pint/1¼ cups
- **meringues** or **meringue baskets**, 4

## tools

- Chopping board
- Small sharp knife
- 3 mixing bowls
- Whisk
- Large metal spoon

*meringue basket*

## COOK'S TIPS

- This dessert gets its name from the English school Eton College, where it is served at the annual summer picnic.
- Do not leave the mess to chill for more than about 12 hours or it will go mushy.
- This is a great way of using up leftover bits of meringue.

1 Remove the green leaves from the top of the strawberries by twisting and pulling them out (known as hulling).

2 Slice the fruit. Set aside a few pretty slices for decoration, then put the rest into a bowl. Adult supervision is required.

3 Sprinkle the strawberry slices with the elderflower cordial or fruit juice. Cover the bowl and chill in the refrigerator for about 2 hours.

4 In a clean bowl, whisk the cream until it has thickened and is standing up in soft peaks.

5 Put the meringues in a bowl and use your hands to crush them into small pieces. Reserve a handful for decoration.

6 Add the strawberries, cordial or juice and most of the meringue to the cream and fold in gently using a large metal spoon.

7 Spoon into serving dishes and chill until required. Before serving, decorate with the reserved strawberries and meringue.

# Chocolate banana fools

You certainly won't be a fool if you make these scrummy desserts. They are very easy and a wonderful treat when you feel in need of something sweet.

*serves* 4

## ingredients

- **dark (bittersweet) chocolate**, 115g/4oz, chopped
- **fresh custard**, 300ml/½ pint/1¼ cups
- **bananas**, 2

## tools

- Heatproof bowl
- Medium pan (optional)
- Mixing bowl
- Large metal spoon
- Chopping board
- Small sharp knife

1 Put the chocolate in a heatproof bowl and melt in the microwave on high power for 1–2 minutes. Alternatively, place over a pan of barely simmering water, making sure the water doesn't touch the base of the bowl. Heat until the chocolate has melted. Adult supervision is required.

2 Remove the bowl from the pan (if using), stir, then set aside to cool.

3 Pour the custard into a mixing bowl and partially fold in the melted chocolate using a large metal spoon. Do not mix it in completely – aim to create a rippled effect.

4 Peel and slice the bananas and gently stir these into the chocolate and custard mixture, taking care not to over-stir or you will lose the rippled effect.

5 Spoon the fool into four glasses and chill for 30–60 minutes, until thick, before serving.

## COOK'S TIP

▶ To make chocolate decorations, line a baking sheet with baking parchment. Melt about 50g/2oz chopped chocolate in a heatproof bowl in the microwave, with adult supervision. Spoon into an icing bag and pipe shapes such as hearts on to the parchment. Chill until set, then peel away the shapes.

 = Watch out! Sharp or electrical tool in use.  = Watch out! Heat is involved.

★★★ nice and challenging | *time to cook:* **20 minutes** | *preparation:* **30 minutes**

# Banana and apricot trifle

This trifle is perfect if you are having a party – if it's a sleepover you will be sneaking down for leftovers!

*serves* 6–8

## ingredients

- **apricot**, **lemon** or **tangerine jelly (gelatine)**, ¼ packet
- **apricot conserve**, 60ml/4 tbsp
- **ginger cake**, 175–225g/6–8oz
- **bananas**, 3
- **fresh custard**, 300ml/½ pint/1¼ cups
- **sugar**, 90g/3½oz/½ cup, plus extra for sprinkling
- **double (heavy) cream**, 300ml/½ pint/1¼ cups

*bananas*

## tools

- 2 heavy pans
- Wooden spoon
- Small sharp knife
- Chopping board
- Baking sheet
- Foil
- Rolling pin
- Mixing bowl
- Whisk

1 Put the jelly, apricot conserve and 60ml/4 tbsp water in a heavy pan and heat, stirring once or twice, until all the jelly dissolves. Adult supervision is required. Set aside until cool.

2 Cut the ginger cake into cubes and place in a deep serving bowl or dish.

3 Cut two of the bananas into thick slices. Adult supervision is required.

4 Pour the cooled jelly mixture over the cake. Arrange the banana slices on top of the jelly, then pour over the custard. Chill for 1–2 hours, until the custard is set.

5 To make the caramel, cover a baking sheet with foil. Ask an adult to help you gently heat the sugar with 60ml/4 tbsp water in a heavy pan until the sugar has dissolved. Increase the heat and boil without stirring until just golden. Take great care. Pour on to the foil and leave until hard. Break into pieces.

6 Place the cream in a bowl and whisk until it stands in soft peaks.

7 Spread the cream over the custard, then cut the reserved banana into slices and arrange on top of the cream with the caramel pieces. Serve the trifle immediately.

# Summer fruit cheesecake

Making this creamy, sweet cheesecake involves several easy stages, but it tastes and looks so good it is well worth the effort and time it requires.

serves 8–10

## ingredients

- **butter**, 175g/6oz/¾ cup
- **digestive biscuits (graham crackers)**, 225g/8oz

for the topping

- **lemons**, 2, rind and juice
- **gelatine**, 11g/scant ½oz sachet
- **cottage cheese**, 225g/8oz/1 cup
- **soft cream cheese**, 200g/7oz/scant 1 cup
- **condensed milk**, 400g/14oz can
- **strawberries**, 450g/1lb/4 cups, hulled
- **raspberries**, 115g/4oz/1 cup

## tools

- **Pencil**
- **20cm/8in round, loose-bottomed, non-stick, spring-clip cake tin (pan)**
- **Baking parchment**
- **Scissors**
- **2 medium pans**
- **Blender or food processor**
- **Spoon**
- **Heatproof bowl**
- **Sieve (strainer)**
- **Chopping board**
- **Sharp knife**
- **Palette knife**

## COOK'S TIPS

▶ If you don't have a blender or food processor, you can create biscuit (cookie) crumbs by placing the biscuit pieces in two plastic sandwich bags, one inside the other for extra strength. Hold the top and gently bash or roll with a rolling pin until you have crumbs.

biscuits

▶ Lots of people think gelatine is tricky to use, but it is actually easy as long as you follow a few simple rules: always add gelatine to the liquid, never the other way round or it will turn lumpy and be unusable; make sure that the gelatine and the liquid are the same temperature or it will turn stringy; always add the gelatine gradually, stirring it into the liquid well each time so it is completely combined before you add a little more.

1 With a pencil, draw around the base of a 20cm/8in round, loose-bottomed, non-stick spring-clip cake tin on to baking parchment. Cut out the parchment circle and use to line the base of the tin.

2 To make the base, put the butter in a pan and melt over a low heat. Break the biscuits in pieces, put them in a blender or food processor and blend until they are crumbs (see Cook's Tips). Stir into the butter. Adult supervision is required.

3 Tip the buttery crumbs into the cake tin and use a spoon to spread the mixture in a thin, even layer over the base, pressing down well with the back of the spoon. Put the tin in the refrigerator while you make the topping.

4 To make the topping, put the lemon rind and juice in a bowl. Sprinkle over the gelatine. With adult supervision, stand the bowl in a pan of water. Heat until the gelatine has all melted. Stir, remove the bowl from the pan and leave to cool.

 = Watch out! Sharp or electrical tool in use.

 = Watch out! Heat is involved.

5 Drain the cottage cheese in a sieve, then transfer to a blender or food processor and blend for 20 seconds. Add the cream cheese and condensed milk and blend again until smooth. Adult supervision is required.

6 Pour in the dissolved gelatine mixture and blend once more.

7 On a chopping board, roughly chop half the strawberries. Adult supervision is required. Scatter over the base with half the raspberries, reserving the rest for decoration.

8 Pour the cheese mixture over the fruit. Level the top with the back of a spoon. Cover and chill in the refrigerator overnight, until set.

9 Loosen the edges of the cheesecake with a palette knife. Stand the tin on a can and open the clip at the side of the tin. Allow the tin to slide down. Put the cheesecake on a serving plate and decorate with the reserved fruit.

# Fruit fondue

A scrumptiously healthy way to eat up lots of fruit, this dessert is perfect for sharing with family and friends as everyone will enjoy helping themselves.

*serves* 6

## ingredients

- **fresh custard**, 425g/15oz/2 cups
- **milk chocolate**, 75g/3oz, broken into squares
- **eating apples**, 3
- **bananas**, 3
- **satsumas** or **clementines**, 3
- **strawberries**, 175g/6oz
- **seedless grapes**, medium-sized bunch

## tools

- ✱ Medium pan
- ✱ Wooden spoon
- ✱ Chopping board
- ✱ Small sharp knife

## COOK'S TIP

► For ease and safety for younger cooks, add the chocolate to a tub of custard. With adult supervision, microwave on Full Power (100%) for 1½ minutes, or until the chocolate has melted. Stir well.

1 Pour the custard into a medium pan and add the chocolate. Heat gently, stirring constantly for about 5 minutes, until the chocolate has melted. Alternatively, melt the chocolate into the custard in the microwave (see Cook's Tip). Adult supervision is required. Cool slightly.

2 Meanwhile, cut the apple into quarters. Carefully cut away the core and then cut the apple into bitesize pieces. Adult supervision is required.

3 Slice the bananas thickly and break the satsumas or clementines into segments.

4 Remove the stalks and leaves from the strawberries by twisting and pulling them out (known as hulling). Break the grapes off their stalks.

5 Pour the warm chocolate custard into a medium serving bowl and stand on a large plate.

6 Arrange the fruit around the bowl on the plate and serve with fondue forks, standard fork or cocktail sticks (toothpicks), for spearing and dipping the fruit.



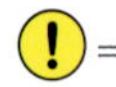 = Watch out! Sharp or electrical tool in use. (!) = Watch out! Heat is involved.

# Cantaloupe melon salad

This simple salad is a lovely way to use fragrant summer melons and strawberries. It makes a refreshing dessert to serve after a meaty barbecue.

*serves* 4

## ingredients

- **cantaloupe melon**, ½
- **strawberries**, 115g/4oz/1 cup
- **icing (confectioners') sugar**, 15ml/1 tbsp, plus extra for dusting

cantaloupe melon

## tools

- Small metal spoon
- Chopping board
- Large sharp knife
- Non-stick baking sheet or shallow ovenproof dish
- Sieve (strainer) or tea strainer
- Oven gloves

## COOK'S TIP

▶ 'Dusting' means to sift a fine layer of powder, such as icing sugar, over food and is often used as a way of decorating desserts. For a light dusting of sugar it's easier to use a tea strainer than a large sieve.

1 Ask an adult to preheat the grill (broiler) to high. On a chopping board, scoop out the seeds from the half melon using a small spoon.

2 Cut the melon in half lengthways. Adult supervision is required. Stand the melon pieces skin-side down on the board.

3 Carefully remove the skin by running the knife close to the skin. Cut the flesh into wedges. Arrange on a serving plate.

4 Remove the stalks and leaves from the strawberries by twisting and pulling them out (known as hulling). Cut in half.

5 Arrange the fruit in a single layer, cut-side up, on a baking sheet or in a shallow ovenproof dish and dust with the icing sugar (see Cook's Tip).

6 Grill the strawberries for 4–5 minutes, until the sugar starts to bubble. Adult supervision is required.

7 Place the caramelized strawberries on top of the melon, then dust everything with icing sugar and serve immediately.

# Chocolate puffs

Everybody loves chocolate profiteroles or éclairs, and choux pastry is quite easy to make, as long as you have good strong arm muscles!

serves 4–6

## ingredients

- **water**, 150ml/¼ pint/⅔ cup
- **butter**, 50g/2oz/¼ cup
- **plain (all-purpose) flour**, 65g/2½oz/generous ½ cup, sifted
- **eggs**, 2, lightly beaten

### for the filling and icing

- **double (heavy) cream**, 150ml/¼ pint/⅔ cup
- **icing (confectioners') sugar**, 225g/8oz/1½ cups
- **unsweetened cocoa powder**, 15ml/1 tbsp
- **water**, 30–60ml/2–4 tbsp

## tools

- Medium pan
- Wooden spoon
- Electric mixer
- 2 baking sheets
- 2 metal spoons
- Oven gloves
- Palette knife
- Wire rack
- Large mixing bowl
- Piping (pastry) bag fitted with a plain or star nozzle (tip)
- Small mixing bowl

## COOK'S TIPS

- As the pastry cooks, the water in the dough turns to steam and puffs up the pastry so, when making, don't let the water boil before the butter fully melts or some of this essential water will evaporate and be lost.
- When adding the flour, beat only until the paste begins to leave the sides of the pan; over-beating makes it oily.
- Eggs lighten the pastry and should be added a little at a time. The mixture will be slightly lumpy at first, but beat vigorously after each addition until the egg and paste are thoroughly mixed together. This will ensure you have a smooth, glossy texture.
- If you are short of time, instead of a wooden spoon use an electric mixer (with adult supervision) to beat the mixture. Be very careful not to over-mix the paste or you will ruin it.

1 **To make the puffs,** put the water in a medium pan, add the butter and heat gently until the butter melts. Increase the heat to high. Adult supervision is required when using heat.

2 As soon as the water and butter mixture boils, tip in all the flour at once. The easiest way to do this is to tip the flour on to a piece of paper so you can pour it in quickly.

3 Beat the ingredients with a wooden spoon until the mixture leaves the sides of the pan and comes together in a ball. It should be quite stiff. Leave to cool slightly in the pan.

4 Preheat the oven to 220°C/425°F/Gas 7.

5 Add the eggs, a little at a time. Beat well each time with a wooden spoon or electric mixer, until the mixture is thick and glossy (you may not need to use all of the egg to achieve this). Adult supervision is required.

6 Dampen two baking sheets with a light sprinkling of cold water.

 = Watch out! Sharp or electrical tool in use. (!) = Watch out! Heat is involved.

7 Place walnut-sized spoonfuls of the mixture on the baking sheets, leaving some space between them in case they spread. Bake for 25–30 minutes, until they are golden brown and well risen.

8 Ask an adult to remove from the oven and carefully lift them on to a rack with a palette knife. Make a small hole in each with the handle of a wooden spoon. Leave until cold.

9 To make the filling, whisk the cream in a bowl until thick. Put it into a piping bag fitted with a plain or star nozzle. Push the nozzle into the hole in each puff and squirt a little cream inside.

10 To make the icing, mix the icing sugar and cocoa in a small bowl. Add enough water to make a thick icing. Spread a spoonful of icing on each puff and serve immediately.

# Chocolate heaven

Get those cold hands wrapped round a steaming mug of creamy hot chocolate, and then dunk home-made chocolate-tipped biscuits (cookies) in it…perfect!

serves 2 (makes 10 biscuits)

## ingredients

### for the hot chocolate

- **milk**, 600ml/1 pint/2½ cups
- **drinking chocolate powder**, 90ml/6 tbsp, plus a little extra for sprinkling
- **sugar**, 30ml/2 tbsp, or more, to taste
- **aerosol whipped cream**, 2 large squirts (optional)

### for the choc-tipped biscuits

- **soft margarine**, 115g/4oz/½ cup, plus extra for greasing
- **icing (confectioners') sugar**, 45ml/3 tbsp, sifted
- **plain (all-purpose) flour**, 150g/5oz/1¼ cups
- **vanilla extract**, a few drops
- **plain (semisweet) chocolate**, 75g/3oz

## tools

- 2 small pans
- Whisk
- 2 non-stick baking sheets
- Large mixing bowl
- Wooden spoon
- Piping (pastry) bag fitted with a star nozzle (tip)
- Oven gloves
- Palette knife
- Wire rack
- Small heatproof bowl

## VARIATIONS

• Make the same quantity of round biscuits if you prefer, and dip half of each biscuit in melted chocolate.

• To melt the chocolate quickly, put it in a heatproof bowl and cook in the microwave on Full Power (100%) for 60–90 seconds, or until it has melted. Adult supervision is required.

• Try adding an Arabian twist to the hot chocolate by gently bashing a couple of cardamom pods with a rolling pin and putting them in the pan with the cold milk. With adult supervision, bring the milk to the boil, then fish out the cardamom pods with a slotted spoon and stir in the chocolate powder and sugar. Alternatively, add a spicy kick by bashing a whole green chilli and using that instead of the cardamom pods, so its spicy flavour goes into the milk as it heats up.

cardamom pods

1 **To make the hot chocolate**, put the milk in a small pan and bring to the boil. Add the chocolate powder and sugar and bring it back to the boil, whisking. Adult supervision is required.

2 Divide between two mugs. Top with a squirt of cream, if you like.

3 **To make the choc-tipped biscuits**, preheat the oven to 180°C/350°F/Gas Mark 4.

4 Lightly grease two baking sheets. Put the margarine and icing sugar in a large mixing bowl and beat them together until creamy. Mix in the flour and vanilla extract.

5 Put the biscuit mixture in a large piping bag fitted with a large star nozzle and pipe 10–13cm/4–5in lines on the greased baking sheets, spaced apart a little.

 = Watch out! Sharp or electrical tool in use.  = Watch out! Heat is involved.

6 Bake in the oven for 15–20 minutes, until pale golden. Ask an adult to remove from the oven. Allow to cool slightly before lifting on to a wire rack with a palette knife. Leave to cool on the rack completely.

7 Put the chocolate in a heatproof bowl. Stand the bowl over a pan of hot water and leave to melt. Do not allow the base of the bowl to touch the water. Adult supervision is required.

8 Dip both ends of each of the cooled cookies in turn in the melted chocolate, so that about 2.5cm/1in is coated. Gently shake to remove any excess chocolate.

9 Place the cookies on the wire rack and leave for about 15 minutes for the chocolate to set.

10 Serve the biscuits with the hot chocolate. If you have any biscuits left over, place in an airtight container, where they will keep for 2–3 days.

# Fresh orange squash

This delicious drink is much healthier than store-bought ones. It will keep in the refrigerator for a few days.

*makes about 4 glasses*

## ingredients

- **caster (superfine) sugar**, 90g/3½oz/scant ½ cup
- **large oranges**, 6
- **still** or **sparkling mineral water**, to serve

## tools

- Small heavy pan
- Wooden spoon
- Chopping board
- Medium sharp knife
- Juice squeezer or juicing machine
- Large jug (pitcher)

*oranges*

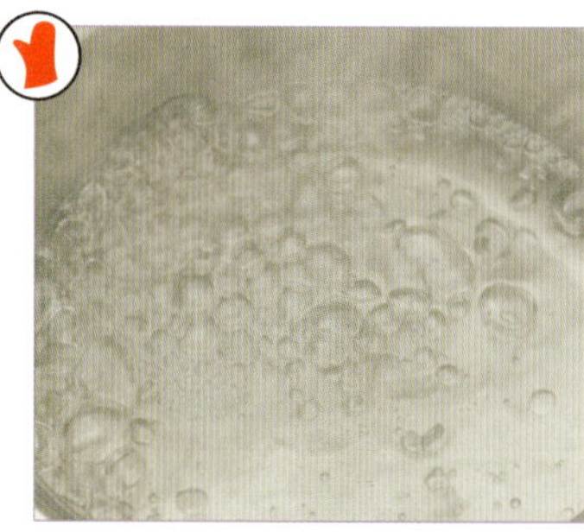

1 Put the sugar in a small, heavy pan with 100ml/3½fl oz/scant ½ cup water. Heat gently, stirring carefully until the sugar has dissolved. Bring to the boil and boil rapidly for 3 minutes. Adult supervision is required.

2 Carefully remove the pan from the heat and leave the syrup to cool.

3 Meanwhile, cut the oranges in half and squeeze the juice from all the pieces. You can do this in a juicer or using a juicing machine, if you have one. Adult supervision is required.

4 Pour the orange juice into a large jug. You should have about 550ml/18fl oz/2½ cups.

5 Mix the cooled sugar syrup into the jug of orange juice, then chill in the refrigerator.

6 To serve, pour some of the drink into a jug or individual glasses and dilute to taste with still or sparkling mineral water. Drop in some ice cubes and serve with straws.

## VARIATION

- This recipe also works well with fresh lemon juice in place of the orange juice and will make delicious bubbly lemonade if you add sparkling mineral water. You may need to add a little extra sugar to taste.

 = Watch out! Sharp or electrical tool in use.  = Watch out! Heat is involved.

# Ruby red lemonade

A colourful twist on lemonade, this scrumptious drink is made with vibrant blueberries or blackberries.

*makes about 6 glasses*

## ingredients

- **blackberries** or **blueberries**, 350g/12oz/3 cups
- **golden caster (superfine) sugar**, 130g/4½oz/scant ¾ cup
- **ice cubes**
- **sparkling mineral water**, to serve

## tools

- Juicing machine or a sieve (strainer) and a large bowl
- Small heavy pan
- Wooden spoon
- Jug (pitcher)

*blueberries*

1 Examine the blackberries or blueberries carefully, removing any tough stalks or leaves from the fruit, and then wash them thoroughly. Allow the fruit to dry.

2 Push through a juicing machine, if you have one, or through a sieve set over a large bowl. Adult supervision is required.

3 Put the sugar in a small, heavy pan with 100ml/3½fl oz/scant ½ cup water. Heat gently, stirring carefully until the sugar has dissolved. Bring to the boil and boil rapidly for 3 minutes. Adult supervision is required.

4 Remove the pan from the heat and leave the syrup to cool.

5 Mix the strained fruit juice with the syrup in a jug. The mixture will keep well in the refrigerator for a few days.

6 For each serving, pour about 50ml/2fl oz/¼ cup fruit syrup into a glass and add ice. Serve topped up with sparkling mineral water.

## COOK'S TIP

► If you happen to have loads of berries, it makes sense to make lots of this syrup and freeze it in single portions in ice cube trays. Then you simply have to tip a couple of cubes into a glass and top up with water for a really cool drink.

# Totally tropical

This gorgeous juice makes use of the best naturally sweet tropical fruit. It is packed with vitamins and is a good way to help you on your way to eating five a day.

makes 2 glasses

## ingredients

- **small pineapple**, ½
- **seedless white grapes**, small bunch
- **mango**, 1
- **mineral water** (optional)
- **fruit straws**, to decorate (see Cook's Tip)

## tools

- **Chopping board**
- **Large sharp knife**
- **Small sharp knife**
- **Blender or food processor**
- **Metal spoon**
- **Spatula**

mango

### COOK'S TIP

► To make fruit straws to garnish your glasses, simply push bitesize pieces of fruit, such as grape, mango and pineapple, on to a drinking straw.

grapes

1 Ask an adult to help you slice the base and top off the pineapple. Stand it upright on a chopping board. Carefully cut away the skin from the pineapple by 'sawing' down. Using the tip of a small, sharp knife carefully cut out the 'eyes' (rough dark round pieces).

2 Cut the pineapple in half and in half again down its length and cut away the tough core; discard. Roughly chop half the flesh. Remove the grapes from their stalks and put in a blender or food processor with the pineapple.

3 Place the mango flat on the board, with the long, flat stone that runs across the middle of the mango standing upright. Carefully cut downwards along the stone (pit) using a sharp knife, keeping as close to the stone as possible. Adult supervision is required.

4 Turn the mango over and repeat on the other side. Discard the stone. Scoop out the flesh with a spoon and add to the blender or food processor.

5 Blend, scraping the mixture down from the side with a spatula. Adult supervision is required.

6 Pour the fruit purée into glasses and top up with mineral water, if using. Serve immediately with fruit straws (see Cook's Tip), if you like.



(!) = Watch out! Sharp or electrical tool in use.  = Watch out! Heat is involved.

# Fruit punch

This lovely recipe is great for any party, picnic or just for when you are in need of a summer cooler. Serve in a punch bowl or a big jug.

serves 6

## ingredients

- **orange juice**, 300ml/½ pint/1¼ cups
- **pineapple juice**, 300ml/½ pint/1¼ cups
- **small pineapple**, ½
- **fresh cherries**, 6
- **tropical fruit juice**, 300ml/½ pint/1¼ cups
- **lemonade (lemon-flavoured soda)**, 475ml/16fl oz/2 cups

## tools

- ✱ **2 ice cube trays**
- ✱ **Chopping board**
- ✱ **Medium sharp knife**
- ✱ **Spoon**
- ✱ **Large jug (pitcher)**

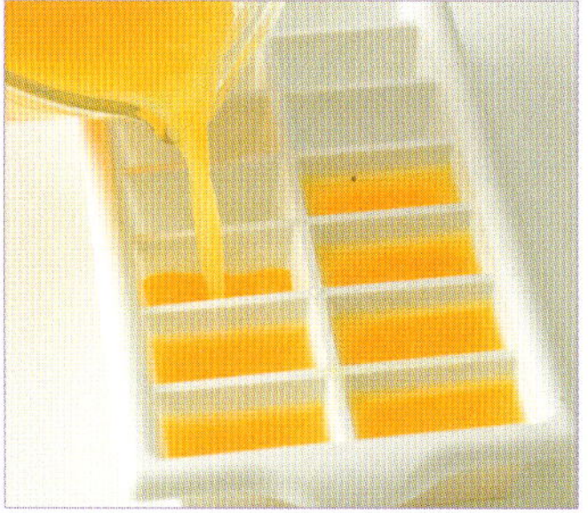

1 Pour the orange juice and pineapple juice into two separate ice cube trays and freeze until solid.

2 Place the pineapple on its side and cut off the base. Cut two thick slices across the width, then cut into eight pieces and reserve. Adult supervision is required.

3 Rinse the cherries and dry with kitchen paper. With adult supervision, make a slit in the bottom of each cherry, so they can sit on the rims of the glasses.

4 Mix together the tropical fruit juice and lemonade in a large jug with a spoon.

5 Turn out some of the ice cubes by flexing the plastic and put a mixture of each flavour in each glass. Pour the fruit punch mixture over.

6 Decorate the glasses with the pineapple slices and cherries and serve immediately.

VARIATION

• Use a combination of your favourite fruit juices, such as pomegranate and raspberry juice ice cubes, with apple juice and lemonade. Or try mango juice and coconut juice (available from most big supermarkets) ice cubes with pineapple juice and lemonade.

pineapple juice

# What a smoothie

An exquisite blend of raspberries and orange mixed with yogurt makes a great after-school pick-you-up.

*makes* 2–3 *glasses*

## ingredients

- **raspberries**, 250g/9oz/1⅓ cups
- **natural (plain) yogurt**, 200ml/7fl oz/ scant 1 cup
- **freshly squeezed orange juice**, 300ml/½ pint/1¼ cups

*orange juice*

*raspberries*

## tools

- **Blender, food processor or sieve (strainer)**
- **Spatula**
- **Bowl (optional)**
- **Spoon (optional)**

1 Chill two or three tall glasses, the raspberries, yogurt and orange juice in the refrigerator for about 1 hour.

2 Place the raspberries and yogurt in a blender or food processor. Blend thoroughly until smooth, scraping the mixture down with a spatula, if necessary. Adult supervision is required.

3 Alternatively, if you don't have a blender or food processor, or don't like the little raspberry seeds in your drink, press the raspberries through a sieve, collecting the purée in a bowl positioned below.

4 Add the yogurt to the raspberry purée in the bowl and stir to combine thoroughly.

5 Add the orange juice to the raspberry and yogurt mixture and process for another 30 seconds or stir until combined if you have pressed the raspberries through a sieve. Adult supervision is required.

6 Pour the smoothie into the chilled glasses and serve immediately with straws, if you like.

## COOK'S TIP

▶ This is delicious poured over crushed ice. If you have a processor or blender that is strong enough (check manufacturer's instructions), blend (with adult help) until crushed. Or, wrap some ice cubes in a clean dish towel and bash with a rolling pin until crushed.

 = Watch out! Sharp or electrical tool in use. = Watch out! Heat is involved.

# Strawberry and apple cooler

This fragrant, sweet drink was invented for enjoying on long, lazy summer days in the garden. It is best served well-chilled.

*makes* 2 *tall glasses*

## ingredients

- **ripe strawberries**, 300g/11oz/2½ cups
- **small**, **crisp eating apples**, 2
- **vanilla syrup**, 10ml/2 tsp
- **crushed ice** (see Cook's Tip on opposite page)

*apples*

*strawberries*

## tools

- **Chopping board**
- **Medium sharp knife**
- **Juicer, blender or food processor**
- **Sieve (strainer, optional)**
- **Jug (pitcher, optional)**
- **Spoon**

1 Pick out a few pretty strawberries and reserve. Remove the stalks and leaves from the other strawberries by slicing them off (with adult supervision) or twisting them out (known as hulling).

2 On a chopping board, cut the apples into quarters, carefully cut out the core and roughly chop. Adult supervision is required.

3 Push the fruits through a juicer, if you have one, or blend in a blender or food processor until smooth. Adult supervision is required. If you want it to be super-smooth, push the mixture through a sieve into a jug positioned below.

4 Stir the vanilla syrup into the collected juice in the blender or jug.

5 Half-fill two tall serving glasses with crushed ice. Add straws or stirrers and position the reserved strawberries (slicing them, if you like) in with the ice, saving a couple for the top, if you like.

6 Pour over the juice and top the drink with the reserved strawberries. Serve immediately.

## COOK'S TIPS

- If you can't find vanilla syrup, add a few drops of vanilla extract to 10ml/2 tsp honey.
- Try freezing the mixture in ice cube trays. Then simply pile into chilled glasses and wait until they start to thaw a little.

# Rainbow juice and fruit slush

Fruity flavours are great for making drinks such as rainbow juice, a stripy medley of tropical goodness, or fruit slush, a blend of semi-frozen blueberry and orange.

*makes 6 glasses*

## ingredients

for the rainbow juice

- **kiwi fruit**, 8
- **small pineapple**, 1
- **strawberries**, 250g/9oz/generous 1 cup, stalks and leaves removed

for the puppy love

- **oranges**, 2
- **blueberries**, 250g/9oz/2¼ cups
- **caster (superfine) sugar**, 50g/2oz/4 tbsp

kiwi fruit

## tools

- **Chopping board**
- **Small sharp knife**
- **Blender or food processor**
- **Spatula**
- **2 small bowls**
- **Spoon**
- **Juicer or sieve (strainer)**
- **Large bowl (optional)**
- **Non-metallic freezer container**
- **Fork**

## COOK'S TIPS

▶ To peel a pineapple, ask an adult to help you cut the top and base off the fruit. Stand the pineapple upright on the board and cut down with a 'sawing' action to remove large strips of skin. Cut out any remaining 'eyes' (small dark, rough pieces) with the tip of a sharp knife, and chop or slice. Alternatively, you can get wonderful gadgets that gouge out a continuous coil of pineapple flesh, leaving the shell and core intact.

▶ For an extra-cool drink, chill or semi-freeze the prepared fruit and the glasses before blending.

pineapple

1 **To make the rainbow juice**, cut away the peel from the kiwis using a sharp knife. Cut away the skin from the pineapple (see Cook's Tip), then halve and remove the core. Roughly chop the flesh. Adult supervision is required.

2 Put the pineapple in a blender or food processor and add 30ml/2 tbsp water. Process to a smooth purée, scraping the mixture down from the side with a spatula, if necessary. Adult supervision is required. Tip into a small bowl.

3 Add the kiwi fruit to the blender and blend until smooth. Tip into a separate bowl.

4 In a clean blender, blend the strawberries until smooth. Adult supervision is required.

5 Pour the strawberry purée into three glass tumblers. Carefully spoon the kiwi fruit purée into the glasses to form a separate layer. Spoon the pineapple purée over the kiwi fruit and serve with spoons or thick straws.

6 **To make the puppy love**, using a small, sharp knife, carefully cut away the skin and pith from the oranges, then cut the oranges into 8–10 chunky wedges. Adult supervision is required.

 = Watch out! Sharp or electrical tool in use.  = Watch out! Heat is involved.

7 Reserve a few blueberries, then push the rest through a juicer, alternating them with the orange wedges. Adult supervision is required. If you don't have a juicer, push the fruit through a sieve placed over a large bowl.

8 Add the sugar and 300ml/½ pint/1¼ cups cold water to the juice and stir until the sugar has dissolved. Pour into a shallow, non-metallic freezer container and freeze for 1–2 hours, or until the juice is beginning to freeze all over.

9 Use a fork to break up any solid areas of the mixture and tip into a blender or food processor. Blend until smooth and slushy. Spoon the drink into glasses and serve, topped with blueberries or other fruit.

# Vanilla milkshake

You could open your very own diner with this recipe, serving the best vanilla shakes in town.

*makes 2 glasses*

## ingredients

- **vanilla pod (bean)**, 1 (see Fact File)
- **full cream (whole) milk**, 400ml/14fl oz/1⅔ cups
- **single (light) cream**, 200ml/7fl oz/scant 1 cup
- **vanilla ice cream**, 4 scoops

*vanilla pods and extract*

## tools

- **Small sharp knife**
- **Small pan**
- **Slotted spoon**
- **Chopping board**
- **Blender or food processor**
- **Ice cream scoop**

*full cream milk*

1 Using a sharp knife, score the vanilla pod down the centre and open out along the cut. Place the milk in a small pan, add the vanilla pod and bring slowly to the boil. Adult supervision is required.

2 When the milk has reached boiling point, remove from the heat. Leave to stand until the milk is cold (known as infusing).

3 Remove the vanilla pod from the cooled milk with a slotted spoon and carefully scrape out the seeds with the tip of a small sharp knife.

4 Transfer the vanilla seeds to the blender or food processor with the milk and cream. Blend until well combined. Adult supervision is required.

5 Add the vanilla ice cream to the blender or food processor and blend well for 30 seconds, or until the mixture is deliciously thick and frothy.

6 Pour the milkshake into two large glasses. Add ice cubes, if you like, and serve immediately with stirrers and straws, if you like.

## FACT FILE

**VANILLA**

You will usually find vanilla pods in the spice section of supermarkets. They have an intense flavour, so you only need a small amount. You can use 10ml/2 tsp vanilla extract instead, if you like.

 = Watch out! Sharp or electrical tool in use. = Watch out! Heat is involved.

# Strawberry shake

If you like strawberries, then you will love this drink. If you have wild strawberries it will be all the more delicious!

*makes* 2 *glasses*

## ingredients

- **ripe strawberries**, 400g/14oz/ 3½ cups,
- **icing (confectioners') sugar**, 30–45ml/2–3 tbsp, sifted
- **Greek (US strained plain)** or **natural (plain) yogurt**, 200g/7oz/scant 1 cup
- **single (light) cream**, 60ml/4 tbsp

*Greek yogurt*

## tools

- **Sieve (strainer)**
- **Kitchen paper**
- **Small sharp knife (optional)**
- **Blender or food processor**
- **Spatula**

1 Pick out a couple of the prettiest strawberries and reserve. Remove the stalks and leaves from the other strawberries by slicing them off or pulling them out (known as hulling). Adult supervision is required.

2 Place the strawberries in a blender or food processor with 30ml/2 tbsp of the icing sugar.

3 Blend the mixture to a smooth purée, scraping the mixture down from the side with a spatula, if necessary. Adult supervision is required.

4 Keep the pretty green leaves on the reserved strawberries. Carefully slice them in half using a small sharp knife. Adult supervision is required.

5 Add the yogurt and cream to the blender and blend again until smooth and frothy. Check the sweetness, adding a little sugar if necessary.

6 Pour the milkshake into two medium-sized glasses. Top with the sliced strawberries and serve immediately with straws, if you like.

### COOK'S TIP

► You can replace the strawberries with other fruits if they are not in season. Try using fresh bananas instead to make another very popular milkshake.

*banana*

# Candystripe

This wickedly indulgent drink combines blended strawberries with a marshmallow-flavoured cream.

*makes* **4** *large glasses*

## ingredients

- **white** and **pink marshmallows**, 150g/5oz
- **full cream (whole) milk**, 500ml/17fl oz/generous 2 cups
- **redcurrant jelly**, 60ml/4 tbsp
- **strawberries**, 450g/1lb/4 cups
- **double (heavy) cream**, 60ml/4 tbsp
- **extra strawberries** and **marshmallows**, to decorate

## tools

- **2 medium heavy pans**
- **Wooden spoon**
- **Blender or food processor**
- **Spatula**
- **Tablespoon**
- **Jug (pitcher)**
- **Teaspoon**

1 With adult supervision, put the marshmallows in a heavy pan with half the milk. Heat gently, stirring, until the marshmallows have melted. Leave to stand until cool.

2 Heat the jelly in the other pan for 4 minutes, until melted. Set aside.

3 Remove the green stalks from the strawberries by twisting them off (known as hulling). Put them in a blender or food processor and process until smooth, scraping down the sides with a spatula if necessary. Adult supervision is required.

4 Stir 10ml/2 tsp of the strawberry purée into the jelly. Cover and set aside at room temperature.

5 Pour the remaining purée into a jug and stir in the marshmallow mixture, the cream and the remaining milk.

6 Cover and chill the milkshake and four large glasses in the refrigerator for at least 1 hour.

7 To serve, use a teaspoon to drizzle lines of the strawberry syrup down the insides of the glasses – this creates a candystripe effect when filled. Fill the glasses with the milkshake.

8 Serve topped with the extra marshmallows and strawberries and drizzle with any leftover strawberry syrup.

★★★ nice and challenging | *time to cook:* **4 minutes** | *preparation:* **10 minutes**

# Banoffee high

Rich, creamy and full of banana and toffee flavour, this drink is a real treat. Keep any leftover syrup for spooning over ice cream.

*makes* 4 *tall glasses*

## ingredients

- **large bananas**, 4
- **milk**, 600ml/1 pint/ 2½ cups
- **vanilla sugar**, 15ml/1 tbsp
- **ice cubes**, 8

*for the toffee syrup*

- **light muscovado (brown) sugar**, 75g/3oz/scant ½ cup
- **double (heavy) cream**, 150ml/¼ pint/⅔ cup

*muscovado sugar*

## tools

- Small heavy pan
- Wooden spoon
- Blender or food processor
- Large mixing bowl
- Whisk
- Tablespoon

*banana*

1 **To make the toffee syrup**, put the sugar in a pan with 75ml/5 tbsp water. Heat gently, stirring until the sugar dissolves. Add 45ml/ 3 tbsp of the cream and simmer for 4 minutes. Remove from the heat and leave to cool for 30 minutes. Adult supervision is required.

2 Peel the bananas, then break them into large pieces. Place the pieces in a blender or food processor with the milk, vanilla sugar, ice cubes and a further 45ml/3 tbsp of the cream. Blend for 1 minute, until smooth and frothy. Adult supervision is required.

3 Pour the remaining cream into a large, clean bowl and whisk gently until thickened and standing in soft peaks.

4 Add half the toffee syrup to the banana milkshake and blend, then pour into glasses.

### COOK'S TIP

▶ To make vanilla sugar, place a vanilla pod in a jar of caster (superfine) sugar and leave for 1 day.

5 Drizzle more syrup around the insides of the glasses. Spoon the cream over the top and drizzle with any remaining syrup. Serve immediately.

# Teatime treats

Yummy – it's teatime! Usually reserved for weekends when you have more time, teatime is a great excuse to eat all your favourite sandwiches, cakes and biscuits. Making your own adds to the enjoyment, and means you can make whatever combination of treats you want.

# Drop scones

Also known as griddlecakes and Scotch pancakes, these make a delectable breakfast or snack served with butter and drizzled with honey.

makes 8–10

## ingredients

- **butter**, 25g/1oz/2 tbsp, diced, plus extra for greasing
- **plain (all-purpose) flour**, 115g/4oz/1 cup
- **bicarbonate of soda (baking soda)**, 5ml/1 tsp
- **cream of tartar**, 5ml/1 tsp
- **egg**, 1, beaten
- **milk**, about 150ml/¼ pint/⅔ cup
- **butter** and **honey**, to serve

## tools

- **Griddle (grill) pan or heavy frying pan**
- **Sieve (strainer)**
- **Large mixing bowl**
- **Wooden spoon**
- **Wooden spatula**
- **Clean dish towel**

1 Lightly grease a griddle pan or heavy frying pan with butter. Sift the flour, bicarbonate of soda and cream of tartar together into a large mixing bowl.

2 Add the butter and rub it into the flour with your fingertips until the mixture resembles fine, evenly textured breadcrumbs.

3 Make a well in the centre of the flour mixture, then stir in the egg with a wooden spoon.

4 Add the milk a little at a time, stirring it in each time to check the consistency. Add just enough milk to give the batter the consistency of double (heavy) cream.

5 Heat the griddle or frying pan to a medium heat. Drop spoonfuls of the batter on to it. Cook for 3 minutes, until bubbles rise to the surface and burst. Adult supervision is required.

6 Turn the scones over with a spatula and cook for 2–3 minutes more, until golden underneath.

### COOK'S TIP

▶ Placing the cooked drop scones in a clean folded dish towel while you cook the remaining batter helps to keep them soft and moist until you are ready to serve them.

7 Place the cooked scones between the folds of a clean dish towel while you cook the remaining batter in the same way. Serve warm, with butter and honey.

 = Watch out! Sharp or electrical tool in use. (!) = Watch out! Heat is involved.

# Buttermilk scones

These deliciously light scones (biscuits) are a favourite for afternoon tea, served fresh from the oven and spread with butter and home-made jam.

*makes about 12 large or 18 small scones*

## ingredients

- **plain (all-purpose) flour**, 450g/1lb/4 cups
- **salt**, 2.5ml/½ tsp
- **bicarbonate of soda (baking soda)**, 5ml/1 tsp
- **butter**, 50g/2oz/¼ cup, at room temperature
- **caster (superfine) sugar**, 15ml/1 tbsp
- **small (medium) egg**, 1, lightly beaten
- **buttermilk**, about 300ml/½ pint/1¼ cups
- **butter** and **jam**, to serve

## tools

- 2 baking trays
- Sieve (sifter)
- Large mixing bowl
- Metal spoon
- Rolling pin
- Fluted cutter
- Oven gloves
- Wire rack

1 Preheat the oven to 220°C/425°F/Gas 7. Grease two baking trays.

2 Sift the flour, salt and bicarbonate of soda into a large mixing bowl, lifting the sieve up high. Add the cubed butter and rub it in with your fingertips until the mixture resembles fine breadcrumbs.

3 Add the sugar and mix in well. Make a well in the middle and add the egg and enough buttermilk to make a soft dough.

4 Turn the dough on to a lightly floured work surface and knead lightly into shape. Roll out to about 1cm/½in thick with a floured rolling pin.

5 Stamp out 12 large or 18 small scones with a fluted cutter, gathering the trimmings and re-rolling as necessary. Arrange on baking trays, spacing apart.

6 Bake for 15–20 minutes, until risen and golden brown, asking an adult to reverse the position of the trays halfway through.

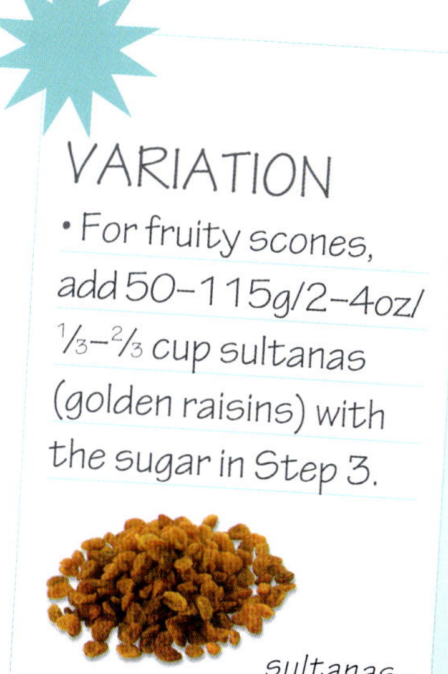

VARIATION

- For fruity scones, add 50–115g/2–4oz/⅓–⅔ cup sultanas (golden raisins) with the sugar in Step 3.

sultanas

7 Ask an adult to remove from the oven, transfer to a wire rack and leave to cool slightly. Serve warm.

# Buttermilk pancakes

It is traditional to have these pancakes with honey, but they also taste good American-style, with crispy fried bacon and a generous drizzle of maple syrup.

*makes about 6*

## ingredients

- **plain (all-purpose) flour**, 150g/5oz/1¼ cups
- **baking powder**, 2.5ml/½ tsp
- **eggs**, 3
- **buttermilk**, 120ml/4fl oz/½ cup
- **oil**, for frying
- **honey**, to serve

## tools

- Sieve (strainer)
- Large mixing bowl or food processor
- Wooden spoon (optional)
- Large, heavy frying pan or griddle
- Small bowl
- Tablespoon
- Fish slice (spatula) or palette knife
- Clean dish towel

1 Sift the flour and baking powder into a large bowl or food processor.

2 Add the eggs and beat with a wooden spoon or pulse to mix. Still beating or pulsing, pour in just enough buttermilk to make a thick, smooth batter. Adult supervision is required.

3 Heat a pan or griddle, then add enough oil to coat the base. Swirl the oil around to coat the base, then pour off any excess oil. Adult supervision is required.

4 Drop three or four tablespoonfuls of the mixture, spaced slightly apart, on to the pan or griddle.

5 Cook the pancakes over a medium heat for about 1 minute, until the bottoms are golden brown. Carefully flip the pancakes over with a fish slice or palette knife and cook for a further 1 minute until both sides are golden brown and cooked. Adult supervision is required.

### FACT FILE

**BUTTERMILK**

Originally a product left over after making butter, nowadays buttermilk is made from skimmed milk with a special bacterial 'culture' to give it the same tangy flavour.

6 Place the cooked pancakes between the folds of a clean dish towel while you cook the remaining batter in the same way. Serve warm, with honey.

 = Watch out! Sharp or electrical tool in use.

 = Watch out! Heat is involved.

# French toast

Also known as eggy bread, this makes a delicious breakfast, brunch or teatime treat. This version is made with a special Italian bread called panettone.

*serves* 4

## ingredients

- **panettone**, 4 large slices
- **eggs**, 2 large
- **butter**, 50g/2oz/¼ cup
- **fresh berries**, to serve
- **caster (superfine) sugar**, 30ml/2 tbsp

## tools

- Chopping board
- Serrated bread knife
- Small bowl
- Fork or whisk
- Shallow dish
- Large non-stick frying pan
- Fish slice (spatula) or palette knife
- Sieve (strainer) or colander

1 On a chopping board cut the slices of bread in half (if you have small slices, leave as they are). Adult supervision is required.

2 Break the eggs into a small bowl. Use a fork or whisk to whisk lightly until well combined, then transfer to a shallow dish.

3 With adult supervision heat the butter in a frying pan.

4 Dip the bread in the egg one to coat on both sides. Add to the pan. Fry for 2–3 minutes on each side, turning over with the fish slice until golden brown. Adult supervision is required.

5 Wash the berries in a sieve or colander, drain and pat dry with kitchen paper.

6 Drain the cooked toast on kitchen paper and dust with sugar. Scatter over the prepared berries and serve immediately.

## VARIATION

• Make a simple fruit compote to serve with the toast by mixing soft fruits, such as raspberries, blueberries and strawberries, with sugar to taste. Add a little fruit juice or cordial (syrup) mixed with a little water, cover and leave to soak for 30 minutes.

*blueberries*

# Banana muffins

Don't throw out nearly black bananas lurking in the fruit bowl. They will be perfect for these moist muffins.

*makes* 12

## ingredients

- **plain (all-purpose) flour**, 225g/8oz/2 cups
- **baking powder**, 5ml/1 tsp
- **bicarbonate of soda (baking soda)**, 5ml/1 tsp
- **salt**, a pinch
- **ground cinnamon**, 2.5ml/½ tsp
- **grated nutmeg**, 1.5ml/¼ tsp
- **large ripe bananas**, 3
- **egg**, 1
- **soft dark brown sugar**, 50g/2oz/¼ cup
- **vegetable oil**, 50ml/2fl oz/¼ cup, plus extra for greasing
- **raisins**, 40g/1½oz/⅓ cup

*bananas*

## tools

- 12-hole muffin tin (pan), plus muffin cases, if liked
- Sieve (strainer)
- 2 large mixing bowls
- Fork or wooden spoon
- 2 metal spoons
- Oven gloves
- Wire rack

1 Preheat the oven to 190°C/375°F/Gas 5. Lightly grease a 12-hole muffin tin, or position paper cases in the holes, if using.

2 Sift together the flour, baking powder, bicarbonate of soda, salt, cinnamon and nutmeg into a large mixing bowl, lifting the sieve high. Set aside.

3 Put the bananas in a separate large mixing bowl.

4 Mash the bananas to a fine pulp with a fork or with a wooden spoon.

5 Add the egg, sugar and oil to the mashed bananas and beat with a wooden spoon to combine thoroughly.

6 Add the dry ingredients to the banana mixture in the bowl and beat in gradually with a wooden spoon. It is important not to over-mix the mixture until it is smooth – it should look a bit 'knobbly'.

7 With the wooden spoon, gently stir in the raisins until just combined. Do not over-mix.

8 Spoon the mixture into the muffin tins or cases with metal spoons, filling them about two-thirds full.

9 Bake for 20–25 minutes, until the tops spring back when touched lightly with your finger. Ask an adult to remove from the oven, cool slightly in the tin, then transfer to a wire rack to cool completely before serving.

 = Watch out! Sharp or electrical tool in use.

 = Watch out! Heat is involved.

# Double choc chip muffins

What better way to enjoy teatime than with this ultimate chocolate treat, which can be eaten warm from the oven or cold.

*makes* 16

## ingredients

- **plain (all-purpose) flour**, 400g/14oz/3½ cups
- **baking powder**, 15ml/1 tbsp
- **unsweetened cocoa powder**, 30ml/2 tbsp, plus extra for dusting (optional)
- **muscovado (molasses) sugar**, 115g/4oz/⅔ cup
- **eggs**, 2
- **sour cream**, 150ml/¼ pint/⅔ cup
- **milk**, 150ml/¼ pint/⅔ cup
- **sunflower oil**, 60ml/4 tbsp
- **white chocolate**, 175g/6oz, chopped into small pieces
- **dark (semisweet) chocolate**, 175g/6oz, chopped into small pieces)

## tools

- 16 muffin cases
- 16-hole muffin tin (pan)
- Sieve (strainer)
- Large mixing bowl
- Wooden spoon
- Small bowl
- Fork
- 2 metal spoons
- Oven gloves
- Wire rack

1 Preheat the oven to 180°C/350°F/Gas 4. Place paper muffin cases in a 16-hole muffin tin.

2 Sift the flour, baking powder and cocoa into a large mixing bowl, lifting the sieve high to add air to the flour. Stir in the sugar. Make a well in the centre of the mixture using your fingers.

3 In a small bowl, beat the eggs with the sour cream, milk and oil, with the fork, then stir into the well in the dry ingredients. Beat well, gradually incorporating all the surrounding flour mixture to make a thick and creamy batter.

4 Stir the white and dark chocolate pieces into the batter mixture.

5 Spoon the mixture into the cases with two metal spoons, filling them almost to the top. Bake for 25–30 minutes, until well risen and firm to the touch.

6 Ask an adult to remove from the oven and cool in the tin slightly before moving to a wire rack to cool completely. Dust with cocoa powder to serve, if you like.

### COOK'S TIP

► If you don't have sour cream, you could use natural (plain) yogurt instead. Or, use double (heavy) cream or extra milk.

*sour cream*

# Banana gingerbread

This sticky treat improves with keeping. You can store it in a container for up to two months – if you can bear to leave it that long.

*makes* 12 *squares*

## ingredients

- **butter**, 75g/3oz/6 tbsp, and for greasing
- **ripe bananas**, 3, mashed
- **plain (all-purpose) flour**, 200g/7oz/1¾ cups
- **bicarbonate of soda (baking soda)**, 10ml/2 tsp
- **ground ginger**, 10ml/2 tsp
- **rolled oats**, 175g/6oz/1½ cups
- **muscovado (molasses) sugar**, 50g/2oz/¼ cup
- **golden (light corn) syrup**, 150g/5oz/⅔ cup
- **egg**, 1, beaten
- **icing (confectioners') sugar**, 75g/3oz/¾ cup
- **preserved stem ginger**, chopped, to decorate (optional)

preserved stem ginger

## tools

- **18 x 28cm/7 x 11in cake tin (pan)**
- **2 small mixing bowls**
- **Fork**
- **Large mixing bowl**
- **Sieve (strainer)**
- **Wooden spoon**
- **Small heavy pan**
- **Skewer**
- **Oven gloves**
- **Medium sharp knife**
- **Chopping board**

1 Preheat the oven to 160°C/325°F/Gas 3. Lightly grease and line a 18 x 28cm/7 x 11in cake tin.

2 Put the bananas in a small mixing bowl and mash with the fork. Sift the flour, bicarbonate of soda and ground ginger into the large bowl. Stir in the oats.

3 Put the sugar, butter and syrup in a pan. Heat gently for a few minutes, stirring occasionally, until the ingredients are melted and well combined. Adult supervision is required.

4 Stir into the flour mixture. Beat in the egg and mashed bananas.

5 Spoon into the tin, level the surface, and bake for about 1 hour, or a skewer comes out clean when it is inserted. Adult supervision is required.

6 Ask an adult to remove from the oven. Cool in the tin, then turn out. Cut into squares.

7 Meanwhile, sift the icing sugar into the remaining bowl and stir in just enough water to make a smooth, runny glaze.

8 Drizzle the glaze over each square of gingerbread and top with pieces of chopped ginger, if you like.

 = Watch out! Sharp or electrical tool in use.  = Watch out! Heat is involved.

 give it a try | time to cook: 45 minutes | preparation: 15 minutes

# Bilberry teabread

This lovely light sponge has a crumbly topping. Try serving it cold for tea or picnics, or warm with custard.

*makes 8 pieces*

## ingredients

- **butter**, 50g/2oz/¼ cup, plus extra for greasing
- **caster (superfine) sugar**, 175g/6oz/scant 1 cup
- **egg**, 1, at room temperature
- **milk**, 120ml/4fl oz/½ cup
- **plain (all-purpose) flour**, 225g/8oz/2 cups
- **baking powder**, 10ml/2 tsp
- **salt**, 2.5ml/½ tsp
- **fresh bilberries** or **blueberries**, 275g/10oz/2½ cups

### for the topping

- **caster (superfine) sugar**, 115g/4oz/generous ½ cup
- **plain (all-purpose) flour**, 40g/1½oz/⅓ cup
- **ground cinnamon**, 2.5ml/½ tsp
- **butter**, 50g/2oz/¼ cup, cut into pieces

## tools

- 23cm/9in baking dish or tin (pan)
- 2 large mixing bowls
- Electric mixer or wooden spoon
- Wooden spoon
- Sieve (strainer)
- Skewer
- Oven gloves
- Large sharp knife
- Chopping board

1 Preheat the oven to 190°C/375°F/Gas 5. Lightly grease a 23cm/9in baking dish or tin.

2 Put the butter and sugar in a bowl and beat together with an electric mixer or wooden spoon until pale and creamy. Adult supervision is required.

3 Add the egg and beat to combine, then mix in the milk until combined.

4 Sift over the flour, baking powder and salt, and stir with a wooden spoon just enough to blend the ingredients. Add the bilberries or blueberries and stir gently.

5 Transfer the mixture to the dish or tin.

6 To make the topping, place the sugar, flour, cinnamon and butter in a mixing bowl. Using your fingertips, rub in the butter until the mixture resembles breadcrumbs. Sprinkle over the mixture in the dish or tin.

7 Bake the teabread in the oven for about 45 minutes, or until a skewer inserted in the centre comes out clean.

8 Ask an adult to remove from the oven and leave to cool slightly. Turn out and cut into squares. Serve warm or cold.

# Carrot cake

It may sound funny adding vegetables to a cake but some, like carrots, give a lovely taste.

*serves* 10–12

## ingredients

- **sunflower oil**, 150ml/¼ pint/⅔ cup, plus extra for greasing
- **self-raising (self-rising) flour**, 225g/8oz/2 cups
- **baking powder**, 10ml/2 tsp
- **soft brown sugar**, 150g/5oz/1 scant cup
- **ready-to-eat dried figs**, 115g/4oz, chopped
- **carrots**, 225g/8oz, grated
- **small ripe bananas**, 2, mashed
- **eggs**, 2

*for the topping*

- **cream cheese**, 175g/6oz/¾ cup
- **icing (confectioners') sugar**, 175g/6oz/1½ cups, sifted
- **small coloured sweets (candies)**, **chopped nuts** or **grated chocolate**, to decorate

*carrots*

### COOK'S TIPS

▶ Because this cake contains moist vegetables and fruit and is topped with a cream cheese icing, it will not keep longer than a week and is best stored in an airtight container in the refrigerator, although it is so tasty it probably won't last that long!

▶ Dried figs add a lovely chewy texture to the cake, as well as making it healthier by adding fibre, which is very good for you. Figs are sold in most supermarkets and specialist dried fruit stores.

*dried figs*

## tools

- 18cm/7in round, loose-based cake tin (pan)
- Pencil
- Baking parchment
- Scissors
- Sieve (strainer)
- 2 large mixing bowls
- 2 wooden spoons
- Small mixing bowl
- Fork
- Palette knife
- Skewer
- Oven gloves
- Wire rack

1 Lightly grease a 18cm/7in cake tin with sunflower oil. Draw around the base of the tin on to baking parchment. Cut out the circle and use to line the base of the tin.

2 Preheat the oven to 180°C/350°F/Gas 4. Sift the flour, baking powder and sugar into a large bowl. Mix well with a wooden spoon, then stir in the figs.

3 Using your hands, squeeze as much liquid out of the grated carrots as you can and add to the flour mixture. Add the mashed bananas and stir to combine.

4 Lightly beat the eggs and oil together in a small mixing bowl with a fork, then pour them into the flour mixture. Beat everything together well with a wooden spoon.

 = Watch out! Sharp or electrical tool in use.  = Watch out! Heat is involved.

5 Transfer to the tin and level the top with a palette knife. Cook for 1–1¼ hours, until a skewer comes out clean. Ask an adult to remove from the tin. Cool on the wire rack.

6 **To make the topping,** put the cream cheese and icing sugar in a large mixing bowl. Beat together with a clean wooden spoon, to make a thick icing. This may take a few minutes.

7 Spread the icing over the top of the cake once it has completely cooled. Decorate the top of the icing with small coloured sweets, chopped nuts or grated chocolate.

8 Transfer to a serving dish, cut into small wedges and serve immediately.

# Simple chocolate cake

Every chef needs a good chocolate cake recipe, and this can be yours. For special occasions, top with whipped cream.

*serves* 6–8

## ingredients

- **butter** or **oil**, for greasing
- **dark (semisweet) chocolate**, 115g/4oz, broken into squares
- **milk**, 45ml/3 tbsp
- **unsalted butter**, 75g/3oz/6 tbsp
- **soft light brown sugar**, 200g/7oz/ scant 1 cup
- **eggs**, 3
- **self-raising (self-rising) flour**, 200g/7oz/1¾ cups
- **unsweetened cocoa powder**, 15ml/1 tbsp

### for the buttercream and topping

- **unsalted butter**, 75g/3oz/6 tbsp
- **icing (confectioners') sugar**, 175g/6oz/1½ cups
- **unsweetened cocoa powder**, 15ml/1 tbsp
- **vanilla extract**, 2.5ml/½ tsp
- **icing sugar** and **unsweetened cocoa powder**, for dusting

## tools

- **2 x 18cm/7in round cake tins (pans)**
- **Baking parchment**
- **Heatproof bowl**
- **Medium pan**
- **2 mixing bowls**
- **Electric mixer or wooden spoon**
- **Sieve (strainer)**
- **Large metal spoon**
- **Skewer**
- **Oven gloves**
- **Wire rack**
- **Mixing bowl**
- **Wooden spoon**

1 Preheat the oven to 180°C/350°F/Gas 4. Grease two 18cm/7in cake tins. Line with baking parchment.

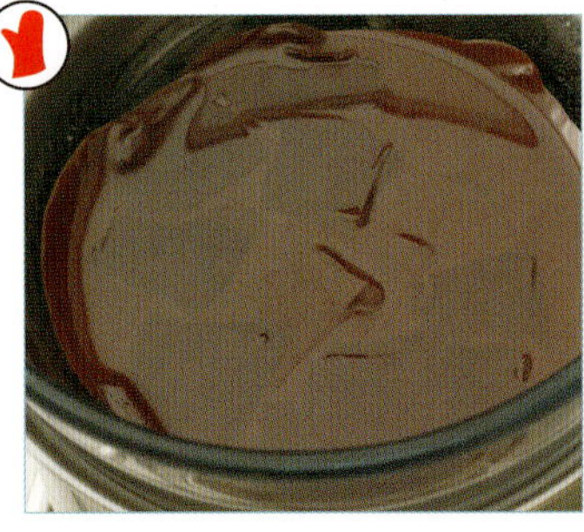

2 Melt the chocolate with the milk in a heatproof bowl set over a pan of barely simmering water. Cool. Adult supervision is required.

3 Put the butter and sugar in a mixing bowl and beat together until pale and creamy with an electric mixer (adult supervision is required) or wooden spoon. Add the eggs, one at a time, beating well after each addition. Stir in the chocolate mixture.

4 Sift the flour and cocoa over the mixture and fold in with a metal spoon until evenly mixed. Transfer the mixture to the tins and level the surface. Bake for 35–40 minutes, until a skewer pushed into the middle of the cake comes out clean.

5 Ask an adult to remove from the oven. Cool slightly in the tins before turning out on to a wire rack to cool completely.

6 **To make the buttercream**, beat the butter, icing sugar, cocoa powder and vanilla extract together in a clean bowl until the mixture is smooth.

7 Sandwich the cake layers together with the buttercream. Dust the top with a mixture of sifted icing sugar and cocoa before serving.

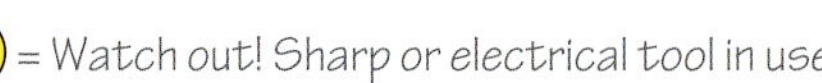
= Watch out! Sharp or electrical tool in use.

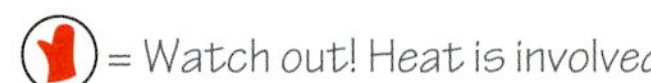
= Watch out! Heat is involved.

# Luscious lemon cake

This sugar-crusted cake is soaked in a lemon syrup, so it stays moist and delicious.

flour

serves 10

## ingredients

- **butter**, 250g/9oz/generous 1 cup, plus extra for greasing
- **caster (superfine) sugar**, 225g/8oz/generous 1 cup
- **eggs**, 5
- **plain (all-purpose) flour**, 275g/10oz/2½ cups, sifted
- **baking powder**, 10ml/2 tsp
- **salt**, a pinch

### for the sugar crust

- **lemon juice**, 60ml/4 tbsp
- **golden (light corn) syrup**, 15ml/1 tbsp
- **sugar**, 30ml/2 tbsp

lemons

## tools

- 1kg/2¼lb loaf tin (pan)
- Baking parchment
- Large mixing bowl
- Electric mixer or wooden spoon
- Sieve (strainer)
- 2 metal spoons
- Skewer
- Oven gloves
- Small heavy pan

1 Preheat the oven to 180°C/350°F/Gas 4. Grease and line a loaf tin.

2 Beat the butter and sugar using an electric mixer (adult supervision is required) or wooden spoon, until pale and creamy. Gradually beat in the eggs.

3 Sift the flour, baking powder and salt into the bowl and fold in.

4 Spoon into the tin, level the surface and bake for 40–50 minutes, until a skewer pushed into the middle comes out clean. Adult supervision is required.

5 Ask an adult to remove from the oven. Stab a skewer right the way through in several places.

6 Put the lemon juice and syrup in a small, heavy pan and heat gently, stirring, until the syrup melts. Adult supervision is required.

7 Add the sugar to the pan and immediately spoon over the cake, so the syrup soaks through but leaves some sugar crystals on the top.

8 Allow to cool before removing from the tin and serving.

# Lemon meringue cakes

Everyone, especially grown-ups, are impressed by people who can make a good meringue and this easy recipe reveals exactly how to do it.

makes 18

## ingredients

- **butter**, 115g/4oz/½ cup
- **caster (superfine) sugar**, 200g/7oz/scant 1 cup
- **eggs**, 2
- **self-raising (self-rising) flour**, 115g/4oz/1 cup
- **baking powder**, 5ml/1 tsp
- **lemons**, 2, grated rind
- **lemon juice**, 30ml/2 tbsp
- **egg whites**, 2

## tools

- 2 x 9-hole bun tins (muffin pans)
- 18 paper cake cases
- 2 large mixing bowls
- Electric mixer or wooden spoon
- 3 metal spoons
- Balloon whisk (optional)
- Oven gloves
- Wire rack

eggs

1 Preheat the oven to 190°C/375°F/Gas 5. Stand the paper cases in the bun tins.

2 Put the butter in a bowl and beat with an electric mixer (adult supervision is required) or spoon until soft. Add 115g/4oz/½ cup of the sugar and continue to beat until smooth and creamy.

3 Beat in the eggs, flour, baking powder, half the lemon rind and all the lemon juice. Mix well to combine thoroughly.

4 Divide the cake mixture between the paper cases using two metal spoons. Fill the cases to near the top of the paper.

5 Put the egg whites in a clean mixing bowl and whisk with a balloon whisk or clean electric mixer until they stand in soft peaks when the whisk is lifted. Adult supervision is required.

6 Stir in the remaining caster sugar and lemon rind with a spoon.

VARIATION

• Use a mixture of oranges and lemons, for a sweeter taste, or use only oranges.

7 Put a spoonful of the meringue mixture on top of each cake. Cook for 20–25 minutes, until the meringue is crisp and brown.

8 Ask an adult to remove from the oven and cool in the tin slightly before cooling completely on a wire rack. Serve hot or cold.

 = Watch out! Sharp or electrical tool in use. = Watch out! Heat is involved.

# Orange and apple rockies

You may know these classic cakes as 'rock' cakes. They are a fantastic teatime treat to throw together at a moment's notice.

*makes* 24

## ingredients

- **self-raising (self-rising) flour**, 225g/8oz/2 cups
- **margarine**, 115g/4oz/½ cup
- **oil**, for greasing
- **large eating apple**, 1
- **ready-to-eat dried apricots**, 50g/2oz/⅓ cup
- **sultanas (golden raisins)**, 50g/2oz/⅓ cup
- **small orange**, 1, grated rind
- **demerara (raw) sugar**, 75g/3oz/⅓ cup
- **egg**, 1
- **milk**, 15ml/1 tbsp

## tools

- Large mixing bowl
- 2 non-stick baking sheets
- Pastry brush
- Peeler
- Chopping board
- Small sharp knife
- Small bowl
- Fork
- Wooden spoon
- Wire rack

1 Put the flour into a large mixing bowl and rub in the margarine with your fingertips until the mixture resembles breadcrumbs. Set aside.

2 Preheat the oven to 190°C/375°F/Gas 5 and brush two baking sheets with a little oil.

3 Peel the apple, then cut it into quarters. Remove the core. Chop the apricots. Adult supervision is required.

4 Stir the apple and apricots into the flour mixture with the sultanas and orange rind. Reserve 30ml/2 tbsp of the sugar and stir the rest into the mixture.

5 Beat the egg and milk in a small bowl with a fork. Stir into the flour mixture with a wooden spoon until just beginning to bind together.

6 Drop spoonfuls, well spaced apart, on to the baking sheets. Sprinkle with the reserved sugar.

VARIATION

• Try replacing the apricots with other dried fruit, such as prunes, figs, mango or banana chips, or add chocolate chips.

7 Bake for 12–15 minutes, until golden and firm. Ask an adult to remove from the oven and transfer to a wire rack to cool. Serve warm or cold with butter.

# Pecan squares

Halved pecan nuts are mixed with sugar and honey and baked in a pastry crust in this sweet treat. Serve on its own or with cream.

*makes* **36**

## ingredients

- **butter** or **oil** for greasing
- **plain (all-purpose) flour**, 225g/8oz/2 cups
- **salt**, a pinch
- **sugar**, 115g/4oz/½ cup
- **cold butter** or **margarine**, 225g/8oz/1 cup, cubed
- **egg**, 1, lightly beaten
- **lemon**, 1, finely grated rind

### for the topping

- **butter**, 175g/6oz/¾ cup
- **clear honey**, 75g/3oz/⅓ cup
- **sugar**, 50g/2oz/¼ cup
- **soft dark brown sugar**, 115g/4oz/½ cup
- **whipping cream**, 75ml/5 tbsp
- **pecan halves**, 450g/1lb/4 cups

## tools

- **37 x 27 x 2.5cm/ 14½ x 10½ x 1in Swiss (jelly) roll tin**
- **Sieve (strainer)**
- **Large mixing bowl**
- **Wooden spoon**
- **Fork or palette knife**
- **Oven gloves**
- **Small heavy pan**
- **2 baking sheets**
- **Large sharp knife**

1 Preheat the oven to 190°C/375°F/Gas 5. Lightly grease the tin.

2 Sift the flour and salt into a large mixing bowl. Stir in the sugar. Add the butter or margarine and rub into the flour and sugar with your fingertips until the mixture resembles chunky breadcrumbs.

3 Add the egg and lemon rind and blend well with a fork or palette knife until the mixture just holds together.

4 Spoon the mixture into the tin. With floured fingertips, press into an even layer. Prick the pastry all over with a fork, cover and chill for 10 minutes.

5 Bake for 15 minutes. Ask an adult to remove from the oven.

6 **To make the topping**, put the butter, honey and both kinds of sugar in a small, heavy pan. Melt over a low heat, stirring frequently. Increase the heat and boil, without stirring, for 2 minutes. Adult supervision is required.

7 Remove from the heat and stir in the cream and pecans. Pour over the pastry crust. Ask an adult to return to the oven. Bake for 25 minutes, until set. Ask an adult to remove from the oven. Cool.

8 Invert on to a baking sheet, place another baking sheet on top and invert again. Cut into squares.

= Watch out! Sharp or electrical tool in use.

= Watch out! Heat is involved.

# Rich chocolate cookie slice

Refrigerator cookies are cool! Simply mix all the ingredients together then let them chill while you get on with something else.

*makes about* 10

## ingredients

- **unsalted butter**, 130g/4¼oz/½ cup, plus extra for greasing
- **plain (semisweet) chocolate**, 150g/5oz
- **milk chocolate**, 150g/5oz
- **digestive biscuits (graham crackers)**, 90g/3½oz
- **white chocolate**, 90g/3½oz

*plain, milk and white chocolate*

## tools

- ✱ 450g/1lb loaf tin (pan)
- ✱ Baking parchment
- ✱ Heatproof bowl
- ✱ Chopping board
- ✱ Large sharp knife
- ✱ Medium heavy pan
- ✱ Wooden spoon
- ✱ Clear film (plastic wrap)

1 Lightly grease the loaf tin and line the base and sides with baking parchment, making sure it comes up over the top.

2 Break the dark and milk chocolate into small, pieces and place in a heatproof bowl. With adult supervision, chop the butter and add to the bowl.

3 Set the bowl over a pan of simmering water (take care not to let the water touch the base of the bowl) and stir with a until melted. Cool for 20 minutes. Adult supervision is required.

4 Meanwhile, break the digestive biscuits into quite small pieces with your fingers.

5 Finely chop the white chocolate. Adult supervision is required. Stir into the melted chocolate with the biscuits.

6 Turn into the tin and pack down gently. Cover with clear film and chill for 2 hours, or until set. Turn out, remove the paper and slice.

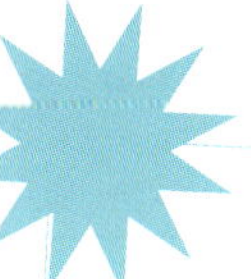

## VARIATION

• There are lots of ways you can vary this recipe. Try different kinds of chocolate, such as ginger, hazelnut, honey and almond, peanut or mocha; add chopped dried fruit, such as apricots, mangoes, cranberries or dried blueberries; or vary the biscuits, using gingersnaps, chocolate chip cookies, Rich Tea or macaroons.

# Chewy flapjacks

Not only are these classic cereal bars super-easy to make, but they will also give you energy to keep going through the busiest of days!

*makes* 18

## ingredients

- **unsalted butter**, 250g/9oz/generous 1 cup
- **large orange**, 1, finely grated rind
- **golden (light corn) syrup**, 225g/8oz/⅔ cup
- **light muscovado (brown) sugar**, 75g/3oz/⅓ cup
- **rolled oats**, 375g/13oz/3¾ cups

*orange rind*

## tools

- **28 x 20cm/11 x 8in shallow baking tin (pan)**
- **Baking parchment**
- **Large heavy pan**
- **Wooden spoon**
- **Oven gloves**
- **Chopping board**
- **Medium sharp knife**

1 Preheat the oven to 180°C/350°F/Gas 4. Line the base and sides of the tin with baking parchment.

2 Put the butter, orange rind, syrup and sugar in a large, heavy pan and heat gently, stirring occasionally until the butter has melted. Adult supervision is required.

3 Add the oats to the pan and stir to mix thoroughly. Tip the mixture into the tin and spread into the corners in an even layer.

4 Bake for 15–20 minutes until just beginning to colour around the edges. (The mixture will still be soft but will harden as it cools).

5 Ask an adult to remove the tin from the oven and leave the mixture to cool in the tin for a few minutes before marking the mixture into squares or bars.

6 Leave to cool completely, then turn out on to a board and cut along the scored lines.

## COOK'S TIPS

- Don't be tempted to overcook flapjacks or they'll turn crisp and dry and lose their chewy texture.
- It is important to score the flapjacks while they are still warm, or they may be hard to cut later.

 = Watch out! Sharp or electrical tool in use. = Watch out! Heat is involved.

# Peanut and jam cookies

These nutty jam cookies are a twist on the original American peanut butter cookie and are a real hit with kids and adults alike at any time of the day.

makes 20–22

## ingredients

- **crunchy peanut butter** (with no added sugar), 227g/8oz jar
- **unsalted butter**, 75g/3oz/ 6 tbsp, at room temperature, diced
- **caster (superfine) sugar**, 90g/3½oz/½ cup
- **light muscovado (brown) sugar**, 50g/2oz/¼ cup
- **large (US extra large) egg**, 1, beaten
- **self-raising (self-rising) flour**, 150g/5oz/1¼ cups
- **seedless raspberry jam**, 250g/9oz/ scant 1 cup

## tools

- 3–4 baking sheets
- Baking parchment
- Large mixing bowl
- Electric mixer or wooden spoon
- Sieve (sifter)
- Fork
- Oven gloves
- Palette knife
- Wire rack
- Teaspoon

1 Preheat the oven to 180°C/350°F/ Gas 4. Line three or four baking sheets with baking parchment.

2 Put the peanut butter and unsalted butter in a large mixing bowl and beat together with a wooden spoon or electric mixer (adult supervision is required) until well combined and creamy.

3 Add the caster and muscovado sugars and mix well. Add the egg and blend well. Sift in the flour and mix to a stiff dough.

4 Roll the dough into walnut-size balls between the palms of your hands. Place the balls on the prepared baking sheets and gently flatten each one with a fork to make a rough-textured cookie with a ridged surface. (Don't worry if the dough cracks slightly.)

5 Bake for 10–12 minutes, or until cooked but not browned. Using a palette knife, transfer to a wire rack to cool.

6 Spoon jam on to one cookie and top with a second. Continue to sandwich the rest in this way.

## VARIATION

• If you don't like raspberry jam, you could use another flavour, such as strawberry, plum or apricot. Alternatively, leave out the jam altogether and simply serve the cookies on their own.

# Triple chocolate cookies

You'll find these chocolatey treats so hard to resist you'll want to eat them as soon as they come out of the oven – just take care not to burn your fingers!

*makes* 12 *large cookies*

## ingredients

- **milk chocolate**, 90g/3½oz
- **white chocolate**, 90g/3½oz
- **dark (bittersweet) chocolate**, 300g/11oz
- **unsalted butter**, 90g/3½oz/7 tbsp, plus extra for greasing
- **vanilla extract**, 5ml/1 tsp
- **light muscovado (brown) sugar**, 150g/5oz/¾ cup
- **self-raising (self-rising) flour**, 150g/5oz/1¼ cups
- **macadamia nut halves**, 100g/3½oz/ scant 1 cup

## tools

- Chopping board
- Large sharp knife
- 2 baking sheets
- Baking parchment
- Large heatproof bowl
- Medium pan
- Wooden spoon
- 2 tablespoons
- Oven gloves
- Palette knife
- Wire rack

1 On a chopping board, roughly chop the milk and white chocolate into small pieces and set aside. Adult supervision is required.

2 Preheat the oven to 180°C/350°F/Gas 4. Grease the baking sheets and line with baking parchment.

3 Chop 200g/7oz of dark chocolate into chunks. Dice the butter. Set aside.

4 Break up the remaining dark chocolate and place in a heatproof bowl set over a pan of simmering water. Stir until melted. Adult supervision is required.

5 Remove from the heat and stir in the butter, then the vanilla extract and muscovado sugar. Add the flour and mix gently.

6 Add half the dark chocolate chunks, all the milk and white chocolate and the nuts and mix well.

7 Using two tablespoons, spoon 12 dollops of the mixture onto the baking sheets, spaced well apart to allow for spreading. Press the remaining dark chocolate chunks into the top of each cookie.

8 Bake the cookies for about 12 minutes until just beginning to colour. Ask an adult to remove from the oven and leave the cookies to cool on the baking sheets. Using the palette knife, lift the cookies on to a wire rack to cool completely before serving.

 = Watch out! Sharp or electrical tool in use. (!) = Watch out! Heat is involved.

# Chocolate caramel nuggets

Inside each of these crumbly, buttery biscuits (cookies) lies a soft-centred chocolate-coated caramel, which softens as it cooks and makes an oozy surprise filling.

*makes* 12

## ingredients

- **self-raising (self-rising) flour**, 150g/5oz/1¼ cups
- **unsalted butter**, 90g/3½ oz/7 tbsp, chilled and diced, plus extra for greasing
- **caster (superfine) sugar**, 50g/2oz/¼ cup
- **egg yolk**, 1
- **vanilla extract**, 5ml/1 tsp
- **soft-centred chocolate caramels**, 14
- **icing (confectioners') sugar** and **unsweetened cocoa powder**, for dusting

## tools

- Food processor
- Clear film (plastic wrap)
- Large baking sheet
- Rolling pin
- 5cm/2in round cookie cutter
- Oven gloves
- Palette knife
- Wire rack

VARIATION

• You could use pieces of fudge instead of chocolate caramels, if you like.

1 Put the flour and butter in a food processor and process until the mixture resembles fine breadcrumbs. Adult supervision is required.

2 Add the sugar, egg yolk and vanilla extract to the food processor and process to a smooth dough.

3 Wrap the dough in clear film and chill for 30 minutes. Preheat the oven to 200°C/400°F/Gas 6. Grease a baking sheet.

4 Roll out the dough thinly on a floured surface and cut out 28 rounds using a 5cm/2in cutter.

5 Place one chocolate caramel on a dough round, then lay a second round on top. Pinch the edges of the dough together so that the caramel is completely enclosed, then place on the baking sheet. Make the remaining biscuits in the same way.

6 Bake the biscuits for about 10 minutes, until pale golden.

7 Ask an adult to remove the tray from the oven, transfer the biscuits to a wire rack with a palette knife and leave to cool. Serve dusted with icing sugar and cocoa powder.

# Party food

It's party time! Whether it's your birthday, Easter, Christmas or you simply have something special to celebrate, it's always fun to rustle up some scrummy treats for all your friends. Better still, get a couple of them over to help you make it all – just make sure you don't eat it all before the others arrive!

# Crazy rainbow popcorn

Before you start, you'll need to take a trip to a good cookshop to get special colourings. Once you have them you will have loads of fun making deliciously crazy corn!

*serves* 10–15

## ingredients

- **vegetable oil**, 15ml/1 tbsp
- **popcorn kernels**, 175g/6oz (see Fact File)
- **green**, **red** and **yellow powdered food colourings** (see Cook's Tip)
- **red cheese**, such as **red Leicester** or **Cheddar**, 50g/2oz, grated
- **green cheese**, such as **sage Derby**, 50g/2oz, grated

*red Leicester cheese*

## FACT FILE

### POPCORN

Completely natural and good for you, popcorn is the ideal snack food. It is also inexpensive and lots of fun to cook as it cracks and pops in the pan. The kernels of the corn are naturally hard and come in two main varieties – yellow and white. The yellow type tends to pop to a larger size than the white kind, so is often used in cinemas (movie theaters), but the white kernels tend to have more flavour. Either can be used in this colourful recipe.

*popcorn kernels*

## tools

- ✱ Large heavy pan
- ✱ Wooden spoon
- ✱ 3 or 4 plastic sandwich or freezer bags
- ✱ Small spoon or knife
- ✱ Large mixing bowl
- ✱ Grater

1 Put the oil and popcorn kernels in a pan and stir to coat the kernels in oil. Cover with a lid and cook for about 5 minutes, until you hear the corn starting to pop. Do not remove the lid. Shake the pan a few times. Adult supervision is required.

2 When you hardly hear any popping at all, ask an adult to remove the pan from the heat and remove the lid. Put small amounts of popcorn in a few plastic sandwich or freezer bags (use as many bags as there are different colourings).

3 Use a tiny spoon or the tip of a knife to add a small amount of food colouring to each of the bags of popcorn. You can choose what colours you use and how much popcorn you want to make a particular colour.

4 Close the bags and hold each in turn in one hand. Shake and tap with the other hand, tossing the popcorn inside the bag to coat it evenly in the colouring. As you colour each batch, tip it into a large serving bowl.

 = Watch out! Sharp or electrical tool in use. = Watch out! Heat is involved.

5 When all the popcorn is coloured, transfer it all to a large mixing bowl. Add both types of grated cheese to the coloured corn. Carefully toss the mixture together with your hands and serve the popcorn immediately.

## COOK'S TIP

► You must use powdered food colouring as the liquid type will turn the popcorn soggy. You will find the powdered kind in specialist cake decorating shops.

# Cheese and potato twists

If you like cheese sandwiches, then you'll love these delicious cheesy twists. They are lovely served warm or cold at any party, so make lots as they are sure to go!

*makes* 12

## ingredients

- **potatoes**, 225g/8oz, peeled, diced and boiled
- **strong white bread flour**, 225g/8oz/2 cups
- **easy bake dried yeast**, 5ml/1 tsp
- **salt**, a pinch
- **lukewarm water**, 150ml/¼ pint/⅔ cup
- **red Leicester** or **Cheddar cheese**, 175g/6oz/1½ cups, finely grated
- **olive oil**, 10ml/2 tsp, for greasing

## tools

- ✱ **Potato masher**
- ✱ **Sieve (strainer)**
- ✱ **Large mixing bowl**
- ✱ **Large chopping board or tray**
- ✱ **Non-stick baking sheet**
- ✱ **Oven gloves**

1 Mash the potatoes and set aside. Sift the flour into a bowl and add the yeast and a pinch of salt. Stir in the potatoes and rub with your fingers until it resembles breadcrumbs.

2 Make a well in the centre and pour in the water. Bring the mixture together with your hands.

3 Knead for 5 minutes on a floured surface. Return to the bowl, cover with a damp cloth and leave to rise in a warm place for 1 hour, until doubled in size.

4 Turn out on to the work surface and re-knead the dough for a few seconds. Divide into 12 pieces and shape into balls.

5 Scatter the cheese over a clean surface, such as a large chopping board or tray. Roll each ball of dough in the cheese.

6 Roll each roll on a dry surface to form a long sausage shape. Fold the two ends together and twist the bread. Lay these on a baking sheet.

## COOK'S TIP

▶ You can't beat making your own bread, but you could also try using a bread mix and adding mashed potato.

7 Cover with a damp cloth and leave to rise in a warm place for 30 minutes.

8 Preheat the oven to 220°C/425°F/Gas 7. Bake for 10–15 minutes, until risen and golden. Ask an adult to remove from the oven and serve.

 = Watch out! Sharp or electrical tool in use.  = Watch out! Heat is involved.

# Sandwich shapes

Try using a selection of different shaped cutters to make these sandwiches. You could also use different coloured breads to give a white layer topped with a brown layer.

*serves* 4–6

## ingredients

- **white bread**, 8 slices
- **brown (whole-wheat) bread**, 8 slices
- **butter** or **margarine**, for spreading
- **shredded lettuce**, **radishes** and **mustard cress**, to garnish

*ham and cheese filling*

- **ham**, 4 thin slices
- **Cheddar cheese**, 8 thin slices

*chicken and mayonnaise filling*

- **roast chicken breast**, 4 thin slices
- **mayonnaise**, for spreading

## tools

- **Butter knife**
- **A selection of different-shaped cookie cutters**

1 Lay the slices of bread out on a work surface and lightly spread one side with softened butter or margarine with a knife.

2 **To make the ham and cheese sandwiches,** put a slice of ham on four slices of the bread, then put two slices of cheese on top of the ham.

3 **For the chicken and mayonnaise sandwiches,** put a slice of chicken on four of the remaining slices of bread and spread a little mayonnaise on top.

4 Use the remaining eight slices of bread to make the sandwich lids. Press down lightly on the top pieces to secure.

5 Using a selection of differently shaped cookie cutters, such as fish, rabbits, teddy bears, stars or hearts, stamp out shapes from the sandwiches by placing the cutter on the sandwich and pushing down. Try to stamp out two or more shapes from each to avoid any waste. (You can eat the leftovers!)

## VARIATION

• You can make tasty sandwich shapes with any favourite fillings. Try egg mayonnaise, tuna mayonnaise or cheese and tomato.

6 Arrange the sandwiches on a serving plate and garnish with a little shredded lettuce, radishes and mustard and cress around the edges. Serve straight away or cover well with clear film (plastic wrap) and chill for 2–3 hours until needed.

# Mini burgers 'n' buns

Instead of serving these burgers with normal chips, go for the healthier option of cucumber strips. You could also try carrot and pepper strips for colourful burgers.

## COOK'S TIPS

► To make fresh breadcrumbs, take a chunk of stale bread and grate it with a coarse grater. Alternatively, blend in a blender or food processor for a few seconds. Adult supervision is required. For crisp crumbs, spread the fresh ones out on a baking sheet and grill (broil) for about 2 minutes, shaking the sheet halfway through. Adult supervision is required.

► Instead of using a round cutter, you could make funny shapes out of the cheese with novelty cutters for themed parties, such as Easter, Halloween or Christmas.

► Although mini burgers are ideal for parties, you could make four larger burgers for a family meal using this recipe.

*bread*

makes 8

## ingredients

- **small onion**, 1
- **minced (ground) steak** or **beef**, 225g/8oz
- **egg**, 1
- **fresh breadcrumbs**, 25g/1oz/½ cup (see Cook's Tips)
- **tomato purée (paste)**, 15ml/1 tbsp
- **small soft bread rolls**, 8
- **Cheddar cheese**, 4 slices
- **ketchup**, to serve
- **lettuce** and **cherry tomatoes**, to garnish

### for the cucumber strips

- **cucumber**, 1

*cucumber*

## tools

- **Foil**
- **2 chopping boards**
- **Medium sharp knife**
- **Large mixing bowl**
- **Wooden spoon**
- **Tongs**
- **Small round cutter**
- **Large serrated knife**

1 Ask an adult to preheat the grill (broiler) to medium-hot. Line a grill (broil) pan with foil. Peel the onion and finely chop it on a chopping board using a sharp knife. Adult supervision is required.

2 Put the meat in a bowl and add the egg, onion, breadcrumbs and tomato purée. Using a wooden spoon, mix all the ingredients together until they are evenly combined.

3 Wet your hands. Take a small handful of mixture, shape it into a round and flatten it slightly. Do this until all the mixture is used up. Place the burgers on the grill pan.

4 Cook for 5 minutes. Carefully turn over with a pair of tongs, then put the burgers back under the grill for another 5–8 minutes until cooked through. Adult supervision is required.

 = Watch out! Sharp or electrical tool in use. (!) = Watch out! Heat is involved.

5 Meanwhile, **make the cucumber strips**. Cut the cucumber in half lengthwise, then slice into two or three pieces. Cut these pieces into thin strips. Adult supervision is required.

6 Stamp out four cheese rounds using a round cutter on a chopping board. With adult supervision, use a serrated knife to carefully cut open the bread rolls on the same board.

7 Place the bottom halves of the rolls on serving plates and place a cheese round on top. Dollop a little ketchup on top.

8 Put the burgers on top of the ketchup and place the bread lids on top. Serve with the strips, lettuce and tomatoes.

# Mini ciabatta pizzas

These tasty little pizzas are perfect for any party. Experiment with different types of bread and toppings to discover your favourite combinations.

serves 8

## ingredients

- **red (bell) peppers**, 2
- **yellow (bell) peppers**, 2
- **ciabatta bread**, 1 loaf
- **prosciutto**, 8 slices
- **mozzarella cheese**, 150g/5oz
- **ground black pepper**
- **tiny basil leaves**, to garnish

Prosciutto

## tools

- ✷ **Chopping board**
- ✷ **Medium sharp knife**
- ✷ **Large bowl**
- ✷ **Large serrated knife**
- ✷ **Oven gloves**

1 Ask an adult to preheat a grill (broiler). Halve the peppers. Remove their seeds.

2 Place the peppers on a grill (broiler) rack. Grill until they are beginning to turn black. Place in the bowl, cover and leave for 10 minutes. Peel off the skins. Adult supervision is required.

3 Cut the bread into eight thick slices and toast both sides until golden. (Leave the grill on.) Adult supervision is required.

4 Cut both the peppers and the prosciutto into thick strips and arrange on the toasts. Adult supervision is required.

5 Slice the mozzarella cheese and arrange on top. Grind over black pepper. Grill for 2–3 minutes, until the cheese is bubbling. Adult supervision is required.

6 Ask an adult to remove from the grill. Arrange the fresh basil leaves on top and serve.

## VARIATION

► There are an almost endless number of different toppings you could use. These may include replacing the peppers with sliced fresh tomatoes or whole roasted tomatoes or, for a spicy kick, adding some pepperoni or chopped drained jalepeño peppers.

pepperoni

 = Watch out! Sharp or electrical tool in use. = Watch out! Heat is involved.

# Tortilla squares

Spanish omelette makes a great supper, but if you cut it into small squares, you can enjoy it as a 'nibble' at parties too. Try serving the pieces on cocktail sticks (toothpicks).

serves 6–8

## ingredients

- **olive oil**, 45ml/3 tbsp
- **Spanish onions**, 2, thinly sliced
- **waxy potatoes**, 300g/11oz, cut into 1cm/½in dice
- **shelled broad (fava) beans**, 250g/9oz/1¾ cups
- **chopped fresh thyme**, 5ml/1 tsp
- **large (US extra large) eggs**, 6
- **mixed chopped fresh chives** and **flat leaf parsley**, 45ml/3 tbsp
- **salt** and **ground black pepper**

## tools

- **23cm/9in deep non-stick frying pan with lid**
- **Wooden spoon**
- **Medium pan**
- **Colander or sieve (strainer)**
- **Large mixing bowl**
- **Small mixing bowl**
- **Fork**
- **Fish slice or metal spatula**
- **Plate**
- **Large knife**

1 Heat 30ml/2 tbsp of the oil in a 23cm/9in deep, non-stick frying pan. Add the onions and potatoes and stir to coat. Cover and cook, stirring frequently, for 20–25 minutes, until the potatoes are cooked and the onions are very soft. Adult supervision is required.

2 Meanwhile, two-thirds fill a medium pan with cold water. Add a little salt and bring up to the boil. Add the beans and cook for 5 minutes, until tender. Ask an adult to drain them well and put in the large bowl to cool.

3 When the beans are cool enough to handle, peel off the grey outer skins and throw them away. This is quite fussy, but fun.

4 Add the beans to the pan, together with the thyme. Season, stir well to mix, then cook for a further 2–3 minutes.

5 Beat the eggs and herbs in a bowl. Add to the pan and increase the heat.

6 Cook until the egg browns underneath, pulling it away from the sides of the pan and tilting it to allow the uncooked egg to run underneath. Adult supervision is required.

7 With adult supervision, cover the pan with an upside-down plate and invert the tortilla on to it. Heat the remaining in the pan. Slip the tortilla back into the pan, uncooked-side down, and cook for 3–5 minutes more, until brown. Slide on to a serving plate. Cut into squares and serve.

# Chicken mini-rolls

These small, crispy rolls can be served warm as part of a party buffet or as nibbles. If you want to get ahead, make them the day before, then reheat in the oven.

serves 4

## ingredients

- **filo (phyllo) pastry**, 1 x 275g/10oz packet, thawed if frozen
- **olive oil**, 45ml/3 tbsp, plus extra for greasing
- **fresh flat leaf parsley**, to garnish

### for the filling

- **minced (ground) chicken**, 350g/12oz
- **egg**, 1, beaten
- **ground cinnamon**, 2.5ml/½ tsp
- **ground ginger**, 2.5ml/½ tsp
- **raisins**, 30ml/2 tbsp
- **salt** and **ground black pepper**
- **olive oil**, 15ml/1 tbsp
- **small onion**, 1, finely chopped

## tools

- Large mixing bowl
- Large frying pan
- Wooden spoon
- Baking sheet
- Chopping board
- Small sharp knife
- Pastry brush
- Oven gloves
- Palette knife
- Wire rack

1 First, **make the filling**. Put the chicken, egg, cinnamon, ginger and raisins in a large mixing bowl and season well.

2 Gently heat the oil in a frying pan, add the onion and cook, stirring occasionally, for 5 minutes, until tender. Leave to cool, then add to the bowl. Adult supervision is required.

3 Preheat the oven to 180°C/350°F/Gas 4. Grease the baking sheet. Open the filo pastry and unravel. Cut the pastry into 10 x 25cm/4 x 10in strips. Adult supervision is required.

4 Take one strip, keeping the remainder covered, and brush with oil. Place a small spoonful of the filling about 1cm/½in from the end.

5 Fold the sides inwards to a width of 5cm/2in and roll into a roll shape. Place on the baking tray and brush with oil. Repeat with the remaining ingredients.

6 Bake for 20–25 minutes, until golden brown and crisp. Ask an adult to remove from the oven and transfer to a wire rack. Serve garnished with parsley.

## COOK'S TIP

► Once filo pastry is exposed to the air it dries out fast, so it is important to work quickly once the pastry is opened and always keep the pastry you are not using covered with with clear film (plastic wrap).

 = Watch out! Sharp or electrical tool in use. = Watch out! Heat is involved.

# Falafel

Sesame seeds are used to give a crunchy coating to these tasty chickpea patties. Serve with hummus for dipping.

*serves* 4

## ingredients

- **chickpeas**, 400g/14oz can, drained
- **garlic**, 1 clove, crushed
- **ground coriander**, 5ml/1 tsp
- **ground cumin**, 5ml/1 tsp
- **chopped fresh mint**, 15ml/1 tbsp
- **chopped fresh parsley**, 15ml/1 tbsp
- **spring onions (scallions)**, 2, finely chopped
- **salt** and **ground black pepper**
- **large (US extra large) egg**, 1, beaten
- **sesame seeds**, for coating
- **sunflower oil**, for frying
- **hummus**, to serve

canned chickpeas

parsley

## tools

- Large mixing bowl
- Wooden spoon
- Food processor
- Plate or small mixing bowl
- Large frying pan
- Metal spatula
- 12–14 cocktail sticks (toothpicks)

1 Put the chickpeas, garlic, ground spices, herbs, spring onions, salt and pepper in a large mixing bowl. Add the egg and mix well with a wooden spoon.

2 Place in a food processor and blend until it forms a coarse paste. Adult supervision is required. If the paste seems too soft, chill it for 30 minutes.

3 Wet your hands slightly. Form the chilled chickpea paste into 12–14 balls with your hands, making them about the same size as a walnut.

4 Put the sesame seeds on a plate or in a small bowl, then roll each chickpea ball in turn in the sesame seeds to coat the outsides thoroughly.

5 Heat enough oil to cover the base of a large frying pan. Fry the falafel, in batches if necessary, for 6 minutes, turning once with a spatula. Adult supervision is required.

6 Transfer to a plate lined with kitchen paper to drain and cool slightly. Spear each ball with a cocktail stick and serve with hummus.

## VARIATION

• If you don't want to fry the falafel, you could bake them instead. Simply preheat the oven to 180°C/350°F/Gas 4, place the balls on a greased baking sheet and cook for about 30 minutes, until crisp on the outside.

★★ give it a try | *time to cook:* **12 minutes** | *preparation:* **10 minutes**

# Mini muffins

Mini mouthfuls of delicious treats are bound to win over party guests. Look out for mini muffin tins in good cookshops and department stores.

*makes* 24

## ingredients

- **butter**, 50g/2oz/4 tbsp
- **glacé (candied) cherries**, 50g/2oz/¼ cup
- **ready-to-eat dried apricots**, 50g/2oz/⅓ cup
- **plain (all-purpose) flour**, 200g/7oz/1½ cups
- **baking powder**, 10ml/2 tsp
- **soft light brown sugar**, 50g/2oz/¼ cup
- **milk**, 150ml/¼ pint/⅔ cup
- **egg**, 1, beaten
- **vanilla extract**, 2.5ml/½ tsp

## tools

- ✱ 2 mini muffin tins (pans)
- ✱ 24 petits fours paper cases
- ✱ Small pan
- ✱ Chopping board
- ✱ Medium sharp knife
- ✱ Large mixing bowl
- ✱ Wooden spoon
- ✱ 2 metal teaspoons
- ✱ Oven gloves
- ✱ Wire rack

1 Preheat the oven to 220°C/425°F/Gas 7. Place the cases in the mini muffin tins.

2 Melt the butter in a small pan. Leave to cool. Meanwhile, chop the cherries and apricots into small pieces. Adult supervision is required.

3 Put the flour, baking powder and sugar in a large mixing bowl and add the milk, egg and melted butter. Stir thoroughly with a wooden spoon until the mixture is smooth and well combined. Add the chopped fruit and the vanilla extract and stir to combine thoroughly.

4 Spoon the mixture into the paper cases using two teaspoons so they are about three-quarters full.

5 Bake for 10–12 minutes, until well risen and browned. Ask an adult to remove from the oven, cool slightly in the tin then transfer to a wire rack.

## VARIATION

- To make orange and banana muffins, substitute 2 small mashed bananas for 60ml/2fl oz/¼ cup of the milk. Omit the chopped cherries, apricot and vanilla extract, and add 15ml/1 tbsp grated orange rind.

 = Watch out! Sharp or electrical tool in use. = Watch out! Heat is involved.

# Cupcake faces

Make happy, funny, laughing faces on yummy cakes with a selection of colourful sweets.

*makes* 12

## ingredients

- **margarine**, 115g/4oz/⅔ cup
- **caster (superfine) sugar**, 115g/4oz/⅔ cup
- **self-raising (self-rising) flour**, 115g/4oz/1 cup
- **eggs**, 2

### for the topping

- **butter**, 50g/2oz/¼ cup, cubed
- **icing (confectioners') sugar**, 115g/4oz/1 cup
- **pink food colouring**
- **coated chocolate candies**, 115g/4oz
- **red liquorice bootlaces**, 2
- **dolly (liquorice) mixtures**, 12
- **plain (semisweet) chocolate**, 75g/3oz, broken into pieces

## tools

- 12 paper cake cases
- 12-hole bun tin (muffin pan)
- Large mixing bowl
- Electric mixer or wooden spoon
- 2 metal spoons
- Oven gloves
- Wire rack
- Small mixing bowl
- Sieve (strainer)
- Wooden spoon
- Palette knife
- Small heatproof bowl
- Small heavy pan
- Baking parchment
- Scissors

1 Preheat the oven to 180°C/350°F/Gas 4. Place the paper cases in the bun tin. Put all the cake ingredients in a bowl and beat with an electric mixer (adult supervision is required) or wooden spoon until smooth.

2 Divide the cake mixture among the cases.

3 Cook for 12–15 minutes, until the cakes are well risen and spring back when pressed with a fingertip. Ask an adult to remove from the oven. Leave to cool slightly in the tin then transfer to a wire rack.

4 Meanwhile, **make the topping**. Put the butter in a small mixing bowl. Sift over the icing sugar and beat the mixture until smooth. Stir in a little pink food colouring.

5 Spread the icing over the cakes with a palette knife.

6 Add sugar-coated chocolate candies for eyes, short pieces of liquorice for mouths and dolly mixture for noses.

7 Put the chocolate in a heatproof bowl. Set over a pan of simmering water. Heat until melted. Adult supervision is required.

8 Remove the pan from the heat and stir the melted chocolate. Spoon into a baking parchment piping bag (see page 33).

9 Snip off the tip of the piping bag and draw hair, eye balls, glasses and moustaches on the top of the cakes.

# Puppy faces

These lightly spiced biscuits (cookies) decorated with cute puppy faces are sure to be a huge hit at any birthday party or special occasion, and are fun to make.

makes 10

## ingredients

- **plain (all-purpose) flour**, 100g/3½oz/scant 1 cup
- **rolled oats**, 50g/2oz/ ½ cup
- **mixed (apple pie) spice**, 2.5ml/ ½ tsp
- **unsalted butter**, 50g/2oz/¼ cup, chilled and diced, plus extra for greasing
- **caster (superfine) sugar**, 100g/3½oz/½ cup
- **egg yolk**, 1

### for the decoration

- **apricot jam**, 60ml/4 tbsp
- **ready-to-roll fondant icing**, 250g/9oz
- **round coloured sweets (candies)**, 10
- **black** and **red writing icing tubes**
- **icing (confectioners') sugar**, for dusting

## tools

- Food processor or blender
- Clear film (plastic wrap)
- 1 large non-stick baking sheet
- Rolling pin
- 6cm/2½in cutter
- Oven gloves
- Palette knife
- Wire rack
- Sieve (strainer)
- Small bowl

## COOK'S TIPS

▶ You can make your own royal icing instead of using ready-to-roll icing. This type of icing sets hard to give a good finish, so is perfect for creating designs for biscuits. To make your own, beat 1 egg white for a few seconds with a fork in a large bowl. Mix in 75g/3oz/⅔ cup sifted icing (confectioners') sugar, a little at a time, until the mixture stands in soft peaks and is thick enough to spread. You can then roll it out and use as in the recipe. This makes enough to cover about 10 biscuits, but you can just multiply the quantities if you make more biscuits.

▶ Spreading the biscuits with strained apricot jam helps the icing to stick to the biscuit.

apricot jam

1 Put the flour, oats, mixed spice and butter into a food processor or blender. Blend until it resembles fine breadcrumbs. Add the sugar, egg yolk and 5ml/1 tsp water and blend until the mixture begins to form a ball. Adult supervision is required.

2 Turn out on to a floured surface and knead for 5 minutes until smooth. Form into a ball, wrap in clear film and chill for 30 minutes.

3 Preheat the oven to 200°C/400°F/ Gas 6. Grease a baking sheet.

4 Roll out the dough on a floured surface. Stamp out 10 rounds using a cookie cutter. Transfer to the baking sheet, spacing slightly apart.

5 Bake for 12 minutes, until pale golden.

6 Ask an adult to remove from the oven and transfer to a wire rack with a palette knife. Leave to cool.

7 Press the jam through a sieve into a small bowl. Spread a little jam over each biscuit to within 5mm/¼ in of the edge. Leave until cold.

8 Roll out half the icing very thinly on a surface dusted with icing sugar. Cut out 10 rounds using a 6cm/2½in cutter and lay one over each biscuit.

 = Watch out! Sharp or electrical tool in use.

 = Watch out! Heat is involved.

9 To make the eyes, halve the coloured sweets, brush the icing lightly with water and press the sweets into the biscuits. Use the black writing icing tube to pipe the noses and mouths, then finish with little red tongues.

10 To make the ears, divide the remaining icing into 20 pieces. Roll each piece into a ball and flatten to make a flat pear shape. Brush with water and stick on to either side of the biscuits. Arrange in a single layer and leave to dry.

# Gingerbread people

With this easy gingerbread recipe there are no end of possibilities for the different-shaped biscuits (cookies) you can make.

## COOK'S TIPS

► Chocolate decorations soften biscuits, so you need to eat them on the day you make them or decorate as many biscuits as you will eat and store the rest in an airtight container for up to four days.

► As an alternative, why not use animal-shaped cutters and make a gingerbread farm.

*makes about* 24

## ingredients

- **oil**, for greasing
- **plain (all-purpose) flour**, 225g/8oz/2 cups
- **ground ginger**, 5ml/1 tsp
- **ground cinnamon**, 1.5ml/¼ tsp
- **bicarbonate of soda (baking soda)**, 7.5ml/1½ tsp
- **margarine**, 50g/2oz/4 tbsp
- **soft light brown sugar**, 115g/4oz/⅔ cup
- **golden (light corn) syrup**, 45ml/3 tbsp
- **milk**, 30ml/2 tbsp
- **dark (bittersweet) chocolate**, 75g/3oz
- **coated chocolate candies**, **liquorice**, **sprinkles**, or **any sweets you like**
- **coloured icing pens**

*sprinkles*

*ground ginger*

## tools

- ✱ 2 baking sheets
- ✱ Pastry brush
- ✱ Sieve (strainer)
- ✱ Large mixing bowl
- ✱ Medium heavy pan
- ✱ Wooden spoon
- ✱ Rolling pin
- ✱ Gingerbread men and women cutters
- ✱ Oven gloves
- ✱ Palette knife
- ✱ Wire rack
- ✱ Medium pan
- ✱ Medium heatproof bowl
- ✱ Piping (pastry) bag and a fine plain nozzle (tip) or baking parchment piping bag

1 Brush two baking sheets with a little oil. Sift the flour, spices and bicarbonate of soda into a mixing bowl.

2 Place the margarine, sugar and syrup in a pan and heat gently, until the margarine has melted. Adult supervision is required.

3 Ask an adult to remove the pan from the heat. Pour the mixture into the bowl containing the flour. Add the milk and mix to a firm dough with a wooden spoon. Chill for 30 minutes.

4 Preheat the oven to 160°C/325°F/Gas 3.

5 Lightly knead the dough for 1 minute on a lightly floured surface, until it is pliable. Roll out the biscuit dough to about 5mm/¼in in thickness with the rolling pin. Carefully stamp out gingerbread men and women with cookie cutters.

6 Carefully transfer the biscuits to the oiled baking sheets with a palette knife. Bring the dough trimmings together into a ball and roll out again. Stamp out as many more people as you can until all the dough is used.

7 Cook for 10 minutes, until golden. Ask an adult to remove from the oven and loosen with a palette knife. Set aside to cool and harden a little on the baking sheets. Transfer to the wire rack once cool with the palette knife.

 = Watch out! Sharp or electrical tool in use. (!) = Watch out! Heat is involved.

8 Break the chocolate into pieces and put in a heatproof bowl. Set over a pan of simmering water. Heat until melted. Adult supervision is required.

9 Use some of the chocolate to make clothes. Leave to set.

10 Spoon the remaining chocolate into a piping bag fitted with a small nozzle and pipe faces on all the biscuits. Decorate the biscuits as you like, using any of the candies and chocolates and piping coloured hair on the heads, if you want to.

# Jammy bodgers

These buttery biscuits (cookies) are an absolute classic. Sandwiched with buttercream and a spoonful of strawberry jam, they are perfect for birthday parties.

*serves* 4

## ingredients

- **plain (all-purpose) flour**, 225g/8oz/2 cups
- **unsalted butter**, 175g/6oz/¾ cup, chilled and diced
- **caster (superfine) sugar**, 130g/2½oz/⅔ cup
- **egg yolk**, 1
- **strawberry jam**, 60–75ml/4–5 tbsp

### for the buttercream

- **unsalted butter**, 50g/2oz/¼ cup, at room temperature, diced
- **icing (confectioners') sugar**, 90g/3½oz/ scant 1 cup

### tools

- ✷ Food processor
- ✷ Clear film (plastic wrap)
- ✷ 2 baking sheets
- ✷ Rolling pin
- ✷ 6cm/2½in fluted cookie cutter
- ✷ Heart-shaped cookie cutter, 2cm/¾in in diameter
- ✷ Oven gloves
- ✷ Palette knife
- ✷ Wire rack
- ✷ Medium mixing bowl
- ✷ Wooden spoon
- ✷ Metal spoon

1 Put the flour and butter in a food processor and process until it resembles breadcrumbs. Add the sugar and egg yolk and process until it starts to form a dough. Adult supervision is required.

2 Knead on a floured surface until smooth. Shape into a ball, wrap in clear film and chill for 30 minutes. Preheat the oven to 180°C/350°F/Gas 4.

3 Roll out the dough and cut out rounds with the cookie cutter.

4 Re-roll the trimmings and cut out more rounds until you have 40 in total. Place half the rounds on a baking sheet. Using the heart-shaped cutter, cut out the centres of the remaining rounds. Place the rounds on the other baking sheet.

5 Bake for 12 minutes, until pale golden. Transfer to a wire rack and leave to cool completely.

6 **To make the buttercream**, beat together the butter and sugar in a medium bowl.

7 Using a palette knife, spread a little buttercream on to each whole biscuit. Spoon a little jam on to the the buttercream, then gently press the cut-out cookies on top, so that the jam fills the heart-shaped hole.

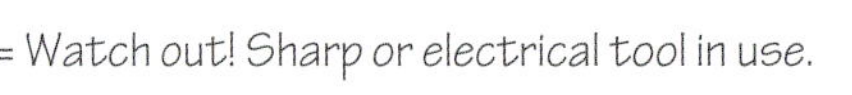
= Watch out! Sharp or electrical tool in use.

= Watch out! Heat is involved.

# Chocolate cookies on sticks

Let your imagination run riot when decorating these chocolatey treats. The only hard bit about this recipe is not eating all the decorations!

*makes* 12

## ingredients

- **milk chocolate**, 125g/4¼oz
- **white chocolate**, 75g/3oz
- **chocolate-coated sweetmeal biscuits (plain cookies)**, 50g/2oz, crumbled into chunks
- **small coloured sweets (candies)**, **chocolate chips** or **chocolate-coated raisins**, to decorate

*chocolate chips*

## tools

- 2 medium heatproof bowls
- 2 medium pans
- Metal spoon
- Baking parchment
- Pencil
- Large baking sheet
- 12 ice lolly (popsicle) sticks
- Piping (pastry) bag

1 Break the milk and white chocolate into pieces and put in separate heatproof bowls. Place each over a pan of simmering water and heat, stirring frequently, until melted. Do not let the bowl touch the water. Adult supervision is required.

2 Meanwhile, carefully draw six 7cm/2¾in rounds and six 9 x 7cm/3½ x 2¾ in rectangles on baking parchment. Invert the parchment on to the large baking sheet.

3 Spoon most of the milk chocolate into the outlines on the paper, reserving one or two spoonfuls for attaching the sticks. Using the back of the teaspoon, carefully spread the chocolate to the edges of the pencilled outlines to make neat shapes.

4 Press the end of a wooden ice lolly stick into each of the shapes, and spoon over a little more melted milk chocolate to cover the top of the sticks. Sprinkle the shapes with the crumbled biscuits while the chocolate is still warm.

5 Pipe over white chocolate squiggles with the piping bag or a spoon, then decorate with coloured sweets, chocolate chips or chocolate-coated raisins. Chill for 1 hour, until set, then carefully peel away the baking parchment.

# Jolly jellies

Jelly (gelatine) is a classic party favourite, and these fun fruity faces make a great alternative to the normal way of serving it.

*serves* 4

## ingredients

- **strawberry jelly (gelatine)**, 150g/5oz packet
- **ripe plums**, 2
- **fromage frais** or **Greek (US strained plain) yogurt**, 175g/6oz
- **dolly (liquorice) mixtures**, 4, cut in half
- **sugar** or **chocolate strands**, 10ml/2 tsp

*plums* *fromage frais*

## tools

- **Small sharp knife or scissors**
- **Large heatproof mixing bowl**
- **Wooden spoon**
- **Chopping board**
- **Medium sharp knife**
- **Teaspoon**
- **4 small bowls or individual pudding moulds**

1 Cut the jelly into pieces with a knife or scissors. Place in a heatproof bowl and ask an adult to pour over 150ml/¼ pint/⅔ cup boiling water. Stir until dissolved, then set aside to cool.

2 On a chopping board, cut the plums in half. Remove the stones (pits) with a teaspoon, then cut four slices for a garnish; reserve the slices. Chop the remaining fruit into pieces. Adult supervision is required.

3 Stir the fromage frais or yogurt into the jelly.

4 Divide the fruit among four small bowls or pudding moulds. Pour over the jelly mixture and chill for 2 hours, until set.

5 Carefully dip the bottoms of the bowls or moulds in a bowl of hot water and turn out on to plates. Decorate with plums for mouths. Push in dolly mixtures for eyes and sugar or chocolate strands for hair.

 = Watch out! Sharp or electrical tool in use. (!) = Watch out! Heat is involved.

# Yogurt lollies

These super-cool lollies (popsicles) are perfect for summer parties. Make plenty in advance as these are so delicious you are likely to quickly run out!

makes 6

## ingredients

- **strawberry yogurt**, 150g/5oz tub
- **milk**, 150ml/¼ pint/⅔ cup
- **strawberry milkshake powder**, 10ml/2 tsp

## tools

- **Measuring jug (cup)**
- **Wooden spoon**
- **6 lolly (popsicle) moulds**
- **6 lolly (popsicle) sticks**
- **Large heatproof bowl**

## COOK'S TIPS

- You can store these lollies for a few weeks in the freezer. Make sure they are tightly covered.
- Try freezing the mixture in an ice cube tray. Then simply pop out a mouthful of frozen yogurt when you feel like it.
- You could make these lollies with any of your favourite flavours. Try banana yogurt with banana milkshake powder or raspberry yogurt with strawberry milkshake powder.

1 In a jug, mix together the strawberry yogurt, milk and strawberry milkshake powder with a wooden spoon. Beat well to blend completely and ensure there are no lumps of milkshake powder.

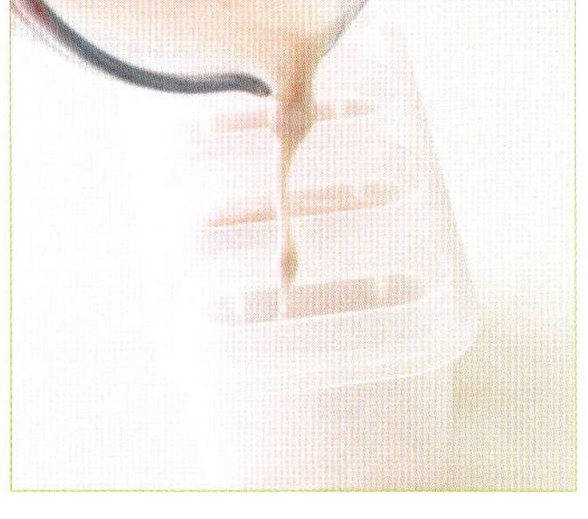

2 Carefully pour the yogurt mixture into six small lolly plastic moulds, filling them to the top. Insert six lolly sticks in the centre of each, then freeze for at least 6 hours or overnight, until firm.

3 Half fill the large heatproof bowl with hot, not boiling, water. Ask an adult to dip the moulds into the hot water, count to 15, then flex the handles and lift out the lollies. Serve immediately.

# Chocolate fudge sundaes

Who needs to go to an ice cream parlour when you can make our very own extra fudgy chocolate sundaes at home! These are perfect for any special occasion.

serves 4

## ingredients

- **vanilla** and **coffee** or **chocolate ice cream**, 4 scoops each
- **small bananas**, 2, peeled and sliced
- **toasted flaked (sliced) almonds**, to serve

*for the chocolate fudge sauce*

- **plain (semisweet) chocolate**, 150g/5oz
- **soft light brown sugar**, 50g/2oz/¼ cup
- **golden (light corn) syrup**, 120ml/4fl/oz/½ cup
- **strong black coffee** or **water**, 45ml/3 tbsp
- **ground cinnamon**, 5ml/1 tsp (optional)
- **whipping cream**, 200ml/7fl oz/scant 1 cup

## tools

- Chopping board
- Large sharp knife
- Small heavy pan
- Wooden spoon
- 4 tall sundae glasses
- Ice cream scoop
- Mixing bowl
- Whisk

1 With adult supervision, roughly chop the chocolate. Set aside.

2 **To make the chocolate fudge sauce**, put the sugar, syrup, coffee or water and cinnamon in a heavy pan. Simmer for 5 minutes, stirring often. Adult supervision is required.

3 Turn off the heat and stir in the chopped chocolate. When melted and smooth, stir in 75ml/3floz/⅓ cup of the cream.

4 Place one scoop of vanilla ice cream into each of four sundae glasses. Top with a scoop of coffee or chocolate ice cream.

5 Whip the cream. Arrange the bananas over the ice cream. Pour a drizzle of fudge sauce over the bananas, then top each with a spoonful of cream.

6 Sprinkle toasted almonds over the cream and serve the sundaes immediately.

## VARIATION

- You could use pistachio ice cream instead of vanilla ice cream, white chocolate instead of plain, water instead of coffee and toasted chopped pistachios instead of almonds.

(!) = Watch out! Sharp or electrical tool in use. (oven glove) = Watch out! Heat is involved.

# Strawberry ice cream

Making your own ice cream is cool! This foolproof recipe is easier than a 'classic' one where you have to make your own custard.

*makes* 900ml/1½ pints/3¾ cups

## ingredients

- **double (heavy) cream**, 300ml/½pint/1¼ cups
- **custard**, 425g/15oz can/1 packet, prepared following the directions
- **strawberries**, 450g/1lb, plus extra to decorate
- **wafers**, to decorate

*strawberries*

## tools

- Large mixing bowl
- Whisk
- Large metal spoon
- Sieve (strainer)
- Blender or food processor
- Large sealable plastic container
- Fork

1 Put the cream in a mixing bowl and whisk until soft peaks form. Using a large metal spoon, fold in the custard.

2 Pull and twist the stalks from the strawberries (known as hulling). Rinse the strawberries in a sieve and pat dry on kitchen paper.

3 Place the strawberries in the blender or food processor and blend until smooth. Adult supervision is required. Pass through the sieve into the cream.

4 Pour the mixture into the sealable container and freeze for 6–7 hours, until semi-frozen.

5 Beat with a fork or blend in a blender or food processor until smooth. Return to the freezer and freeze until solid.

6 Remove from the freezer 10 minutes before serving so that it can soften slightly. Serve with wafers and extra strawberries.

## VARIATION

• To make strawberry ripple ice cream, purée and sift an extra 250g/9oz strawberries into a separate bowl in Step 3. Stir in 30ml/ 2 tbsp icing (confectioners') sugar. Swirl this purée into the half-frozen ice cream in Step 4, then freeze until solid and serve. Or, make the purée from raspberries.

# Balloon cake

Whether it's for a family birthday or a gift for a friend, this smart cake will make a brilliant centrepiece for any party. Leave plenty of time to make it.

*serves* **10–12**

## ingredients

### for the cake

- **butter** or **oil**, for greasing
- **self-raising (self-rising) flour**, 225g/8oz/2 cups
- **baking powder**, 10ml/2 tsp
- **soft butter**, 225g/8oz/1 cup
- **caster (superfine) sugar**, 225g/8oz/1 cup
- **eggs**, 4

### for the decoration

- **buttercream**, 115g/4oz/½ cup (see page 228)
- **apricot jam**, 45ml/3 tbsp, warmed
- **icing (confectioners') sugar**, for dusting
- **marzipan**, 450g/1lb
- **ready-to-roll fondant icing**, 450g/1lb/3 cups
- **red**, **blue**, **green** and **yellow food colouring paste** (see Cook's Tips)
- **royal icing**, 115g/4oz/¾ cup

## tools

- **20cm/8in round loose-based cake tin (pan)**
- **Baking parchment**
- **Pencil**
- **Scissors**
- **Sieve (strainer)**
- **Large mixing bowl**
- **Wooden spoon or electric mixer**
- **Skewer**
- **Oven gloves**
- **Wire rack**
- **Large serrated knife**
- **Sharp knife**
- **Pastry brush**
- **Rolling pin**
- **Piping (pastry) bag fitted with a small star nozzle (tip)**
- **Ribbon and candles**

## COOK'S TIPS

- Colouring pastes are concentrated, which means they won't water down your icing or make it sticky like liquid food colourings can. Look for them in some large supermarkets and cake decorating stores.
- Ready-to-roll fondant icing is also sold as 'easy ice' or 'sugar paste'. It dries out quite quickly once it is exposed to the air, so you need to ice the cake quickly to prevent the icing cracking. Keep any leftover icing wrapped in clear film (plastic wrap) in the refrigerator.

**1** Preheat the oven to 160°C/325°F/Gas 3. Lightly grease a 20cm/8in cake tin. Place the tin on the baking parchment and draw around the base with a pencil. Cut out the circle with scissors and use to line the base of tin.

**2** Sift the flour and baking powder into a large mixing bowl. Add the butter, sugar and eggs. Beat with a wooden spoon or an electric mixer (adult supervision is required) for 2–3 minutes, until pale, creamy and glossy.

**3** Spoon the mixture into the cake tin and level the surface with the back of a spoon. Bake for 30–40 minutes, or until a skewer inserted into the centre of the cake comes out clean. Ask an adult to remove from the oven and turn out on to a wire rack. Cool.

**4** Ask an adult to cut the cake in half and spread one half with buttercream. Sandwich the other half on top and place the cake on a cake board. Brush all over with apricot jam.

**5** On a surface dusted with icing sugar, roll out the marzipan and use to cover the cake. Smooth over the surface and down the sides with your hands. Trim the edges. Adult supervision is required. Brush with water.

 = Watch out! Sharp or electrical tool in use. = Watch out! Heat is involved.

**6** Roll out the fondant icing and use most of it to cover the cake. Trim the edges with the knife, reserving the trimmings. Add the trimmings to the reserved fondant icing, then divide into three. Colour the pieces pink, blue and green.

**7** Draw the outlines of nine balloons on baking parchment. Roll out the coloured fondant icing and cut out three balloons from each colour. Brush one side with water and carefully position on the cake, overlapping the balloons.

**8** Colour the royal icing yellow. Place some in a piping bag and pipe balloon strings or numbers on to the top of the cake.

**9** Place the remaining yellow icing in a piping bag fitted with a small star nozzle and pipe a border around the base. Tie the ribbon around the side of the cake and add the candles.

# Spooky biscuits

These dramatic biscuits (cookies) might scare away guests, leaving all the more for you!

*makes* 28

## ingredients

- **plain (all-purpose) flour**, 225g/8oz/2 cups
- **unsalted butter**, 175g/6oz/ ¾ cup, chilled and diced
- **orange**, 1, finely grated rind
- **light muscovado (brown) sugar**, 130g/4¼ oz/⅔ cup
- **egg yolk**, 1

### for the decoration

- **orange juice**, 30ml/2 tbsp
- **icing (confectioners') sugar**, 200g/7oz/1¾ cups, sifted
- **orange** and **green food colouring pastes**
- **red** and **black writing icing pens**
- **assorted sweets (candies)**

## tools

- **Food processor**
- **Clear film (plastic wrap)**
- **6cm/2½in round cookie cutter**
- **Rolling pin**
- **2 non-stick baking sheets**
- **Oven gloves**
- **Palette knife**
- **Wire rack**
- **Large mixing bowl**
- **Wooden spoon**
- **3 small mixing bowls**
- **Small butter knife**

1 Put the flour, butter, and orange rind into a food processor. Blend until the mixture resembles bread crumbs. Add the sugar and egg yolk and blend until it starts to bind together. Adult supervision is required.

2 Turn out on to a lightly floured surface and knead until it forms a dough.

3 Shape the dough into a ball, wrap it in clear film and chill for 30 minutes.

4 Preheat the oven to 180°C/350°F/Gas 4. Roll out the dough on a floured surface and stamp out rounds using a 6cm/ 2½in round cookie cutter. Re-roll the trimmings and repeat the process.

5 Transfer the rounds to the baking sheets, spacing them slightly apart. Bake for 12–15 minutes, until pale golden. Ask an adult to remove from the oven and transfer to a wire rack with the palette knife to cool.

6 **To decorate the cookies**, put the orange juice in a large mixing bowl and gradually stir in the icing sugar until the mixture has the consistency of thick pouring cream. Divide the mixture among three small bowls. Leave one batch white, colour the other orange and the third green with the colouring paste.

7 Spread the biscuits with the different coloured icings using a butter knife. Using the red and black writing icing pens and various sweets, make vampire faces on the white cookies, witchy faces and hair on the green cookies and pumpkin faces on the orange cookies. Leave to set for 30 minutes.

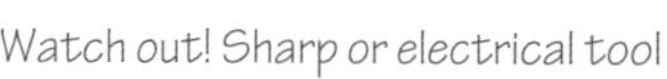
= Watch out! Sharp or electrical tool in use.
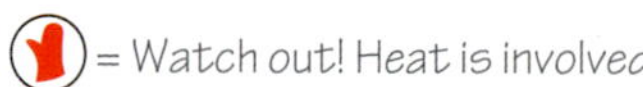
= Watch out! Heat is involved.

# Chocolate witchy apples

You won't want to give these away to the trick or treaters! Better than toffee apples, you could get all your friends at the party to decorate their own.

*makes 6*

## ingredients

- **oil** or **butter**, for greasing
- **small apples**, 6
- **milk chocolate**, 250g/8oz
- **round sweets (candies)**, 12
- **liquorice bootlaces**
- **ice cream cones**, 6
- **jewel-coloured sweets** (optional)

*apples*

## tools

- Baking sheet
- Baking parchment
- Vegetable peeler
- 6 wooden skewers or lolly (popsicle) sticks
- Heatproof bowl
- Medium pan
- Wooden spoon

1 Lightly grease a baking sheet with oil or butter and line with a piece of baking parchment.

2 Peel the apples with a vegetable peeler and thoroughly dry them on kitchen paper. Press a wooden skewer or lolly stick into the core of each one. Adult supervision is required.

3 Put the chocolate in a heatproof bowl set over a pan of barely simmering water (take care not to let the water touch the base of the bowl). Leave to melt for about 5 minutes. Remove the bowl from the pan and stir the chocolate gently with a wooden spoon. Adult supervision is required.

4 Tilt the bowl to collect a deep pool of chocolate on one side of the bowl. Dip each apple in the chocolate, coating the outside completely (reserve any leftover chocolate in the bowl). Place each apple on the lined baking sheet. Leave for about 30 minutes, until the chocolate is almost set.

5 One at a time, hold the apples by the sticks. Press two round sweets into the chocolate on each apple to make the witch's eyes. Use a small piece of a liquorice bootlace to make a smile, and attach longer pieces to the top of the apple to make hair. Repeat with the other apples.

6 Use a little of the remaining melted chocolate to attach the cone to the top of the apple, for a hat. If you like, use a little more melted chocolate to attach jewel-coloured sweets to the cone, for decoration.

# Jack-o'-lantern cake

This spooky cake is guaranteed to be popular at your next Halloween party. Cook it the day before so you don't need to rush and the icing will have time to dry.

serves 8–10

## ingredients

- **plain (all-purpose) flour**, 175g/6oz/½ cups
- **baking powder**, 12.5ml/2½ tsp
- **salt**, a pinch
- **butter**, 115g/4oz/½ cup, at room temperature, plus extra for greasing
- **caster (superfine) sugar**, 225g/8oz/generous 1 cup
- **egg yolks**, 3, at room temperature, well beaten
- **grated lemon rind**, 5ml/1 tsp
- **milk**, 175ml/6fl oz/¾ cup

for the cake covering

- **icing (confectioners') sugar**, 500g/1¼lb/5 cups, plus extra for dusting
- **egg white**, 1
- **liquid glucose**, 30ml/2 tbsp (see Cook's Tip)
- **orange** and **black food colouring pastes**

flour, sugar and butter

## COOK'S TIP

► Liquid glucose is sometimes referred to as glucose syrup. It is a thick, clear liquid used for sweetening a number of desserts, cakes and sweets. It differs from sugar in that it does not form sugar crystals when it is used, giving a smoother result. This is especially important when you want a nice smooth icing, or when you are making ice cream. To make it easier to measure, warm the syrup or the spoon slightly before measuring, so it doesn't stick.

## tools

- ✱ **20cm/8in round loose-based cake tin (pan)**
- ✱ **Pencil**
- ✱ **Baking parchment**
- ✱ **Scissors**
- ✱ **Sieve (strainer)**
- ✱ **2 large mixing bowls**
- ✱ **Electric mixer or wooden spoon**
- ✱ **2 metal spoons**
- ✱ **Skewer**
- ✱ **Oven gloves**
- ✱ **Wire rack**
- ✱ **Rolling pin**
- ✱ **Small sharp knife**
- ✱ **Pastry brush**

1 Preheat the oven to 190°C/375°F/Gas 5. Grease the cake tin. Using a pencil draw around the tin on to baking parchment. Cut out the circle and use it to line the base of the tin.

2 Sift together the flour, baking powder and salt into a mixing bowl.

3 Using an electric mixer (adult supervision is required) or wooden spoon, beat the butter and sugar until pale and creamy.

4 Gradually beat in the egg yolks, then add the lemon rind. Fold in the flour mixture in three batches, alternating with the milk, using a large metal spoon. Spoon into the prepared tin.

5 Bake for 35–40 minutes until golden brown and a skewer comes out clean when inserted into the centre. Ask an adult to remove from the oven. Cool in the tin for 5 minutes, then turn out on to a wire rack to cool.

6 **For the cake covering**, sift 500g/1¼lb/5 cups of the icing sugar into another bowl. Make a well in the centre and add 1 egg white and the liquid glucose. Mix, then add the food colouring. Mix to form a dough.

= Watch out! Sharp or electrical tool in use. = Watch out! Heat is involved.

7 Transfer the icing dough to a clean work surface dusted generously with icing sugar and knead briefly until pliable and the dough is an even shade of orange.

8 Add some more icing sugar to the work surface. Dust a rolling pin with icing sugar, then roll out the icing to about 5mm/¼in in thickness and to form a circle large enough to cover the top and sides of the cake.

9 Drape the icing over the rolling pin, lift over the cake and position. Smooth over the edges and sides with your hands and trim around base, reserving the excess icing. Adult supervision is required.

10 Put the excess icing back in the bowl and add a small amount of black food colouring paste. Mix well until evenly coloured, then transfer to the work surface and roll out thinly. Cut two triangles for the eyes, a slightly smaller triangle for the nose and a jagged shape for the teeth. Cut small shapes for the hair.

11 Brush the undersides of the shapes with a little water and arrange the icing on top of the cake.

# Creamy fudge

Fudge is an old-fashioned treat that makes a perfect gift for birthdays or celebrations such as Christmas. You could make some decorative gift boxes to give it in.

makes 900g/2lb

## ingredients

- **unsalted butter**, 50g/2oz/4 tbsp, plus extra for greasing
- **granulated sugar**, 450g/1lb/2 cups
- **double (heavy) cream**, 300ml/½ pint/ 1¼ cups
- **milk**, 150ml/¼ pint/⅔ cup
- **water**, 45ml/3 tbsp

### flavourings

- **dark (bittersweet)** or **milk chocolate dots**, 225g/8oz/1 cup
- **almonds**, **hazelnuts**, **walnuts** or **brazil nuts**, 115g/4oz/1 cup, chopped
- **glacé (candied) cherries**, **dates** or **dried apricots**, 115g/4oz/½ cup, chopped

glacé cherries

## tools

- **20cm/8in shallow square tin (pan)**
- **Large heavy pan**
- **Cup**
- **Wooden spoon**
- **Large sharp knife**

1 Grease the tin. Put the butter, sugar, cream, milk, and water into a pan. Heat very gently, until the sugar has dissolved. Fill a cup with cold water. Bring the mixture to a rolling boil. Spoon a small amount into the water. If you can roll it into a soft ball, then it is ready. If not, boil and test again in a few minutes. Adult supervision is required.

2 If you are making chocolate-flavoured fudge, add the chocolate dots to the mixture at this stage. Stir well.

3 Remove the pan from the heat and beat with a wooden spoon until the mixture starts to thicken and become opaque. Adult supervision is required.

4 Just before this stage has been reached, add the nuts, glacé cherries or dried fruit. Beat well.

5 Carefully pour into the tin. Leave until cool. Using the knife, score small squares and leave in the tin until quite firm. Turn out and cut into squares. Adult supervision is required.

### COOK'S TIP

► There are different stages when you are boiling sugar, depending on what you are making, that tell you when the mixture is ready. If you go beyond the required stage the sugar will set too firmly. This recipe uses the 'soft ball' method.

 = Watch out! Sharp or electrical tool in use. = Watch out! Heat is involved.

# Stripy biscuits

Try these pretty biscuits (cookies) with vanilla ice cream or chocolate mousse. You will have great fun moulding them around a spoon handle to get the special shape.

white chocolate

makes 25

## ingredients

- **butter** or **oil**, for greasing
- **white chocolate**, 50g/2oz, melted
- **red** and **green food colouring dusts** or **pastes**
- **egg whites**, 2
- **caster (superfine) sugar**, 90g/3½oz/⅓ cup
- **plain (all-purpose) flour**, 50g/2oz/½ cup
- **unsalted butter**, 50g/2oz/4 tbsp, melted

## tools

- 2 non-stick baking sheets
- Baking parchment
- 2 small bowls
- 2 piping (pastry) bags fitted with plain nozzles (tips)
- Large mixing bowl
- Whisk
- Sieve (strainer)
- Teaspoon
- Palette knife
- Oven gloves
- 2–3 wooden spoons
- Wire rack

1 Preheat the oven to 190°C/375°F/Gas 5. Grease and line two non-stick baking sheets.

2 Put half the chocolate in one bowl, and the other half in another. Add red food colouring to one and green to the other and mix. Fill two piping bags with each and fold down the tops.

3 Put the egg whites in a large mixing bowl and whisk until they form stiff peaks. Gradually add the sugar, whisking well after each addition, to make a thick meringue.

4 Sift in the flour and add the melted butter. Fold in gently until the mixture is smooth.

5 Drop teaspoonfuls of the mixture on to the baking sheets and spread into rounds with a palette knife.

6 Pipe zigzags of green and red chocolate over each. Bake for 3–4 minutes, until pale golden. Ask an adult to loosen with the palette knife and return to the oven for a few seconds.

7 With adult supervision, take one biscuit out of the oven and roll it around a spoon handle. Leave it for a few seconds to set. Repeat to make the remaining biscuits.

8 Remove the set biscuits from the spoon handles and leave to cool completely on the wire rack.

# Christmas tree angels

These edible tree decorations will make any Christmas party complete. Hang them on the tree before guests arrive and give them as 'going home presents'.

*makes* 20–30

## ingredients

- **demerara (raw) sugar**, 90g/3½oz/ scant ½ cup
- **golden (light corn) syrup**, 200g/7oz/1 cup
- **ground ginger**, 5ml/1 tsp
- **ground cinnamon**, 5ml/1 tsp
- **ground cloves**, 1.5ml/¼ tsp
- **unsalted butter**, 115g/4oz/½ cup, cut into pieces, plus extra for greasing
- **bicarbonate of soda (baking soda)**, 10ml/2 tsp
- **egg**, 1, beaten
- **plain (all-purpose) flour**, 500g/1¼lb/4½ cups, sifted

### for the decoration

- **egg white**, 1
- **icing (confectioners') sugar**, 175–225g/ 6–8oz/1½–2 cups, sifted
- **silver** and **gold balls**

## VARIATIONS

• You could use this lightly spiced biscuit (cookie) dough to make any number of shaped biscuits, including Christmas trees, stars, teddy bears, elephants – the only limit is what shape cookie cutters you happen to have.

• Don't restrict yourself to gold and silver balls when decorating the biscuits – you can add any small sweets (candies) you like, or why not try sprinkling over coloured or chocolate sprinkles.

## tools

- **2 baking sheets**
- **Baking parchment**
- **Large heavy pan**
- **Wooden spoon**
- **Large heatproof bowl**
- **Sieve (strainer)**
- **Rolling pin**
- **Plain round cookie cutter**
- **Small sharp knife**
- **Drinking straw**
- **Oven gloves**
- **Wire rack**
- **Palette knife**
- **Fork**
- **Small mixing bowl**
- **Piping (pastry) bag fitted with a plain nozzle (tip)**
- **Fine ribbon or thread**

1 Preheat the oven to 160°C/ 325°F/Gas 3. Grease and line two baking sheets. Put the sugar, syrup, ginger, cinnamon and cloves in a pan. Bring up to the boil, stirring. Remove from the heat. Adult supervision is required.

2 Put the butter in a large heatproof bowl and pour over the sugar mixture. Add the bicarbonate of soda and stir until the butter has melted. Beat in the egg, then the flour. Mix, then knead on a floured surface to form a smooth dough.

3 Divide the dough into four pieces and roll out one at a time, between sheets of baking parchment, to a thickness of about 3mm/⅛in. Keep the unrolled dough in a plastic bag until needed to prevent it drying out.

4 Stamp out medium rounds with the cutter. With adult supervision, cut off two segments from either side of the round to give a body and two wings. Place the wings, round-side down, behind the body and press together.

5 Roll a small piece of dough for the head, place at the top of the body and flatten with your fingers. Using the end of the drinking straw, stamp out a hole through which ribbon can be threaded when they are cooked.

 = Watch out! Sharp or electrical tool in use. (!) = Watch out! Heat is involved.

6 Place the biscuits on the baking sheets. Bake for 10–15 minutes until golden brown. Ask an adult to remove from the oven. Leave to cool slightly on the sheets, then transfer to a wire rack with the palette knife. Cool completely.

7 **To make the decoration**, beat the egg white with a fork in a small mixing bowl. Whisk in enough icing sugar to make an icing that forms soft peaks when you lift the fork from the mixture.

8 Put the icing in a piping bag fitted with a plain writing nozzle and decorate the biscuits with simple designs, such as stripes on the dress or wings, hair, faces, zigzags on the wings, or whatever you like.

9 Press silver and gold balls into the icing, in whatever patterns you like, before the icing has set. Leave to set for about 15 minutes.

10 Finally, thread loops of fine ribbon through the holes in the tops of the biscuits, so they can be hung up on a tree.

# Mince pies

Although you need to make mincemeat in advance, it is well worth using your own rather than store-bought varieties as it tastes so much better.

*makes* 12

## ingredients

- **butter**, for greasing
- **icing (confectioners') sugar**, for dusting (optional)

### for the mincemeat

- **tart cooking apples**, 500g/1¼lb, peeled, cored and finely diced
- **ready-to-eat dried apricots**, 115g/4oz/½ cup, coarsely chopped
- **dried mixed fruit**, 900g/2lb/5⅓ cups
- **whole blanched almonds**, 115g/4oz/1 cup, chopped
- **shredded suet**, 175g/6oz/1 cup
- **muscovado (molasses) sugar**, 225g/8oz/generous 1 cup
- **orange**, 1, grated rind and juice
- **lemon**, 1, grated rind and juice
- **ground cinnamon**, 5ml/1 tsp
- **grated nutmeg**, 2.5ml/½ tsp
- **ground ginger**, 2.5ml/½ tsp
- **orange juice**, 120ml/4fl oz/½ cup

### for the pastry

- **plain (all-purpose) flour**, 225g/8oz/2 cups
- **salt**, 2.5ml/½ tsp
- **caster (superfine) sugar**, 15ml/1 tbsp
- **butter**, 150g/5oz/⅔ cup
- **egg yolk**, 1
- **grated orange rind**, 5ml/1 tsp

## tools

- 2 large glass mixing bowls
- 2 metal spoons
- Sterilized glass jars
- 12-hole bun tin (muffin pan)
- Rolling pin
- 7.5cm/3in round cutter
- 5cm/2in round cutter
- Teaspoon
- Pastry brush
- Oven gloves
- Wire rack

## COOK'S TIPS

► Once opened, store jars of mincemeat in the refrigerator and use within 4 weeks. Unopened, it will keep for 1 year.

► Before potting, you need to 'sterilize' the jars. To do this, wash the jars in hot, soapy water, rinse and turn upside down to drain. Stand on a baking sheet lined with kitchen paper. Rest any lids on top. Place in a cold oven, then heat to 100°C/225°F/Gas ¼ and bake for 30 minutes. Leave to cool slightly before filling.

1 **To make the mincemeat**, put the apples, apricots, dried fruit, almonds, suet and sugar in a large glass mixing bowl and stir together with a large spoon until everything is thoroughly combined.

2 Add the orange and lemon rind and juice, cinnamon, nutmeg, ginger and orange juice and mix well. Cover the bowl with a clean dish towel and leave to stand in a cool place for 2 days, stirring occasionally.

3 Spoon the mincemeat into cool sterilized jars, pressing down well, and being very careful not to trap any air bubbles. Cover and seal. Store the jars in a cool, dark place for at least 4 weeks before using.

4 **To make the pastry**, sift the flour and salt into a large bowl and stir in the sugar. Rub in the butter until the mixture resembles crumbs. Stir in the egg yolk and orange rind and gather into a ball. Chill for 30 minutes.

5 Preheat the oven to 220°C/425°F/Gas 7 and grease the 12-hole bun tray. Roll out the pastry on a lightly floured surface to about 3mm/⅛in thick and, using a 7.5cm/3in cutter, cut out 12 rounds.

 = Watch out! Sharp or electrical tool in use. = Watch out! Heat is involved.

6 Press the rounds into the prepared bun tray, crinkling the edge, if you like. Gather up the pastry offcuts, form into a ball and roll out again, cutting slightly smaller rounds to make 12 lids.

7 Spoon mincemeat into each case (shell), dampen the edges of the pastry and top with a pastry lid. Gently push down on the lid to make a good seal. Make a small slit in each pie with a small sharp knife.

8 Bake in the oven for 15–20 minutes, until the tops are light golden brown. Ask an adult to remove from the oven. Transfer to a wire rack to cool slightly and serve dusted with sugar, if desired.

# Easter biscuits

These delicious spiced cookies will go down really well after Easter lunch. Yummy!

*makes about* 18

## ingredients

- **unsalted butter**, 175g/6oz/¾ cup, at room temperature, diced
- **caster (superfine) sugar**, 115g/4oz/generous ½ cup
- **lemon**, 1, finely grated rind
- **egg yolks**, 2
- **plain (all-purpose) flour**, 225g/8oz/2 cups
- **currants**, 50g/2oz/¼ cup

*currants*

### for the topping

- **marzipan**, 400g/14oz/¾ cup
- **icing (confectioners') sugar**, 200g/7oz/1¾ cups, sifted, plus extra for dusting
- **3 different-coloured food colouring pastes**
- **mini sugar-coated chocolate Easter eggs**

## tools

- **Large mixing bowl**
- **Wooden spoon or electric mixer**
- **Rolling pin**
- **9cm/3½in round or fluted cookie cutter**
- **Palette knife**
- **2 large non-stick baking sheets**
- **6cm/2½in round or fluted cookie cutter**
- **Oven gloves**
- **Wire rack**
- **Mixing bowl**
- **3 small bowls**
- **3 teaspoons**

1 Preheat the oven to 180°C/350°F/Gas 4. Put the butter, sugar and lemon rind in a large mixing bowl and beat with a wooden spoon or electric mixer (adult supervision is required) until pale and creamy.

2 Beat in the egg yolks, then stir in the flour.

3 Add the currants and mix to a firm dough. If it is a little soft, chill in the refrigerator until firm.

4 Roll out the dough to just under 5mm/¼in thick. Using a 9cm/3½in cutter, stamp out rounds. Place the rounds on the baking sheets.

5 **To make the topping,** roll out the marzipan on a surface dusted with icing sugar to just under 5mm/¼in thick.

6 Use a 6cm/2½in cutter to stamp out enough rounds to cover the biscuits. Place a marzipan round on top of each biscuit.

7 Ask an adult to put the biscuits in the oven and bake for 12 minutes, until just golden. Ask an adult to remove from the oven. Leave for 5 minutes to cool on the baking sheets, then transfer to a wire rack.

8 Put the sugar in a bowl and add enough water to mix to a spreadable consistency. Divide among three bowls and add food colouring to each.

9 Divide the biscuits into three and spread with icing. Press eggs on top and leave to set.



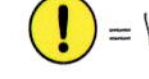 = Watch out! Sharp or electrical tool in use. = Watch out! Heat is involved.

 give it a try | *time to cook:* **5 minutes** | *preparation:* **10 minutes**

# Chocolate birds' nests

These are a real delight to make and lovely to give as Easter gifts or to serve at an Easter party. You could also rustle them up at other times of the year, too.

*makes* 12

## ingredients

- **milk chocolate**, 200g/7oz
- **unsalted butter**, 25g/1oz/2 tbsp, diced
- **shredded wheat breakfast cereal**, 90g/3½oz (*see* Variation)
- **small pastel-coloured, sugar-coated chocolate eggs**, 36

## tools

- **12-hole bun tin (muffin pan)**
- **12 paper cake cases**
- **Medium heatproof bowl**
- **Medium pan**
- **Wooden spoon**
- **Teaspoon**

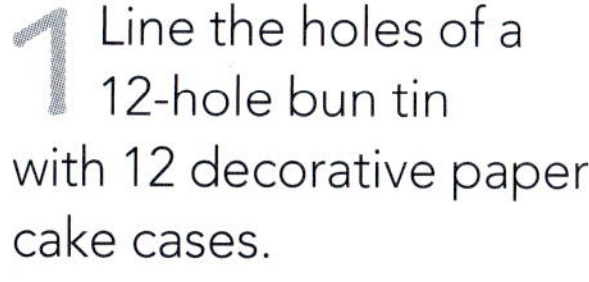

1 Line the holes of a 12-hole bun tin with 12 decorative paper cake cases.

2 Break the milk chocolate into pieces. With adult supervision, put it in a heatproof bowl with the butter and place over a pan of simmering water.

3 Stir occasionally until melted. Remove the bowl from the heat and leave to cool for a few minutes. Adult supervision is required.

4 Meanwhile, crumble the shredded wheat. Stir into the melted chocolate until the cereal is completely coated.

5 Divide the mixture evenly among the paper cases, pressing it down gently with the back of a metal spoon.

6 Make an indentation in the centre. Put three eggs into each and leave to set in the refrigerator for about 2 hours.

## VARIATION

• Replace the shredded wheat cereal with any other favourite cereal, such as Rice Krispies, Cheerios, Corn Flakes, Bran Flakes or Shreddies. If the cereal is small, leave as it is, otherwise crumble as in recipe.

# Nutritional notes

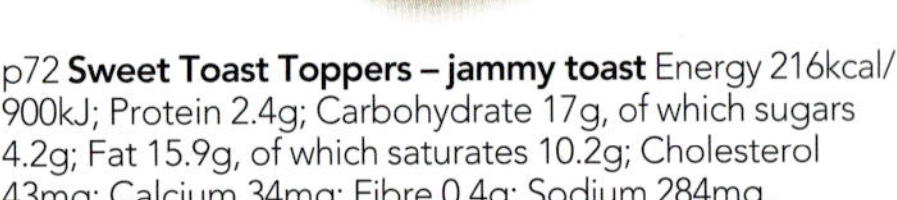

p40 **Hummus** Energy 226kcal/940kJ; Protein 6.5g; Carbohydrate 11.6g, of which sugars 0.4g; Fat 17.4g, of which saturates 2.4g; Cholesterol 0mg; Calcium 81mg; Fibre 3.5g; Sodium 153mg.

p41 **Speedy Sausage Rolls** Energy 91kcal/378kJ; Protein 2.3g; Carbohydrate 7.1g, of which sugars 0.5g; Fat 6.1g, of which saturates 2.7g; Cholesterol 11mg; Calcium 19mg; Fibre 0.2g; Sodium 171mg.

p42 **Eggstra Special Sandwich Selection – egg and cress filling** Energy 155kcal/649kJ; Protein 4.7g; Carbohydrate 13.4g, of which sugars 0.8g; Fat 9.6g, of which saturates 3.5g; Cholesterol 77mg; Calcium 54mg; Fibre 0.5g; Sodium 222mg.

p42 **Eggstra Special Sandwich Selection – egg and tuna filling** Energy 114kcal/484kJ; Protein 7.9g; Carbohydrate 13.7g, of which sugars 0.8g; Fat 3.6g, of which saturates 0.8g; Cholesterol 70mg; Calcium 43mg; Fibre 0.4g; Sodium 200mg.

p44 **Ham and Mozzarella Calzone** Energy 686kcal/2877kJ; Protein 34.8g; Carbohydrate 70.2g, of which sugars 3.5g; Fat 31.5g, of which saturates 15.6g; Cholesterol 183mg; Calcium 453mg; Fibre 2.7g; Sodium 769mg.

p45 **Tomato and Cheese Pizza** Energy420kcal/1761kJ; Protein 7.6g; Carbohydrate 49.8g, of which sugars 7.8g; Fat 22.6g, of which saturates 2.2g; Cholesterol 2mg; Calcium 133mg; Fibre 3.4g; Sodium 130mg.

p46 **Cheese and Ham Tarts** Energy 100kcal/419kJ; Protein 3.2g; Carbohydrate 9.6g, of which sugars 1.3g; Fat 5.6g, of which saturates 1.2g; Cholesterol 21mg; Calcium 59mg; Fibre 0.4g; Sodium 101mg.

p47 **Spicy Sausage Tortilla** Energy 273kcal/1136kJ; Protein 9.9g; Carbohydrate 18.9g, of which sugars 4.5g; Fat 17.8g, of which saturates 6.4g; Cholesterol 105mg; Calcium 142mg; Fibre 1.8g; Sodium 292mg.

p48 **Popeye's Pie** Energy 611kcal/2544kJ; Protein 20.8g; Carbohydrate 46.8g, of which sugars 4.7g; Fat 38.7g, of which saturates 23.1g; Cholesterol 145mg; Calcium 667mg; Fibre 6.4g; Sodium 1054mg.

p50 **Tomato and Pasta Salad** Energy 309kcal/1303kJ; Protein 8.6g; Carbohydrate 45g, of which sugars 3.6g; Fat 11.8g, of which saturates 1.3g; Cholesterol 0mg; Calcium 23mg; Fibre 2.3g; Sodium 16mg.

p51 **Chicken Pasta Salad** Energy 373kcal/1575kJ; Protein 32g; Carbohydrate 44g, of which sugars 3.7g; Fat 8.9g, of which saturates 2.6g; Cholesterol 69mg; Calcium 138mg; Fibre 3.4g; Sodium 419mg.

p52 **Mozzarella and Avocado Salad** Energy 613kcal/2554kJ; Protein 18.8g; Carbohydrate 38.3g, of which sugars 6.7g; Fat 43.8g, of which saturates 12.7g; Cholesterol 33mg; Calcium 232mg; Fibre 4.6g; Sodium 240mg.

p53 **Tuna and Bean Salad** Energy 294kcal/1235kJ; Protein 27.4g; Carbohydrate 23.9g, of which sugars 4.9g; Fat 10.5g, of which saturates 1.7g; Cholesterol 33mg; Calcium 105mg; Fibre 8.4g; Sodium 714mg.

p54 **Confetti Salad** Energy 276kcal/1150kJ; Protein 4.6g; Carbohydrate 41.9g, of which sugars 5.2g; Fat 9.9g, of which saturates 1.4g; Cholesterol 0mg; Calcium 29mg; Fibre 1.7g; Sodium 8mg.

p55 **Lemony Couscous Salad** Energy 211kcal/879kJ; Protein 6g; Carbohydrate 38.4g, of which sugars 2.8g; Fat 4.5g, of which saturates 0.4g; Cholesterol 0mg; Calcium 42mg; Fibre 1.1g; Sodium 451mg.

p56 **Fabulous Fruit Salad** Energy 162kcal/692kJ; Protein 2.4g; Carbohydrate 38.8g, of which sugars 37.5g; Fat 0.8g, of which saturates 0.2g; Cholesterol 0mg; Calcium 42mg; Fibre 4.1g; Sodium 8mg.

p57 **Yogurt Pots – raspberry and apple purée** Energy 68kcal/291kJ; Protein 4.8g; Carbohydrate 11.3g, of which sugars 11.3g; Fat 1g, of which saturates 0.5g; Cholesterol 1mg; Calcium 158mg; Fibre 2g; Sodium 65mg.

p57 **Yogurt Pots – apricot compote** Energy 139kcal/592kJ; Protein 6.4g; Carbohydrate 28.2g, of which sugars 28.2g; Fat 1.1g, of which saturates 0.4g; Cholesterol 1mg; Calcium 176mg; Fibre 3.7g; Sodium 69mg.

p57 **Yogurt Pots – granola** Energy 758kcal/3169kJ; Protein 19.8g; Carbohydrate 74.9g, of which sugars 35.7g; Fat 44.3g, of which saturates 4.5g; Cholesterol 1mg; Calcium 328mg; Fibre 7.4g; Sodium 101mg.

p58 **Apricot and Pecan Flapjacks** Energy 240kcal/1000kJ; Protein 3.2g; Carbohydrate 18.3g, of which sugars 3.7g; Fat 17.6g, of which saturates 8.1g; Cholesterol 32mg; Calcium 21mg; Fibre 1.9g; Sodium 98mg.

p59 **Date Slices** Energy 211kcal/893kJ; Protein 3.6g; Carbohydrate 43.6g, of which sugars 35.5g; Fat 3.6g, of which saturates 0.5g; Cholesterol 12mg; Calcium 56mg; Fibre 1.3g; Sodium 18mg.

p60 **Butterscotch Brownies** Energy 469kcal/1961kJ; Protein 8.1g; Carbohydrate 48.7g, of which sugars 37.7g; Fat 28.3g, of which saturates 11.4g; Cholesterol 61mg; Calcium 182mg; Fibre 1g; Sodium 151mg.

p61 **Chocolate Thumbprint Cookies** Energy 54kcal/227kJ; Protein 0.7g; Carbohydrate 6.4g, of which sugars 3.5g; Fat 3g, of which saturates 1.8g; Cholesterol 10mg; Calcium 19mg; Fibre 0.2g; Sodium 33mg.

p62 **Peanut Butter Cookies** Energy 154kcal/641kJ; Protein 3.4g; Carbohydrate 13.7g, of which sugars 8.3g; Fat 9.9g, of which saturates 4g; Cholesterol 18mg; Calcium 19mg; Fibre 0.8g; Sodium 71mg.

p63 **Blueberry and Lemon Muffins** Energy 131kcal/552kJ; Protein 3.1g; Carbohydrate 20.3g, of which sugars 8.7g; Fat 4.8g, of which saturates 2.7g; Cholesterol 42mg; Calcium 47mg; Fibre 0.7g; Sodium 52mg.

p66 **Frankfurter Sandwich** Energy 517kcal/2158kJ; Protein 13.7g; Carbohydrate 39.1g, of which sugars 4.1g; Fat 35.4g, of which saturates 13.1g; Cholesterol 75mg; Calcium 52mg; Fibre 4.8g; Sodium 927mg.

p67 **Ciabatta Sandwich** Energy 693kcal/2909kJ; Protein 30.4g; Carbohydrate 74.1g, of which sugars 8.8g; Fat 32.6g, of which saturates 10.7g; Cholesterol 62mg; Calcium 433mg; Fibre 4.4g; Sodium 1380mg.

p68 **Toasted Bacon Sandwich** Energy 587Kcal/2439kJ; Protein 17.5g; Carbohydrate 28.2g, of which sugars 3g; Fat 46.1g, of which saturates 8.5g; Cholesterol 414mg; Calcium 150mg; Fibre 2g; Sodium 587mg.

p69 **Cheesy Treats – croque monsieur** Energy 384kcal/1602kJ; Protein 18.5g; Carbohydrate 22.5g, of which sugars 1.8g; Fat 24.3g, of which saturates 15.4g; Cholesterol 80mg; Calcium 331mg; Fibre 1.8g; Sodium 935mg.

p69 **Cheesy Treats – Welsh rarebit** Energy 334kcal/1390kJ; Protein 15.4g; Carbohydrate 13.9g, of which sugars 1.2g; Fat 23.4g, of which saturates 15g; Cholesterol 66mg; Calcium 404mg; Fibre 0.4g; Sodium 706mg.

p70 **Cheese Toasties** Energy 429kcal/1788kJ; Protein 18.5g; Carbohydrate 24.7g, of which sugars 1.4g; Fat 28.3g, of which saturates 17.2g; Cholesterol 166mg; Calcium 395mg; Fibre 0.8g; Sodium 705mg.

p70 **Stripy Toast** Energy 418kcal/1743kJ; Protein 17g; Carbohydrate 24.7g, of which sugars 1.4g; Fat 27.5g, of which saturates 17.8g; Cholesterol 77mg; Calcium 427mg; Fibre 0.8g; Sodium 715mg.

p72 **Sweet Toast Toppers – jammy toast** Energy 216kcal/900kJ; Protein 2.4g; Carbohydrate 17g, of which sugars 4.2g; Fat 15.9g, of which saturates 10.2g; Cholesterol 43mg; Calcium 34mg; Fibre 0.4g; Sodium 284mg.

p72 **Sweet Toast Toppers – cinnamon toast** Energy 240kcal/1000kJ; Protein 2.8g; Carbohydrate 22.3g, of which sugars 8.6g; Fat 16.2g, of which saturates 10.3g; Cholesterol 43mg; Calcium 42mg; Fibre 0.4g; Sodium 285mg.

p73 **Eggtastic – dippy egg with toast soldiers** Energy 382kcal/1611kJ; Protein 14.7g; Carbohydrate 49.3g, of which sugars 2.6g; Fat 15.6g, of which saturates 7.4g; Cholesterol 213mg; Calcium 140mg; Fibre 1.5g; Sodium 665mg.

p73 **Eggtastic – poached egg on toast** Energy 348kcal/1456kJ; Protein 17.1g; Carbohydrate 26.6g, of which sugars 1.4g; Fat 20.3g, of which saturates 8.7g; Cholesterol 404mg; Calcium 118mg; Fibre 0.8g; Sodium 496mg.

p74 **Egg-stuffed Tomatoes** Energy 398kcal/1644kJ; Protein 7.9g; Carbohydrate 4.3g, of which sugars 4g; Fat 39.1g, of which saturates 6.5g; Cholesterol 223mg; Calcium 69mg; Fibre 1.8g; Sodium 281mg.

p75 **Ham and Tomato Scramble** Energy 350kcal/1456kJ; Protein 14.1g; Carbohydrate 17.1g, of which sugars 4.4g; Fat 25.7g, of which saturates 14.3g; Cholesterol 257mg; Calcium 78mg; Fibre 1.3g; Sodium 689mg.

p76 **Dunkin' Dippers** Energy 221kcal/919kJ; Protein 4.4g; Carbohydrate 11.2g, of which sugars 4.6g; Fat 18g, of which saturates 6.3g; Cholesterol 21mg; Calcium 71mg; Fibre 2.7g; Sodium 230mg.

p78 **Skinny Dips** Energy 444kcal/1870kJ; Protein 33.4g; Carbohydrate 45.9g, of which sugars 10g; Fat 15.1g, of which saturates 8.2g; Cholesterol 99mg; Calcium 159mg; Fibre 3g; Sodium 771mg.

p79 **Chilli Cheese Nachos** Energy 290kcal/1210kJ; Protein 9.6g; Carbohydrate 18.7g, of which sugars 1.4g; Fat 19.7g, of which saturates 7.6g; Cholesterol 24mg; Calcium 236mg; Fibre 2.5g; Sodium 430mg.

p80 **Cheese and Basil Tortillas** Energy 420kcal/1752kJ; Protein 18.2g; Carbohydrate 29.9g, of which sugars 0.6g; Fat 24.8g, of which saturates 13.3g; Cholesterol 56mg; Calcium 480mg; Fibre 1.2g; Sodium 556mg.

p81 **Chicken Pitta Pockets** Energy 349kcal/1472kJ; Protein 20g; Carbohydrate 45.6g, of which sugars 3.9g; Fat 10.9g, of which saturates 1.9g; Cholesterol 22mg; Calcium 149mg; Fibre 3.3g; Sodium 436mg.

p82 **Chunky Veggie Salad** Energy 184kcal/765kJ; Protein 7.2g; Carbohydrate 12g, of which sugars 10.5g; Fat 12.2g, of which saturates 1.9g; Cholesterol 0mg; Calcium 82mg; Fibre 5.1g; Sodium 22mg.

p83 **Chicken and Tomato Salad** Energy 424kcal/1762kJ; Protein 26.9g; Carbohydrate 7.2g, of which sugars 7g; Fat 32.2g, of which saturates 5.2g; Cholesterol 43mg; Calcium 230mg; Fibre 4.4g; Sodium 245mg.

p84 **Country Pasta Salad** Energy 381kcal/1600kJ; Protein 13.3g; Carbohydrate 44.4g, of which sugars 3.8g; Fat 18g, of which saturates 5g; Cholesterol 15mg; Calcium 212mg; Fibre 2.9g; Sodium 341mg.

p85 **Tuna Pasta Salad** 441kcal/1862kJ; Protein 27.4g; Carbohydrate 60.2g, of which sugars 6g; Fat 11.7g, of which saturates 1.8g; Cholesterol 25mg; Calcium 104mg; Fibre 8.2g; Sodium 543mg.

p88 **Chilled Tomato Soup** Energy 218kcal/902kJ; Protein 4.8g; Carbohydrate 7.5g, of which sugars 7.2g; Fat 19g, of which saturates 3.6g; Cholesterol 6mg; Calcium 100mg; Fibre 2.2g; Sodium 104mg.

p89 **Chilled Avocado Soup** Energy 242kcal/1001kJ; Protein 2.8g; Carbohydrate 3g, of which sugars 1.3g; Fat 24.2g, of which saturates 5.2g; Cholesterol 0mg; Calcium 22mg; Fibre 4.6g; Sodium 9mg.

p90 **Broccoli Soup** Energy 100kcal/423kJ; Protein 7.6g; Carbohydrate 14.6g, of which sugars 2.5g; Fat 1.6g, of which saturates 0.3g; Cholesterol 0mg; Calcium 98mg; Fibre 3.6g; Sodium 140mg.

p91 **Chinese Soup** Energy 176kcal/748kJ; Protein 6.3g; Carbohydrate 37.5g, of which sugars 5.6g; Fat 1.2g, of which saturates 0.1g; Cholesterol 0mg; Calcium 66mg; Fibre 3.4g; Sodium 39mg.

p92 **Potato and Pepper Frittata** Energy 374kcal/1563kJ; Protein 16.7g; Carbohydrate 34.9g, of which sugars 11.3g; Fat 19.4g, of which saturates 4.5g; Cholesterol 381mg; Calcium 87mg; Fibre 3.9g; Sodium 162mg.

p93 **Tomato Omelette Envelopes** Energy 488kcal/2027kJ; Protein 26g; Carbohydrate 8.6g, of which sugars 7.9g; Fat 38.2g, of which saturates 15.1g; Cholesterol 434mg; Calcium 226mg; Fibre 2.4g; Sodium 479mg.

p94 **Fiorentina Pizza** Energy 515kcal/2150kJ; Protein 20.9g; Carbohydrate 40.8g, of which sugars 5.2g; Fat 30.8g, of which saturates 11.4g; Cholesterol 104mg; Calcium 415mg; Fibre 3.2g; Sodium 634mg.

p95 **Ham and Pineapple Pizza** Energy 310kcal/1304kJ; Protein 14.4g; Carbohydrate 39.2g, of which sugars 12g; Fat 11.3g, of which saturates 5.1g; Cholesterol 29mg; Calcium 223mg; Fibre 2.7g; Sodium 666mg.

p96 **Mexican Tomato Rice** Energy 552kcal/2305kJ; Protein 12.7g; Carbohydrate 108.3g, of which sugars 4.8g; Fat 7g, of which saturates 1g; Cholesterol 0mg; Calcium 42mg; Fibre 3g; Sodium 10mg.

p97 **Quick and Easy Risotto** Energy 405kcal/1692kJ; Protein 18.3g; Carbohydrate 55.1g, of which sugars 0.2g; Fat 12g, of which saturates 6.5g; Cholesterol 136mg; Calcium 221mg; Fibre 0g; Sodium 425mg.

p98 **Presto Pasta Sauces – basic tomato** Energy 75kcal/313kJ; Protein 0.9g; Carbohydrate 4.4g, of which sugars 4g; Fat 6.2g, of which saturates 2.5g; Cholesterol 9mg; Calcium 15mg; Fibre 1.3g; Sodium 42mg.

p98 **Presto Pasta Sauces – roasted vegetable** Energy 79kcal/329kJ; Protein 1.5g; Carbohydrate 7.5g, of which sugars 7g; Fat 5g, of which saturates 0.8g; Cholesterol 0mg; Calcium 15mg; Fibre 2.5g; Sodium 8mg.

p98 **Presto Pasta Sauces – pesto** Energy 286kcal/1179kJ; Protein 5.8g; Carbohydrate 1.5g, of which sugars 0.7g; Fat 28.6g, of which saturates 5.2g; Cholesterol 10mg; Calcium 147mg; Fibre 1g; Sodium 114mg.

p98 **Presto Pasta Sauces – cream and Parmesan** Energy 283kcal/1169kJ; Protein 5.5g; Carbohydrate 0.8g, of which sugars 0.8g; Fat 30.4g, of which saturates 18.3g; Cholesterol 80mg; Calcium 167mg; Fibre 0g; Sodium 241mg.

p100 **Baked Macaroni Cheese** Energy 523kcal/2202kJ; Protein 20.6g; Carbohydrate 69.7g, of which sugars 6.6g; Fat 19.3g, of which saturates 11.7g; Cholesterol 51mg; Calcium 349mg; Fibre 2.5g; Sodium 349mg.

p101 **Farfalle with Tuna** Energy 459kcal/1949kJ; Protein 25.2g; Carbohydrate 78.6g, of which sugars 7.8g; Fat 7.1g, of which saturates 1.1g; Cholesterol 22mg; Calcium 53mg; Fibre 4.2g; Sodium 756mg.

p102 **Tortellini with Ham** Energy 509kcal/2118kJ; Protein 19.9g; Carbohydrate 26.2g, of which sugars 4.1g; Fat 36.8g, of which saturates 17.5g; Cholesterol 85mg; Calcium 353mg; Fibre 1.9g; Sodium 696mg.

p103 **Spaghetti Carbonara** Energy 707kcal/2964kJ; Protein 32.1g; Carbohydrate 66.4g, of which sugars 4.1g; Fat 36.8g, of which saturates 14.3g; Cholesterol 259mg; Calcium 246mg; Fibre 2.8g; Sodium 949mg.

p104 **Bubble and Squeak** Energy 219kcal/908kJ; Protein 2.5g; Carbohydrate 17.2g, of which sugars 2.5g; Fat 15.9g, of which saturates 1.9g; Cholesterol 0mg; Calcium 33mg; Fibre 2.6g; Sodium 14mg.

p105 **Bean and Tomato Chilli** Energy 309kcal/1302kJ; Protein 16.7g; Carbohydrate 43.7g, of which sugars 14.1g; Fat 8.7g, of which saturates 4.2g; Cholesterol 18mg; Calcium 193mg; Fibre 12.4g; Sodium 1202mg.

p106 **Tuna and Corn Fish Cakes** Energy 329kcal/1382kJ; Protein 17g; Carbohydrate 30.7g, of which sugars 3.9g; Fat 16.3g, of which saturates 2.2g; Cholesterol 25mg; Calcium 27mg; Fibre 1.5g; Sodium 324mg.

p107 **Fast Fishes** Energy 268kcal/1124kJ; Protein 16.4g; Carbohydrate 27.1g, of which sugars 3.8g; Fat 11.2g, of which saturates 1.6g; Cholesterol 48mg; Calcium 99mg; Fibre 2.3g; Sodium 306mg.

p108 **Colourful Chicken Kebabs** Energy 229kcal/951kJ; Protein 18.2g; Carbohydrate 1g, of which sugars 0.7g; Fat 17g, of which saturates 4.4g; Cholesterol 81mg; Calcium 11mg; Fibre 0.2g; Sodium 69mg.

p109 **Sticky Chicken** Energy 109kcal/458kJ; Protein 14.7g; Carbohydrate 1.2g, of which sugars 1.1g; Fat 5.1g, of which saturates 1.4g; Cholesterol 77mg; Calcium 9mg; Fibre 0g; Sodium 222mg.

p110 **Honey Mustard Chicken** Energy 287kcal/1205kJ; Protein 33.9g; Carbohydrate 12.1g, of which sugars 12.1g; Fat 11.8g, of which saturates 3g; Cholesterol 174mg; Calcium 30mg; Fibre 0.7g; Sodium 386mg.

p111 **Yellow Bean Chicken** Energy 327kcal/1367kJ; Protein 30.8g; Carbohydrate 9g, of which sugars 2.5g; Fat 18.9g, of which saturates 3.7g; Cholesterol 48mg; Calcium 40mg; Fibre 2.3g; Sodium 272mg.

p112 **Turkey Patties** Energy 141kcal/596kJ; Protein 24.8g; Carbohydrate 0.8g, of which sugars 0.6g; Fat 4.4g, of which saturates 1.1g; Cholesterol 69mg; Calcium 15mg; Fibre 0.2g; Sodium 62mg.

p113 **Pittas with Lamb Koftas** Energy 609kcal/2568kJ; Protein 35.3g; Carbohydrate 83.8g, of which sugars 5.4g; Fat 17g, of which saturates 7.3g; Cholesterol 87mg; Calcium 230mg; Fibre 3.8g; Sodium 737mg.

p114 **Mexican Tacos** Energy 559kcal/2325kJ; Protein 24.6g; Carbohydrate 26g, of which sugars 3.2g; Fat 39.6g, of which saturates 16g; Cholesterol 77mg; Calcium 322mg; Fibre 3.8g; Sodium 610mg.

p115 **Meatballs in Tomato Sauce** Energy 475kcal/1972kJ; Protein 28.5g; Carbohydrate 15.8g, of which sugars 5.1g; Fat 33.2g, of which saturates 10.7g; Cholesterol 123mg; Calcium 58mg; Fibre 2g; Sodium 131mg.

p116 **Pork Satay** Energy 103kcal/432kJ; Protein 13.1g; Carbohydrate 5.2g, of which sugars 4.4g; Fat 3.5g, of which saturates 0.8g; Cholesterol 33mg; Calcium 20mg; Fibre 0.5g; Sodium 54mg.

p117 **Honey Chops** Energy 550kcal/2278kJ; Protein 17.6g; Carbohydrate 19.1g, of which sugars 18.5g; Fat 45.3g, of which saturates 20.1g; Cholesterol 109mg; Calcium 68mg; Fibre 3.1g; Sodium 217mg.

p120 **Corn and Potato Chowder** Energy 251kcal/1052kJ; Protein 9.7g; Carbohydrate 25.9g, of which sugars 9.3g; Fat 12.9g, of which saturates 4.9g; Cholesterol 18mg; Calcium 128mg; Fibre 5.5g; Sodium 1154mg.

p121 **Carrot Soup** Energy 209kcal/865kJ; Protein 5.6g; Carbohydrate 14.1g, of which sugars 12.5g; Fat 15.2g, of which saturates 8.7g; Cholesterol 27mg; Calcium 123mg; Fibre 6g; Sodium 134mg.

p122 **Super Duper Soup** Energy 131kcal/553kJ; Protein 4.4g; Carbohydrate 23.3g, of which sugars 6.2g; Fat 2.8g, of which saturates 0.5g; Cholesterol 0mg; Calcium 38mg; Fibre 3.3g; Sodium 26mg.

p123 **Tomato and Bread Soup** Energy 285kcal/1194kJ; Protein 5g; Carbohydrate 28g, of which sugars 7.2g; Fat 17.9g, of which saturates 2.5g; Cholesterol 0mg; Calcium 64mg; Fibre 2.6g; Sodium 243mg.

p124 **Boston Baked Beans** Energy 235kcal/997kJ; Protein 19.1g; Carbohydrate 37.4g, of which sugars 13g; Fat 2g, of which saturates 0.5g; Cholesterol 18mg; Calcium 92mg; Fibre 9.5g; Sodium 221mg.

p125 **Courgette and Potato Bake** Energy 248kcal/1032kJ; Protein 4.2g; Carbohydrate 19.1g, of which sugars 7.6g; Fat 17.7g, of which saturates 2.6g; Cholesterol 0mg; Calcium 43mg; Fibre 3.1g; Sodium 18mg.

p126 **Creamy Coconut Noodles** Energy 181kcal/766kJ; Protein 7.2g; Carbohydrate 30.4g, of which sugars 12.3g; Fat 4.3g, of which saturates 1.1g; Cholesterol 8mg; Calcium 115mg; Fibre 3.6g; Sodium 559mg.

p127 **Crunchy Summer Rolls** 106Kcal/445kJ; Protein 3.5g; Carbohydrate 21.2g, of which sugars 4.7g; Fat 0.7g, of which saturates 0.2g; Cholesterol 0mg; Calcium 44mg; Fibre 2.2g; Sodium 10mg.

p128 **Chinese Omelette Parcels** Energy 148kcal/614kJ; Protein 10.4g; Carbohydrate 6.2g, of which sugars 5.4g; Fat 9.3g, of which saturates 2.2g; Cholesterol 190mg; Calcium 152mg; Fibre 3g; Sodium 323mg.

p130 **Raving Ravioli** Energy 710kcal/2962kJ; Protein 19.7g; Carbohydrate 56.1g, of which sugars 3.7g; Fat 51.1g, of which saturates 25.3g; Cholesterol 245mg; Calcium 190mg; Fibre 2.5g; Sodium 125mg.

p132 **Spudtastic – Stir-fried Veg** Energy 328kcal/1380kJ; Protein 8.5g; Carbohydrate 46.3g, of which sugars 7.6g; Fat 12.5g, of which saturates 1.8g; Cholesterol 0mg; Calcium 53mg; Fibre 5.4g; Sodium 1009mg.

p132 **Spudtastic – Red Bean Chillies** Energy 500kcal/2094kJ; Protein 13.1g; Carbohydrate 59g, of which sugars 7.8g; Fat 25.1g, of which saturates 1 5.2g; Cholesterol 48mg; Calcium 139mg; Fibre 8.9g; Sodium 586mg.

p132 **Spudtastic – Cheese and Creamy Corn** Energy 417kcal/1760kJ; Protein 14.5g; Carbohydrate 66.9g, of which sugars 12.9g; Fat 11.4g, of which saturates 6.7g; Cholesterol 28mg; Calcium 232mg; Fibre 3.9g; Sodium 505mg.

p134 **Vegetable Paella** Energy 388kcal/1646kJ; Protein 13.5g; Carbohydrate 78.8g, of which sugars 7.5g; Fat 3.6g, of which saturates 0.9g; Cholesterol 0mg; Calcium 57mg; Fibre 8.5g; Sodium 299mg.

p135 **Fish and Rice Paella** Energy 585kcal/2445kJ; Protein 36.1g; Carbohydrate 60.9g, of which sugars 10.1g; Fat 20.4g, of which saturates 5.6g; Cholesterol 268mg; Calcium 132mg; Fibre 4.2g; Sodium 1055mg.

p136 **Plaice with Tomato Sauce** Energy 334kcal/1391kJ; Protein 22.5g; Carbohydrate 14.2g, of which sugars 4g; Fat 21.1g, of which saturates 2.5g; Cholesterol 0mg; Calcium 90mg; Fibre 1.3g; Sodium 279mg.

p137 **Fish and Cheese Pies** Energy 300kcal/1252kJ; Protein 19.7g; Carbohydrate 18.6g, of which sugars 5.4g; Fat 16.6g, of which saturates 8.3g; Cholesterol 60mg; Calcium 260mg; Fibre 1.8g; Sodium 373mg.

p138 **Tandoori-style Chicken** Energy 202kcal/847kJ; Protein 19.4g; Carbohydrate 11.4g, of which sugars 2.8g; Fat 9g, of which saturates 2.2g; Cholesterol 87mg; Calcium 67mg; Fibre 0.8g; Sodium 63mg.

p140 **Chicken Fajitas** Energy 485kcal/2044kJ; Protein 26g; Carbohydrate 67.4g, of which sugars 15.3g; Fat 14.2g, of which saturates 3.8g; Cholesterol 60mg; Calcium 118mg; Fibre 4g; Sodium 53mg.

p142 **Turkey Croquettes** Energy 404kcal/1698kJ; Protein 19.4g; Carbohydrate 47g, of which sugars 7.7g; Fat 16.7g, of which saturates 2.4g; Cholesterol 73mg; Calcium 93mg; Fibre 3.3g; Sodium 315mg.

p143 **Turkey Surprise Packages** Energy 236kcal/988kJ; Protein 39.2g; Carbohydrate 2.4g, of which sugars 2.3g; Fat 7.7g, of which saturates 2.5g; Cholesterol 90mg; Calcium 25mg; Fibre 1.1g; Sodium 392mg.

p144 **Pork and Pineapple Curry** Energy 187kcal/790kJ; Protein 22.2g; Carbohydrate 15.3g, of which sugars 15.3g; Fat 4.5g, of which saturates 1.6g; Cholesterol 63mg; Calcium 55mg; Fibre 1.2g; Sodium 449mg.

p145 **Thai Pork Patties** Energy 235kcal/976kJ; Protein 21.7g; Carbohydrate 0.1g, of which sugars 0.1g; Fat 16.4g, of which saturates 4.7g; Cholesterol 74mg; Calcium 11mg; Fibre 0.1g; Sodium 79mg.

p146 **Sausage Casserole** Energy 414kcal/1736kJ; Protein 14.2g; Carbohydrate 45.4g, of which sugars 11.4g; Fat 20.8g, of which saturates 7.9g; Cholesterol 30mg; Calcium 107mg; Fibre 6.7g; Sodium 894mg.

p147 **Mini Toads-in-the-hole** Energy 282kcal/1183kJ; Protein 11.5g; Carbohydrate 28.3g, of which sugars 2.9g; Fat 14.6g, of which saturates 4.8g; Cholesterol 119mg; Calcium 131mg; Fibre 1.3g; Sodium 372mg.

p148 **Lamb and Potato Pies** Energy 784kcal/3275kJ; Protein 25.1g; Carbohydrate 74.6g, of which sugars 5.2g; Fat 44.9g, of which saturates 26.1g; Cholesterol 178mg; Calcium 155mg; Fibre 4g; Sodium 345mg

p149 **Shepherd's Pie** Energy 487kcal/2045kJ; Protein 29.4g; Carbohydrate 50.1g, of which sugars 15.2g; Fat 20.2g, of which saturates 8.4g; Cholesterol 69mg; Calcium 55mg; Fibre 5.3g; Sodium 379mg.

p150 **Guard of Honour** Energy 479kcal/1988kJ; Protein 21.4g; Carbohydrate 28.5g, of which sugars 5.5g; Fat 31g, of which saturates 15.9g; Cholesterol 95mg; Calcium 28mg; Fibre 1.1g; Sodium 114mg.

p151 **Lamb Stew** Energy 152kcal/635kJ; Protein 12.3g; Carbohydrate 7.5g, of which sugars 5g; Fat 8.4g, of which saturates 3.3g; Cholesterol 44mg; Calcium 29mg; Fibre 2.2g; Sodium 59mg.

p152 **Steak with Tomato Salsa** Energy 291kcal/1215kJ; Protein 35.3g; Carbohydrate 5g, of which sugars 5g; Fat 14.5g, of which saturates 5.9g; Cholesterol 87mg; Calcium 22mg; Fibre 1.7g; Sodium 110mg.

p153 **Cheesy burgers** Energy 288kcal/1206kJ; Protein 29.9g; Carbohydrate 8.9g, of which sugars 2.6g; Fat 15.1g, of which saturates 6.9g; Cholesterol 118mg; Calcium 83mg; Fibre 0.4g; Sodium 246mg.

p156 **Magic Chocolate Pudding** Energy 480kcal/2025kJ; Protein 10g; Carbohydrate 77.6g, of which sugars 58.3g; Fat 16.7g, of which saturates 10.2g; Cholesterol 34mg; Calcium 227mg; Fibre 3g; Sodium 309mg.

p157 **Rice Pudding** Energy 325kcal/1365kJ; Protein 6.7g; Carbohydrate 56.2g, of which sugars 38.2g; Fat 6.3g, of which saturates 1.9g; Cholesterol 1mg; Calcium 44mg; Fibre 0.5g; Sodium 171mg.

p158 **Lazy Pastry Pudding** Energy 462kcal/1940kJ; Protein 5.4g; Carbohydrate 64.8g, of which sugars 36.2g; Fat 22g, of which saturates 13.8g; Cholesterol 89mg; Calcium 81mg; Fibre 2.8g; Sodium 214mg.

p159 **Plum Crumble** Energy 569kcal/2390kJ; Protein 8.2g; Carbohydrate 80.1g, of which sugars 50.6g; Fat 25.7g, of which saturates 11.3g; Cholesterol 44mg; Calcium 126mg; Fibre 4.8g; Sodium 157mg.

p160 **Lemon Surprise Pudding** Energy 319kcal/1341kJ; Protein 7g; Carbohydrate 43.1g, of which sugars 33.8g; Fat 14.5g, of which saturates 8.1g; Cholesterol 126mg; Calcium 166mg; Fibre 0.4g; Sodium 190mg.

p161 **Baked Bananas** Energy 416kcal/1740kJ; Protein 6.3g; Carbohydrate 50.7g, of which sugars 47.2g; Fat 21.1g, of which saturates 9.5g; Cholesterol 35mg; Calcium 117mg; Fibre 1.9g; Sodium 124mg.

p162 **Banana and Toffee Ice Cream** Energy 455kcal/1909kJ; Protein 6.9g; Carbohydrate 63.2g, of which sugars 56.6g; Fat 21.1g, of which saturates 12.6g; Cholesterol 53mg; Calcium 215mg; Fibre 0.6g; Sodium 178mg.

p163 **Pineapple Sorbet on Sticks** Energy 79kcal/337kJ; Protein 0.5g; Carbohydrate 20.1g, of which sugars 20.1g; Fat 0.2g, of which saturates 0g; Cholesterol 0mg; Calcium 23mg; Fibre 1.2g; Sodium 3mg.

p164 **Strawberry Mousse** Energy 492kcal/2037kJ; Protein 1.8g; Carbohydrate 29.1g, of which sugars 29.1g; Fat 40.3g, of which saturates 25.1g; Cholesterol 103mg; Calcium 61mg; Fibre 0.7g; Sodium 24mg.

p165 **Eton Mess** Energy 526kcal/2182kJ; Protein 3.5g; Carbohydrate 32.8g, of which sugars 32.8g; Fat 40.4g, of which saturates 25.1g; Cholesterol 103mg; Calcium 60mg; Fibre 1.4g; Sodium 53mg.

p166 **Chocolate Banana Fools** Energy 268kcal/1127kJ; Protein 4.1g; Carbohydrate 42.1g, of which sugars 38.1g; Fat 9.6g, of which saturates 4.9g; Cholesterol 3mg; Calcium 81mg; Fibre 1.4g; Sodium 33mg.

p167 **Banana and Apricot Trifle** Energy 452kcal/1893kJ; Protein 4.8g; Carbohydrate 53.8g, of which sugars 44.1g; Fat 25.7g, of which saturates 13.6g; Cholesterol 129mg; Calcium 104mg; Fibre 0.7g; Sodium 77mg.

p168 **Summer Fruit Cheesecake** Energy 472kcal/1969kJ; Protein 11.2g; Carbohydrate 41.3g, of which sugars 29g; Fat 30.1g, of which saturates 18.3g; Cholesterol 85mg; Calcium 188mg; Fibre 1.3g; Sodium 477mg.

p170 **Fruit Fondue** Energy 197kcal/833kJ; Protein 3.8g; Carbohydrate 33.7g, of which sugars 30.2g; Fat 5.4g, of which saturates 2.3g; Cholesterol 4mg; Calcium 107mg; Fibre 1.5g; Sodium 44mg.

p171 **Cantaloupe Melon Salad** Energy 34kcal/144kJ; Protein 0.7g; Carbohydrate 8g, of which sugars 8g; Fat 0.1g, of which saturates 0g; Cholesterol 0mg; Calcium 21mg; Fibre 1.1g; Sodium 8mg.

p172 **Chocolate Puffs** Energy 403kcal/1687kJ; Protein 4.2g; Carbohydrate 48.4g, of which sugars 39.8g; Fat 22.8g, of which saturates 13.6g; Cholesterol 115mg; Calcium 62mg; Fibre 0.6g; Sodium 106mg.

p174 **Chocolate Heaven** Energy 1388kcal/5814kJ; Protein 21.2g; Carbohydrate 171.6g, of which sugars 110.8g; Fat 73.2g, of which saturates 15.3g; Cholesterol 45mg; Calcium 502mg; Fibre 2.4g; Sodium 746mg.

p176 **Fresh Orange Squash** Energy 181kcal/773kJ; Protein 2.9g; Carbohydrate 44.8g, of which sugars 44.8g; Fat 0.3g, of which saturates 0g; Cholesterol 0mg; Calcium 130mg; Fibre 4.3g; Sodium 14mg.

p177 **Ruby Red Lemonade** Energy 119kcal/503kJ; Protein 0.7g; Carbohydrate 30.8g, of which sugars 28.5g; Fat 0g, of which saturates 0g; Cholesterol 0mg; Calcium 12mg; Fibre 1.2g; Sodium 1mg.

p178 **Totally Tropical** Energy 162kcal/692kJ; Protein 2.4g; Carbohydrate 38.9g, of which sugars 37.5g; Fat 0.8g, of which saturates 0.2g; Cholesterol 0mg; Calcium 42mg; Fibre 4.1g; Sodium 8mg.

p179 **Fruit Punch** Energy 111kcal/473kJ; Protein 0.9g; Carbohydrate 27.7g, of which sugars 27.7g; Fat 0.4g, of which saturates 0g; Cholesterol 0mg; Calcium 37mg; Fibre 1.7g; Sodium 17mg.

p180 **What a Smoothie** Energy 94kcal/401kJ; Protein 5.1g; Carbohydrate 17.6g, of which sugars 17.6g; Fat 1g, of which saturates 0.4g; Cholesterol 1mg; Calcium 158mg; Fibre 2.2g; Sodium 68mg.

p181 **Strawberry and Apple Cooler** Energy 78kcal/331kJ; Protein 1.4g; Carbohydrate 18.8g, of which sugars 18.8g; Fat 0.2g, of which saturates 0g; Cholesterol 0mg; Calcium 28mg; Fibre 2.7g; Sodium 24mg.

p182 **Rainbow Juice** Energy 78kcal/332kJ; Protein 1.5g; Carbohydrate 17.8g, of which sugars 17.6g; Fat 0.6g, of which saturates 0g; Cholesterol 0mg; Calcium 39mg; Fibre 2.8g; Sodium 7mg.

p182 **Fruit Slush** Energy 75kcal/319kJ; Protein 1g; Carbohydrate 18.8g, of which sugars 17.1g; Fat 0.1g, of which saturates 0g; Cholesterol 0mg; Calcium 28mg; Fibre 1.7g; Sodium 3mg.

p184 **Vanilla Milkshake** Energy 648kcal/2687kJ; Protein 15.8g; Carbohydrate 36.4g, of which sugars 36.3g; Fat 49.6g, of which saturates 30.8g; Cholesterol 83mg; Calcium 475mg; Fibre 0g; Sodium 205mg.

p185 **Strawberry Shake** Energy 286kcal/1195kJ; Protein 9.1g; Carbohydrate 30.4g, of which sugars 30.4g; Fat 16.2g, of which saturates 8.9g; Cholesterol 17mg; Calcium 217mg; Fibre 2.2g; Sodium 93mg.

p186 **Candystripe** Energy 349kcal/1467kJ; Protein 6.8g; Carbohydrate 54.2g, of which sugars 47.2g; Fat 13.1g, of which saturates 8.2g; Cholesterol 38mg; Calcium 176mg; Fibre 1.3g; Sodium 79mg.

p187 **Banoffee High** Energy 469kcal/1958kJ; Protein 6.9g; Carbohydrate 54.1g, of which sugars 51.8g; Fat 26.3g, of which saturates 16.4g; Cholesterol 72mg; Calcium 213mg; Fibre 1.1g; Sodium 75mg.

p190 **Drop Scones** Energy 60kcal/252kJ; Protein 2g; Carbohydrate 11.1g, of which sugars 1.8g; Fat 1.1g, of which saturates 0.2g; Cholesterol 11mg; Calcium 66mg; Fibre 0.4g; Sodium 56mg.

p191 **Buttermilk Scones** Energy 74kcal/311kJ; Protein 1.7g; Carbohydrate 10.9g, of which sugars 0.7g; Fat 3g, of which saturates 1.8g; Cholesterol 8mg; Calcium 34mg; Fibre 0.4g; Sodium 26mg.

p192 **Buttermilk Pancakes** Energy 90kcal/380kJ; Protein 3.2g; Carbohydrate 18.7g, of which sugars 4.4g; Fat 0.8g, of which saturates 0.2g; Cholesterol 17mg; Calcium 61mg; Fibre 0.6g; Sodium 18mg.

p193 **French Toast** Energy 494kcal/2060kJ; Protein 8.6g; Carbohydrate 44.7g, of which sugars 17.7g; Fat 32.5g, of which saturates 15g; Cholesterol 148mg; Calcium 111mg; Fibre 1.3g; Sodium 287mg.

p194 **Banana Muffins** Energy 152kcal/642kJ; Protein 2.8g; Carbohydrate 29g, of which sugars 13.9g; Fat 3.6g, of which saturates 0.5g; Cholesterol 16mg; Calcium 34mg; Fibre 1g; Sodium 9mg.

p195 **Double Choc Chip Muffins** Energy 281kcal/1183kJ; Protein 4.7g; Carbohydrate 41.3g, of which sugars 21.9g; Fat 11.9g, of which saturates 5.7g; Cholesterol 7mg; Calcium 94mg; Fibre 1.3g; Sodium 40mg.

p196 **Banana Gingerbread** Energy 133kcal/563kJ; Protein 2.3g; Carbohydrate 25.9g, of which sugars 15.2g; Fat 3g, of which saturates 0.5g; Cholesterol 19mg; Calcium 37mg; Fibre 0.7g; Sodium 18mg.

p197 **Bilberry Teabread** Energy 374kcal/1575kJ; Protein 5g; Carbohydrate 66.2g, of which sugars 40.9g; Fat 11.7g, of which saturates 6.9g; Cholesterol 51mg; Calcium 104mg; Fibre 2.1g; Sodium 95mg.

p198 **Carrot Cake** Energy 331kcal/1387kJ; Protein 6.4g; Carbohydrate 41g, of which sugars 24.6g; Fat 16.9g, of which saturates 7g; Cholesterol 73mg; Calcium 63mg; Fibre 1.5g; Sodium 83mg.

p200 **Simple Chocolate Cake** Energy 427kcal/1776kJ; Protein 6.1g; Carbohydrate 29.2g, of which sugars 9.8g; Fat 32.6g, of which saturates 19.6g; Cholesterol 139mg; Calcium 65mg; Fibre 1.4g; Sodium 238mg.

p201 **Luscious Lemon Cake** Energy 420kcal/1757kJ; Protein 6g; Carbohydrate 49.2g, of which sugars 28.3g; Fat 23.6g, of which saturates 14.3g; Cholesterol 153mg; Calcium 70mg; Fibre 0.9g; Sodium 229mg.

p202 **Lemon Meringue Cakes** Energy 123kcal/514kJ; Protein 1.7g; Carbohydrate 16.6g, of which sugars 11.7g; Fat 6g, of which saturates 3.5g; Cholesterol 35mg; Calcium 19mg; Fibre 0.2g; Sodium 54mg.

p203 **Orange and Apple Rockies** Energy 87kcal/366kJ; Protein 1.3g; Carbohydrate 11.6g, of which sugars 4.5g; Fat 4.3g, of which saturates 0.9g; Cholesterol 8mg; Calcium 19mg; Fibre 0.5g; Sodium 42mg.

p204 **Pecan Squares** Energy 245kcal/1016kJ; Protein 2.1g; Carbohydrate 15.5g, of which sugars 10.5g; Fat 19.8g, of which saturates 7.6g; Cholesterol 33mg; Calcium 26mg; Fibre 0.8g; Sodium 71mg.

p205 **Rich Chocolate Cookie Slice** Energy 326kcal/1361kJ; Protein 2.7g; Carbohydrate 29g, of which sugars 23.8g; Fat 23g, of which saturates 13.9g; Cholesterol 33mg; Calcium 44mg; Fibre 0.9g; Sodium 144mg.

p206 **Chewy Flapjacks** Energy 241kcal/1007kJ; Protein 2.7g; Carbohydrate 29.5g, of which sugars 14.3g; Fat 13.2g, of which saturates 7.2g; Cholesterol 30mg; Calcium 18mg; Fibre 1.4g; Sodium 125mg.

p207 **Peanut and Jam Cookies** Energy 170kcal/713kJ; Protein 3.3g; Carbohydrate 21g, of which sugars 15.3g; Fat 8.5g, of which saturates 3.1g; Cholesterol 16mg; Calcium 36mg; Fibre 0.8g; Sodium 92mg.

p208 **Triple Chocolate Cookies** Energy 416kcal/1738kJ; Protein 4.3g; Carbohydrate 47.6g, of which sugars 37.8g; Fat 24.4g, of which saturates 11.8g; Cholesterol 21mg; Calcium 71mg; Fibre 1.6g; Sodium 84mg.

p209 **Chocolate Caramel Nuggets** Energy 149kcal/625kJ; Protein 1.8g; Carbohydrate 18.7g, of which sugars 9.5g; Fat 8g, of which saturates 4.6g; Cholesterol 30mg;Calcium 34mg; Fibre 0.3g; Sodium 58mg.

p212 **Crazy Rainbow Popcorn** Energy 103kcal/430kJ; Protein 2.4g; Carbohydrate 5.7g, of which sugars 0.1g; Fat 7.9g, of which saturates 2g; Cholesterol 6mg; Calcium 50mg; Fibre 0g; Sodium 49mg.

p214 **Cheese and Potato Twists** Energy 231kcal/971kJ; Protein 8.7g; Carbohydrate 26.4g, of which sugars 0.8g; Fat 10.4g, of which saturates 5.2g; Cholesterol 21mg; Calcium 203mg; Fibre 1.2g; Sodium 162mg..

p215 **Sandwich Shapes** Energy 342kcal/1433kJ; Protein 14.6g; Carbohydrate 31.5g, of which sugars 2.2g; Fat 18.2g, of which saturates 7.9g; Cholesterol 50mg; Calcium 136mg; Fibre 1.7g; Sodium 726mg.

p216 **Mini Burgers 'n' Buns** Energy 229kcal/960kJ; Protein 12.9g; Carbohydrate 20.7g, of which sugars 1.5g; Fat 10.8g, of which saturates 5.2g; Cholesterol 54mg; Calcium 148mg; Fibre 0.7g; Sodium 341mg.

p218 **Mini Ciabatta Pizzas** Energy 154kcal/647kJ; Protein 8.6g; Carbohydrate 18.7g, of which sugars 6.2g; Fat 5.4g, of which saturates 2.9g; Cholesterol 16mg; Calcium 106mg; Fibre 2g; Sodium 325mg.

p219 **Tortilla Squares** Energy 177kcal/738kJ; Protein 9.2g; Carbohydrate 15.5g, of which sugars 4.8g; Fat 9.2g, of which saturates 1.9g; Cholesterol 150mg; Calcium 71mg; Fibre 3.7g; Sodium 66mg.

p220 **Chicken Mini-rolls** Energy 467kcal/1963kJ; Protein 27.9g; Carbohydrate 49.6g, of which sugars 6.9g; Fat 19g, of which saturates 3.5g; Cholesterol 132mg; Calcium 109mg; Fibre 2.1g; Sodium 105mg.

p221 **Falafel** Energy 372kcal/1557kJ; Protein 19.3g; Carbohydrate 35.3g, of which sugars 5.8g; Fat 18.1g, of which saturates 2.6g; Cholesterol 48mg; Calcium 280mg; Fibre 8g; Sodium 89mg.

p222 **Mini Muffins** Energy 67kcal/281kJ; Protein 1.4g; Carbohydrate 11.1g, of which sugars 4.8g; Fat 2.2g, of which saturates 1.2g; Cholesterol 13mg; Calcium 25mg; Fibre 0.4g; Sodium 19mg.

p223 **Cupcake Faces** Energy 328kcal/1374kJ; Protein 3.2g; Carbohydrate 42.5g, of which sugars 33.1g; Fat 17.3g, of which saturates 5.4g; Cholesterol 43mg; Calcium 53mg; Fibre 0.6g; Sodium 127mg.

p224 **Puppy Faces** Energy 251kcal/1063kJ; Protein 2.1g; Carbohydrate 52.2g, of which sugars 40.9g; Fat 5.2g, of which saturates 2.8g; Cholesterol 31mg; Calcium 37mg; Fibre 0.7g; Sodium 38mg.

p226 **Gingerbread People** Energy 94kcal/395kJ; Protein 1.2g; Carbohydrate 16.5g, of which sugars 9.3g; Fat 3g, of which saturates 0.7g; Cholesterol 0mg; Calcium 19mg; Fibre 0.4g; Sodium 23mg.

p228 **Jammy Bodgers** Energy 831kcal/3480kJ; Protein 6.4g; Carbohydrate 104.6g, of which sugars 63.9g; Fat 45.9g, of which saturates 28.3g; Cholesterol 162mg; Calcium 119mg; Fibre 1.7g; Sodium 334mg.

p229 **Chocolate Cookies on Sticks** Energy 107kcal/448kJ; Protein 1.5g; Carbohydrate 12.3g, of which sugars 10.9g; Fat 6.1g, of which saturates 3.5g; Cholesterol 2mg; Calcium 43mg; Fibre 0.2g; Sodium 30mg.

p230 **Jolly Jellies** Energy 195kcal/824kJ; Protein 4.9g; Carbohydrate 39.2g, of which sugars 38.9g; Fat 3.2g, of which saturates 2g; Cholesterol 9mg; Calcium 55mg; Fibre 0.3g; Sodium 26mg.

p231 **Yoghurt Lollies** Energy 41kcal/172kJ; Protein 1.9g; Carbohydrate 7.3g, of which sugars 7.3g; Fat 0.6g, of which saturates 0.4g; Cholesterol 2mg; Calcium 68mg; Fibre 0g; Sodium 27mg.

p232 **Chocolate Fudge Sundaes** Energy 595kcal/2498kJ; Protein 6.3g; Carbohydrate 88.1g, of which sugars 85.3g; Fat 26.5g, of which saturates 14.1g; Cholesterol 26mg; Calcium 139mg; Fibre 1.8g; Sodium 144mg.

p233 **Strawberry Ice Cream** Energy 2198kcal/9105kJ; Protein 21.6g; Carbohydrate 110g, of which sugars 93.9g; Fat 183.6g, of which saturates 108.7g; Cholesterol 456mg; Calcium 657mg; Fibre 5.8g; Sodium 290mg.

p234 **Balloon Cake** Energy 574kcal/2413kJ; Protein 5.9g; Carbohydrate 89g, of which sugars 76.2g; Fat 24.1g, of which saturates 5.9g; Cholesterol 74mg; Calcium 82mg; Fibre 1.2g; Sodium 226mg.

p236 **Spooky Cookies** Energy 122kcal/515kJ; Protein 1g; Carbohydrate 18.7g, of which sugars 12.5g; Fat 5.4g, of which saturates 3.4g; Cholesterol 22mg; Calcium 19mg; Fibre 0.3g; Sodium 48mg.

p237 **Chocolate Witchy Apples** Energy 348kcal/1467kJ; Protein 4.3g; Carbohydrate 54.8g, of which sugars 49.9g; Fat 13.8g, of which saturates 8g; Cholesterol 13mg; Calcium 107mg; Fibre 1.7g; Sodium 84mg.

p238 **Jack-o'-lantern Cake** cake Energy 458kcal/1936kJ; Protein 3.8g; Carbohydrate 90.2g, of which sugars 76.9g; Fat 11.6g, of which saturates 6.9g; Cholesterol 88mg; Calcium 93mg; Fibre 0.5g; Sodium 110mg.

p240 **Creamy Fudge** Energy 5886kcal/24635kJ; Protein 40.4g; Carbohydrate 708.8g, of which sugars 704.5g; Fat 340.8g, of which saturates 171g; Cholesterol 540mg; Calcium 874mg; Fibre 14.1g; Sodium 512mg.

p241 **Stripy Biscuits** Energy 47kcal/198kJ; Protein 0.6g; Carbohydrate 6.5g, of which sugars 5g; Fat 2.3g, of which saturates 1.4g; Cholesterol 5mg; Calcium 11mg; Fibre 0.1g; Sodium 22mg.

p242 **Christmas Tree Angels** Energy 147kcal/622kJ; Protein 1.9g; Carbohydrate 28.7g, of which sugars 16g; Fat 3.6g, of which saturates 2.1g; Cholesterol 15mg; Calcium 31mg; Fibre 0.5g; Sodium 45mg.

p244 **Mince Pies** Energy 236kcal/993kJ; Protein 2.5g; Carbohydrate 36.7g, of which sugars 22.4g; Fat 9.8g, of which saturates 5.2g; Cholesterol 37mg; Calcium 43mg; Fibre 1g; Sodium 70mg.

p246 **Easter Biscuits** Energy 285kcal/1197kJ; Protein 2.9g; Carbohydrate 45g, of which sugars 35.4g; Fat 11.6g, of which saturates 5.5g; Cholesterol 43mg; Calcium 48mg; Fibre 0.9g; Sodium 66mg.

p247 **Chocolate Birds' Nests** Energy 214kcal/896kJ; Protein 3.4g; Carbohydrate 24.4g, of which sugars 19g; Fat 12.1g, of which saturates 7.2g; Cholesterol 12mg; Calcium 77mg; Fibre 1g; Sodium 42mg.

# Index

D



E



F

**Picture credits**

The publishers would like to thank the following for permission to reproduce their images: **iStock Images**: 6t (Thomas Perkins); 7 (Ekaterina Monakhova); 8br (Rich Yasick); 8c (Daniel Loiselle); 12bl (Arne Trautmann); 13br (Carrie Bottomley); 17tr (Edd Westmacott); 19cl (Bojan Pavlukovic); 22tl (Daniel Kirkegaard Mouritsen); p184m and 185m (Joao Virissimo).